THE NEW
PRACTICAL
HANDYMAN'S
ENCYCLOPEDIA

THE NEW
PRACTICAL
HANDYMAN'S
ENCYCLOPEDIA
VOLUME 1

THE COMPLETE ILLUSTRATED

(DO IT YOURSELF)

LIBRARY FOR HOME & OUTDOORS

GREYSTONE PRESS/NEW YORK · TORONTO · LONDON

YOUR NEW PRACTICAL HANDYMAN'S ENCYCLOPEDIA

OVER 100 expert authors, artists, designers, and photographers and 15 years of painstaking labor were necessary to produce these 3,564 pages of the most massive and comprehensive do-it-yourself encyclopedia ever created for the home handyman.

• All major building projects—including entire homes, cabins, boats, furniture—were actually constructed from the ground up, photographed in step-by-step detail, drawn to exacting dimensions, thoroughly tested by actual use, and proven to save your building dollars before they were accepted for this work.

• Every home repair—including automobile, television, appliance, electrical, heating and plumbing repairs—was performed with tools, parts and materials available to every home craftsman and requiring no special skills or training.

• Each home modernization project—including room and garage additions, new kitchens and bathrooms, attic and basement finishing —was carefully designed to add beauty, practicality and solid financial value to your home.

• Every home maintenance job—including painting, plastering, furniture refinishing, lawn care, masonry work—was expertly planned to save you substantial time and labor yet produce professional results.

• All hobbies and family fun ideas—including photography, gardening, hi-fi, patios and play areas, barbecues—were created to allow you luxury pleasures at minimum cost.

• In short, in this encyclopedia you will find hundreds of fine projects to bring more fun into your life, to provide more of the good things to make your entire family happy, and to keep you profitably busy for a joyous lifetime!

• A work of this magnitude is only as good as the authors, artists, designers, photographers and editors involved. In the preparation of The New Practical Handyman's Encyclopedia, we were fortunate to utilize the top writing talent developed during the past fifteen years. Our major authors range from specialists who regularly contribute to such famous magazines as Popular Mechanics, Popular Science, Mechanix Illustrated, The Family Handyman, House Beautiful, Woman's Day, Readers Digest and others, plus syndicated newspaper columnists. In addition, most of these authors have produced a multitude of hard cover and paperback books. They are the professionals whose expert advice has helped millions of home owners and do-it-yourselfers enjoy finer homes and a more abundant life. A board of editors, artists, illustrators, designers and photographers with decades of practical experience in do-it-yourself techniques was appointed to organize and edit this practical series of books—the most useful library of how-to information ever assembled.

THE PUBLISHERS

FRANK BOWERS, Editor-In-Chief **LARRY EISINGER**, Consulting Editor
SILVIO LEMBO, Art Editor **HAROLD E. PRICE**, Associate Art Editor
HERB JONAS, Asst. Art Editor

STAFF EDITORS

ADOLPHE BARREAUX **RAY GILL** **DAN BLUE**
ELLENE SAUNDERS

PRODUCTION STAFF

LUCILLE DE SANTIS **LORETTA ANAGNOST** **STEVEN LEMBO** **JULIA BETZ**

STAFF ARTISTS

MIKE GAYNOR **ALEX SANTIAGO** **JOHN SELVAGGIO**
MIKE MONTE **JACK LA CERRA** **JOHN CERVASIO**

CONTRIBUTING AUTHORS

BERNARD GLADSTONE: Home Improvement Editor of The New York Times; author of how-to books.

RICHARD DAY: Author of many books in do-it-yourself field; Contributing Editor of Popular Science Magazine.

R. J. DeCRISTOFORO: Well-known author of how-to books; writer for Mechanix Illustrated, Popular Mechanics; Contributing Editor of Popular Science Magazine.

ANDY LANG: Homes Editor for The Associated Press and nationally syndicated author appearing in over 400 newspapers.

T. H. EVERETT: World famous author, lecturer on gardening and landscaping, former horticulturist with The New York Botanical Garden.

SIMON NATHAN: Renowned writer for Popular Photography and author of books on photography, pioneer of the Simon-wide camera.

BILL BAKER: Author of do-it-yourself furniture books and designer of contemporary kitchens, bathrooms.

HANK SPIES: Homes expert and author; editor for famous Small Homes Council of the University of Illinois.

SEICHO KONZO: Author, heating and air conditioning engineer; former professor at the University of Illinois.

JOHN CAPOTOSTO: Home improvement expert; leading do-it-yourself writer for Mechanix Illustrated, many other national magazines.

TOM RILEY: Feature Writer for Field & Stream, Better Homes & Gardens; author of top-selling how-to-do-it books.

HAL KELLY: Designer of championship racing boats, family runabouts, cruisers, etc.; writer for major boating magazines.

JACK KRAMER: Gardening authority for House Beautiful, Family Circle.

WALTER IAN FISCHMAN: Former Editor of Popular Mechanics; articles in Popular Science, Mechanix Illustrated; author of how-to books.

WAYNE THOMS: Automotive authority; writer for Mechanix Illustrated; author of five books.

DAVID MANNERS: Author of six books; articles in Mechanix Illustrated, Popular Mechanics, Readers Digest.

HENRY CLARK: How-to artist and designer; pioneer expert in do-it-yourself diagrams that make understanding techniques and building projects easy.

ROBERT HERTZBERG: Former Editor-in-Chief of Mechanix Illustrated, electronics authority, TV and radio author.

RUDOLPH MATERN: Famed Architect of hundreds of home designs.

DAVID WENNER: Automotive expert.

ART MARGOLIS: TV Specialist; author of more than 10 books on the subject.

TOM PHILBIN: Former Home and Shop Editor of Mechanix Illustrated; Shop Editor of The Family Handyman Magazine; regularly published writer for Popular Science Magazine.

GLEN WITT: Naval Architect and expert designer of all types of family and sport boats.

JIM MARTENHOFF: Boating Columnist of Miami Herald; winner of Thomas Flemming Award as best boating writer in the U.S.A.

ARTHUR M. WATKINS: Best selling Homes writer, air conditioning and heating engineer, former associate editor of House and Home Magazine.

RALPH TREVES: Writer for Mechanix Illustrated, Popular Science, Family Handyman and Popular Mechanics Magazine. Author of how-to books.

We have listed here only a few of the famous authors who have contributed to your Practical Handyman's Encyclopedia.

CONTENTS OF THIS ENCYCLOPEDIA

The following contents lists only major subjects. For a complete,
cross-referenced index of the entire encyclopedia, see last volume.

CONTENTS OF VOLUME ONE

This type of wall paneling mounts on strips and makes it very easy to decorate. Shelf brackets, picture hooks and similar items easily snap into the strips wherever you wish to place them—they can be easily changed.

KNOW YOUR MATERIALS

Send for catalogs, tour your lumber yard and Home Center

We think of materials as being those items you need to maintain, enhance or modernize your home. All supplies in these areas available to professionals are available to you. The local "lumber yard" is passé; today it's a Home Center where you can buy anything from a washer to a pre-fab garden shed. It's almost routine at our house to walk through these places before starting any project, just to see what's available that will make the job easier to do and better to look at. Many times, the sightseeing leads *to* a project. Once we were able to build an inside brick wall without pouring a concrete foundation because we discovered plastic brick light enough so we could eliminate a footing.

All craftsmen should maintain a file of manufacturer's catalogs. These will keep you up to date on materials and will also tell facts concerning their use and installation. Getting these catalogs is simple—just look through do-it-yourself books and magazines and send away to manufacturers for their literature.

SOME THOUGHTS ON LUMBER

Wood is either "hard" or "soft," but don't take the terms literally; they are botanical catagories that indicate the wood has come from a broad-leafed, deciduous tree (hardwood) or a cone-bearing or evergreen tree (softwood).

Maple, birch, mahogany, walnut, oak are typical hardwoods. Cedar, pine, fir,

QUICK FACTS ON SOME POPULAR WOODS

WOOD	DESCRIPTION	TYPICAL PROJECTS
ASH	Hardwood, heavy, with good strength and open grain, that takes gluing fairly well and is easy to nail—good for turning.	Ball bats, frames for boats, handles for tools, paneling veneer
BIRCH	Hardwood, heavy, with great strength that glues fairly well, but nails poorly. Has close grain and is good for turning. Often mistaken for Maple.	Bowls and plates, furniture, dowels, interior trim
CHERRY	Hardwood, medium weight, with fair strength and a grain that can stand filling. Excellent for gluing and turning.	Cabinet making, furniture, turned projects, handles
GUM	Rates about the middle in hardness, weight, strength and grain. Very good for gluing, nailing and turning. Often a hypocrite wood for walnut.	Use as a substitute wood for walnut—most always stained to resemble something else.
MAHOGANY	Medium hardwood, heavy, with fair strength and open grain. Very good for gluing, nailing and turning. Honduras best, Phillipine cheapest.	Fine mahogany for cabinets, furniture, boats, veneers—others for plywood facings.
MAPLE	Heavy hardwood, strong, with close grain that glues and turns pretty good but is tough to nail. Some species just a little softer.	Good furniture wood, popular for colonial designs, flooring, handles, bowls, wooden ware
OAK	Heavy hardwood with great strength and very open grain that's about the middle of the road for gluing, nailing and turning.	Heavy-duty furniture, boat frames, desks, handles
PINE (harder)	Species of pines that are heavy, strong and semi-hard with fairly open grain. Glues fairly well but is poor for nailing and turning.	Functional applications, some interior finish stock
PINE (softer)	Like the sugar pines that are light in weight, not too strong, soft, close grained. Great for gluing, nailing, and not too bad for turning.	Trim stock, moldings, window and door stock. Functional shelves
REDWOOD	Lightweight wood, soft, with close grain and good strength. Good for gluing, nailing, turning. Redwood burl makes beautiful turnings.	House covering and trim, outdoor furniture, fences, planters, interior wall covering, inside trim
WALNUT	Classified as hardwood of medium weight, strength and grain. Good for gluing and nailing and excellent for turning.	Quality wood for furniture, wall paneling, turnings, gunstocks, cabinetry, novelties

redwood, are typical softwoods. If you have ever worked with mahogany you know that it isn't hard in the sense that it's difficult to cut. Fir is a softwood but not in the sense that you can work it easily with a kitchen knife.

Wood can be "open-grained" or "close-grained." This relates to the cellular structure of the species. Oak is a good example of open-grain wood while maple is a typical species of close-grained woods. This characteristic af-

fects finishing procedures. Open-grained woods require a filler to pack the pores so the finish will be smooth. Close-grained woods do not need filling since a good sanding job produces a smooth finish.

A tree gets bigger by adding layers of wood each year. These "growth rings," which you can count to determine the age of the tree, are what contribute to the grain pattern when the tree is sliced into boards. This pat-

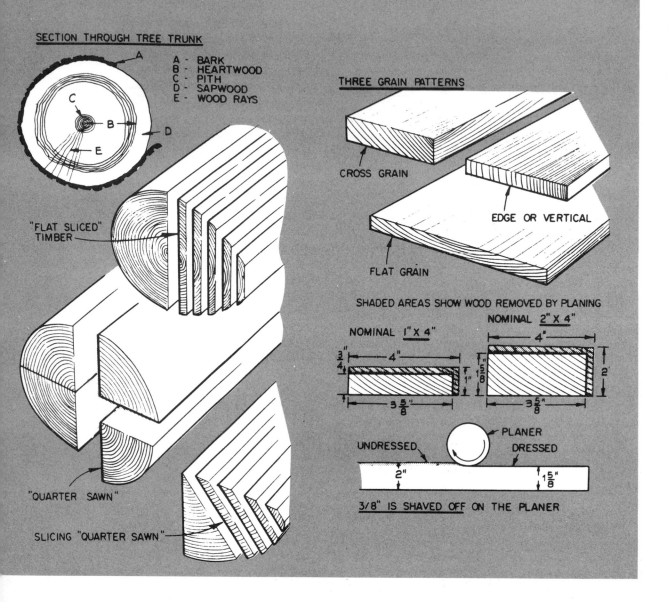

SECTION THROUGH TREE TRUNK

A - BARK
B - HEARTWOOD
C - PITH
D - SAPWOOD
E - WOOD RAYS

"FLAT SLICED" TIMBER

"QUARTER SAWN"

SLICING "QUARTER SAWN"

THREE GRAIN PATTERNS

CROSS GRAIN

EDGE OR VERTICAL

FLAT GRAIN

SHADED AREAS SHOW WOOD REMOVED BY PLANING

NOMINAL 1" X 4"

NOMINAL 2" X 4"

UNDRESSED

PLANER

DRESSED

3/8" IS SHAVED OFF ON THE PLANER

tern can vary from tree to tree in the same species and even from area to area in the same tree but it is still characteristic enough so you can recognize a particular species. How the tree is cut up also effects the grain pattern in the board.

SLICING LOGS

Slicing lengthwise produces wide boards with prominent grain. Milling this way is economical and most yard lumber is produced in this fashion. Quarter sawing is like cutting the log, initially, into four sections that look like giant pieces of quarter-round

molding. The broad sides of the "molding" are then sliced. An even, attractive grain pattern results but since it's an expensive milling technique it's used mostly to get boards from some of the more rare hardwoods.

ROTARY CUTTING

A log can be placed in a giant lathe-like machine and then turned against a knife so long, thin sheets of veneer are peeled off. This is rotary cutting. To make a common type of plywood, an odd number of veneers are placed at right angles to each other and glued together. There are other methods of

BUILDING LUMBER—UTILITY BOARD GRADES

#1 common	adequate for general-purpose work—contains small, tight knots —use on outside trim, door and window frames, siding	#5 common	bottom grade and seldom shipped out of mill locality
#2 common	contains knots and some may not be sound—use for sub-flooring, some siding, "hidden shelves"	B Select and better	tops—hard to find a blemish—use for built-ins, interior trim, cabinet work, furniture
#3 common	more knots and many unsound— also pitch pockets and stains— can be culled for shelving use	C Select	imperfections may be easily covered with paint—can be used as B Select but inspect carefully first
#4 common	worse than #3 so not too useful except for temporary structures, boxes, crates	D Select	low man on the better grade pole—imperfections similar to those in C Select but more of them—use for painted interior work, shelves, etc.

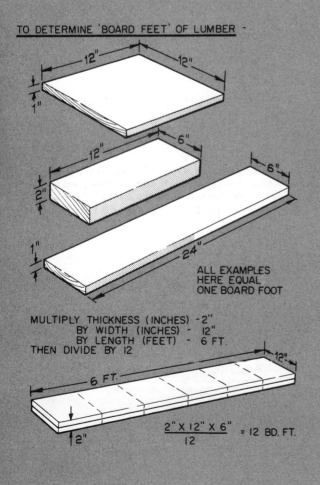

TO DETERMINE 'BOARD FEET' OF LUMBER -

12"   12"
1"

12"   6"
2"

6"
1"   24"

ALL EXAMPLES HERE EQUAL ONE BOARD FOOT

MULTIPLY THICKNESS (INCHES) - 2"
BY WIDTH (INCHES) - 12"
BY LENGTH (FEET) - 6 FT.
THEN DIVIDE BY 12

6 FT.   12"
2"

$$\frac{2" \times 12" \times 6"}{12} = 12 \text{ BD. FT.}$$

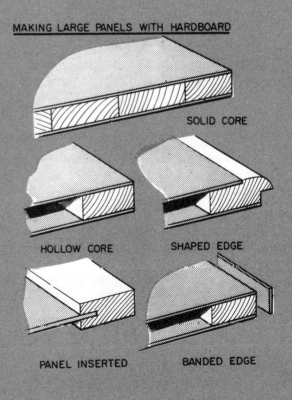

MAKING LARGE PANELS WITH HARDBOARD

SOLID CORE

HOLLOW CORE

SHAPED EDGE

PANEL INSERTED

BANDED EDGE

Outdoor projects call for materials that will hold up in weather. Redwood and cedar are typical woods used. If any gluing is involved, make sure you use a waterproof glue. Also check instructions on how to apply.

For deluxe indoor projects, use the fancier hardwoods available. Since a natural finish is almost standard, such jobs call for much more care and craftsmanship than applied to painted jobs, since mistakes will show.

producing veneers; some of them quite similar to the cutting techniques used to get boards. Each produces a particular grain pattern. You can buy veneers to glue to your projects or to make your own panels. Beautiful slabs (for table-top use, for example) can be produced at home by following the grain-matching techniques shown in

the drawings. You don't have to make the entire panel—just glue the veneer to a plywood panel you buy.

DRYING LUMBER

Wood, when first cut, contains a considerable amount of moisture. If used as is, or allowed to dry in an uncon-

When a propect is going to take a beating, think in terms of durability. Plastic faced material was used both on top and door fronts. Other parts are plywood, carefully stained to match for a pleasing total effect.

If you crave oak paneled walls, relax. You can put it up in big 4x8-ft. sheets. The typical plastic-faced hardboard is factory-finished and wipes clean with a damp cloth. It can be purchased embossed or perforated.

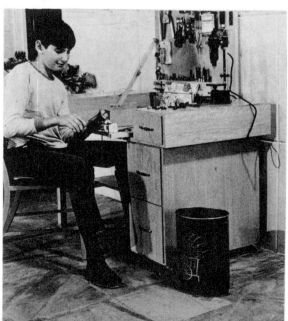

Modern plywood products include items like this fretwork piece that requires nothing but simple framing to create an attractive divider or screen. It can also be used for doors; either a whole door or a part.

You can do your own fancy work with some of the many veneers available if you have the means of pressing them together with glue. Screws you buy, but the press you must make yourself. It is not difficult.

trolled fashion, considerable distortion may result. This is because the moisture content and the wood structure is not uniform. Since you don't want this to occur *after* you have made a project, the moisture content of the wood is reduced to an acceptable minimum before it gets to you.

Mostly, it's done by placing the green wood in storage sheds where the atmosphere can be controled. Steam may be introduced so the moisture content in the wood will become as uniform as possible. This minimizes distortion when the wood is finally dried.

Air-drying is simply a way of stacking wood carefully with spacers between to provide adequate ventilation.

Acoustical tile comes in different sizes and textures. This is a suspended ceiling. The tiles rest on gridwork that hangs from a series of wires that are nailed to the ceiling joists. Manufacturer instructions are simple.

A new floor, easy to put down when working with tile, can change the character of the average room—and quickly. Many brands are available, some with peel-off adhesive backs. This saves you a gluing operation.

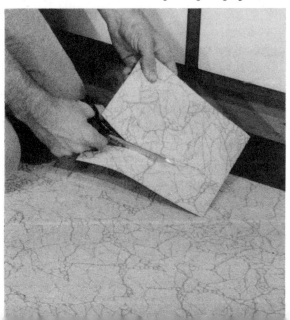

HINTS ON BUYING AND USING

Don't, as we said, buy enough to start your own little lumber yard. Get what you need for the project—let the dealer worry about storage space and possible distortion.

Always buy the cheapest grade that is adequate for the job.

When you plan a small project but want a deluxe finish, you can often save money by buying a lower grade of material and culling out the good sections. For example, by buying a decent grade of pine shelving, you can produce a good amount of clear pine merely by cutting out the knots. Naturally this can't always work. But when you figure the lowest cost pine shelving with knots and compare it to clear stock, you can see that the idea might pay off occasionally.

ACCLIMATE AND SEAL

Whatever wood material you buy, store it for a bit in the area where it will be used. This will let it get accustomed to the new atmosphere so possible slight changes will happen *before* not *after*. This applies to lumber, shaped lumber paneling, plywood panels—even prefinished varieties, acoustical tile, etc. Actually, any material that is porous enough to absorb moisture.

Finishing is important, not just for looks, but for protection. No matter what the project is, even one made from cheap lumber that won't be painted, put a coat of sealer on it.

HOW TO ORDER

Most times, when you order, it pays to specify the lengths you want. Don't ask for X number of feet. Instead, for example, order 8 pieces, 10 feet long or 3 pieces 12 feet long. This, of course, after you have judged your requirements and made a logical decision on most suitable lengths. *Don't*, however, ask for specific sizes for the project; stick to stock sizes. Special cutting by the lumber yard costs money.

PLYWOOD

Plywood is basically a sandwich of veneers. It is, however, available with a solid lumber core, a particleboard core, even a hardboard core. The solid core examples are usually more expensive and often are faced with fancy wood veneers.

Plywood is practical since it gives you large, stable panels, ready to work with. In effect, since the surface coating can be a thin veneer, it makes available greater quantities of rare woods.

The most practical panel for shop use and for many projects is made of fir and is available in 4′ × 8′ sheets. Larger sizes are available—5′ × 9′ for a ping-pong table for example, or a 4′ × 12′ for a boat, but these are usually made available on order.

TYPES OF PLYWOOD

There are many types. The best way to ask for it is to identify it with the project you are planning. There is plywood for underlayment, sheathing, sub-roofing, concrete forms, common grades of shop plywood that you can cut up for shelves and so on. Fir plywood is often used for inside projects but these call for the higher, sanded grades that are free of blemishes on one or both faces.

Common thicknesses are ¼″, ½″ and ¾″ but ⅜″ and ⅝″ can also be obtained. A special 1⅛″ panel, matched on all four edges for continuous runs in any direction is available for subflooring over post and beam construction.

HARDBOARDS

Hardboards are also a wood product and have come a long way since they were first introduced. At one time they were thought of as utility material for drawer bottoms and cabinet dividers and so on. Today they are used for wall paneling—as is, or coated with wood-grained plastics—and can be purchased

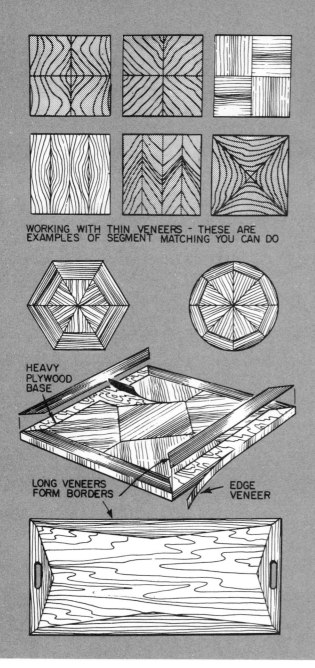

WORKING WITH THIN VENEERS - THESE ARE
EXAMPLES OF SEGMENT MATCHING YOU CAN DO

HEAVY
PLYWOOD
BASE

LONG VENEERS
FORM BORDERS

EDGE
VENEER

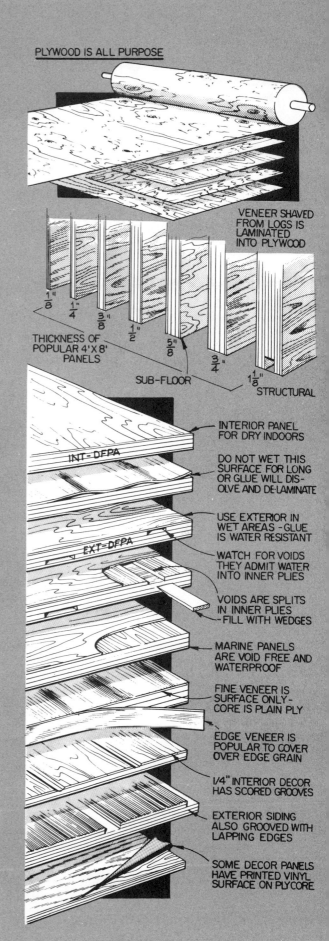

PLYWOOD IS ALL PURPOSE

VENEER SHAVED
FROM LOGS IS
LAMINATED
INTO PLYWOOD

THICKNESS OF
POPULAR 4' X 8'
PANELS

$\frac{1}{8}$" $\frac{1}{4}$" $\frac{3}{8}$" $\frac{1}{2}$" $\frac{5}{8}$" $\frac{3}{4}$" $1\frac{1}{8}$"

SUB-FLOOR

STRUCTURAL

INT - DFPA

INTERIOR PANEL
FOR DRY INDOORS

DO NOT WET THIS
SURFACE FOR LONG
OR GLUE WILL DIS-
OLVE AND DE-LAMINATE

EXT = DFPA

USE EXTERIOR IN
WET AREAS - GLUE
IS WATER RESISTANT

WATCH FOR VOIDS
THEY ADMIT WATER
INTO INNER PLIES

VOIDS ARE SPLITS
IN INNER PLIES
- FILL WITH WEDGES

MARINE PANELS
ARE VOID FREE AND
WATERPROOF

FINE VENEER IS
SURFACE ONLY -
CORE IS PLAIN PLY

EDGE VENEER IS
POPULAR TO COVER
OVER EDGE GRAIN

1/4" INTERIOR DECOR
HAS SCORED GROOVES

EXTERIOR SIDING
ALSO GROOVED WITH
LAPPING EDGES

SOME DECOR PANELS
HAVE PRINTED VINYL
SURFACE ON PLYCORE

embossed or perforated. Marlite is an
example of plastic-coated hardboard
that is available in sheets for cutting
or for use as wall covering. Special
types are available that stand up in
moisture areas. You can, by using special extrusions and caulking, even use
it in a shower.

Perforated hardboards are great for
storage walls. Special pieces of hardware are available so you can hang
most anything. They can even be used
for acoustical purposes when backed
up with a sound-absorbing material—
something to consider when covering
shop walls.

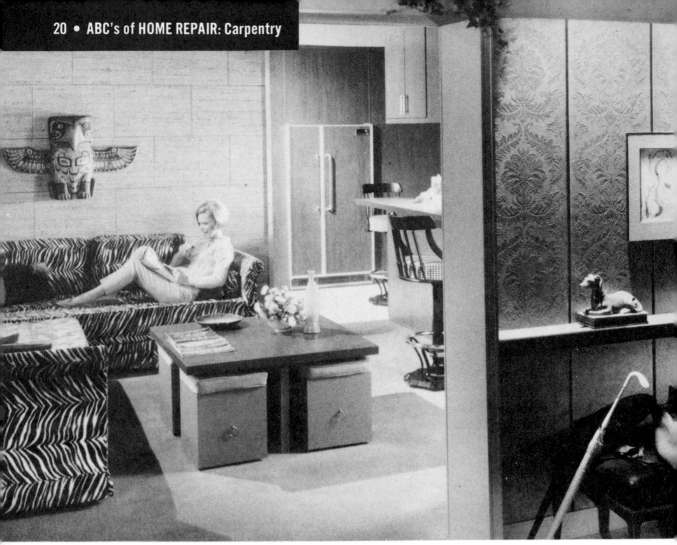

Ma

Modern look is not difficult with new materials. Textured paneling on family room wall has a mar-proof plastic-coated surface and is easily wiped clean with a damp cloth. New materials are very easy to install.

WALLS ARE FOR COVERING

If your existing walls bore you or you are finishing a new room, read on...

More often than not, walls are boring to look at. They serve as a backdrop for furniture when they should actually be adding visual interest, providing dramatic accent or emphasizing the room decor.

One way to alter this situation is to panel them with prefinished paneling, such as hardboard, wood paneling, imitation stone, tiles, wallpapers, fabrics.

For touches of glamor, filigree hardboards offer an excellent choice. Use them in bathrooms, foyers, and bedrooms. Use them for accent paneling, room dividers, and folding screens.

Textured panels may be used in recreation areas, hobby rooms and hallways. Try the embossed panels in dining areas and the marbelized for the bathrooms. Many styles and colors are available. We show some ideas on these pages. Adapt these or create your own.

INSTALLING PANELS

Panels can be installed on existing walls if they are sound and flat, otherwise furring strips will be required. Ordinary tools are all you need although the use of power tools will make the job go faster. To determine the number of panels required, simply add the lengths of the walls and divide by four if your panels are 48″ wide. Deduct half a panel for doors and ¼ panel for windows.

If wood-grained panels are used, they should be arranged for the best grain effect. Line the panels up around the room and arrange them for grain and color sequence. Number the back of the panels with a crayon in the sequence in which you will use them. Condition the panels by leaving them standing in the room for 48 hours prior to installation. This will acclimate them to the room's temperature and humidity.

Panel installation differs slightly depending on the type used. Plywood panels are butted and hardboard is installed with a slight gap at the joints.

The installation of the paneling is not too difficult. Except for areas around doors and windows, the installation is fairly fast. If the walls being covered are fairly flat, the panels can be mounted directly using adhesives. Walls in bad condition will require furring strips. These should run at right angles to the direction of the panel application. Mount them horizontally, 16″ on centers. Furring can be either 1 x 2 lumber or ⅜ x 1⅞ plywood. If necessary, furring should be shimmed to true up the surface. In extreme cases, it may be necessary to use 2 x 3 studs.

BASEMENT WALLS

Masonry walls in basement may pose a problem because of dampness. If conditions warrant, cure the dampness problem with suitable compounds. These are available at hardware and building supply dealers. In addition, you will need a vinyl vapor barrier and insulation between the masonry surface and your wall. Follow the manufac-

A barren entry hall was made elegant by covering these walls with Georgia-Pacific Chateau Pecan panels. Contrasting prefinished dark brown molding was used for trim around doors and edges, a sleek touch.

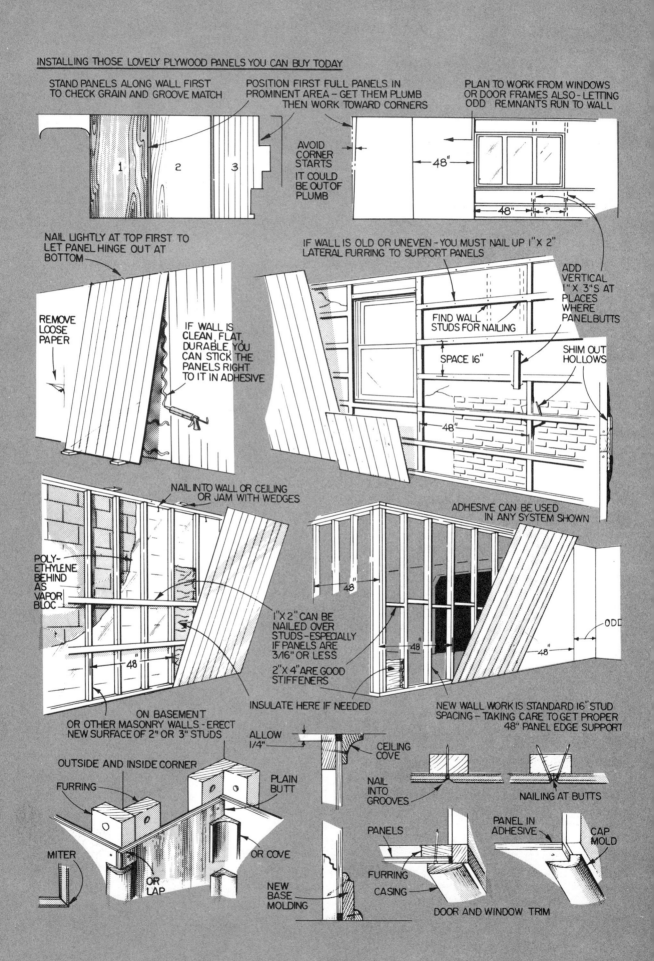

INSTALLING THOSE LOVELY PLYWOOD PANELS YOU CAN BUY TODAY

STAND PANELS ALONG WALL FIRST TO CHECK GRAIN AND GROOVE MATCH

POSITION FIRST FULL PANELS IN PROMINENT AREA – GET THEM PLUMB THEN WORK TOWARD CORNERS

PLAN TO WORK FROM WINDOWS OR DOOR FRAMES ALSO - LETTING ODD REMNANTS RUN TO WALL

AVOID CORNER STARTS IT COULD BE OUT OF PLUMB

48"

48"   ?

NAIL LIGHTLY AT TOP FIRST TO LET PANEL HINGE OUT AT BOTTOM

IF WALL IS OLD OR UNEVEN - YOU MUST NAIL UP 1"X 2" LATERAL FURRING TO SUPPORT PANELS

ADD VERTICAL 1" X 3"S AT PLACES WHERE PANEL BUTTS

REMOVE LOOSE PAPER

IF WALL IS CLEAN, FLAT, DURABLE YOU CAN STICK THE PANELS RIGHT TO IT IN ADHESIVE

FIND WALL STUDS FOR NAILING

SPACE 16"

SHIM OUT HOLLOWS

48"

NAIL INTO WALL OR CEILING OR JAM WITH WEDGES

ADHESIVE CAN BE USED IN ANY SYSTEM SHOWN

POLY-ETHYLENE BEHIND AS VAPOR BLOC

48"

48"

1"X 2" CAN BE NAILED OVER STUDS - ESPECIALLY IF PANELS ARE 3/16" OR LESS

2"X 4" ARE GOOD STIFFENERS

48"

48"

ODD

ON BASEMENT OR OTHER MASONRY WALLS - ERECT NEW SURFACE OF 2" OR 3" STUDS

INSULATE HERE IF NEEDED

NEW WALL WORK IS STANDARD 16" STUD SPACING - TAKING CARE TO GET PROPER 48" PANEL EDGE SUPPORT

OUTSIDE AND INSIDE CORNER

FURRING

PLAIN BUTT

OR COVE

MITER

OR LAP

ALLOW 1/4"

CEILING COVE

NAIL INTO GROOVES

PANELS

FURRING

CASING

NEW BASE MOLDING

NAILING AT BUTTS

PANEL IN ADHESIVE

CAP MOLD

DOOR AND WINDOW TRIM

The first step in paneling a room is to make it ready. Carefully remove all moldings, switch and outlet plates. If molding is in good shape, you can repaint it to match panels. Otherwise, it can be easily replaced.

Remove base with care. Here a telephone line was hidden behind the molding. If possible, tuck the wires behind the wallboard so they won't be accidentally struck by nails or screws. Keep a record of location.

Cardboard templates permit you to cut the wall panels accurately for a perfect fit. Use small pieces of board, taping them into place wherever wall is irregular. Make certain it is exact, checking it as you proceed.

Place the panels in room 48 hours before installation to acclimate them to the room temperature and humidity. Place in order for best grain patterning; number on back for reference, to avoid confusion and save time.

Butt the first panel to the adjacent wall of starting corner. Chances are the corner is not plumb. Mark a plumb line at panel's outside edge and then start first panel parallel to this line. You can fill open area.

When working to an outside corner, cut the panel so it falls just short of the corner about ⅜". Outside corner molding will conceal the joint. Run the molding from floor to ceiling, making certain it is exactly on plumb.

On irregular walls, space furring 16" on center horizontally and 48" on center vertically. Use shims to level off face of strips. It is easier to install hardboard panels with adhesive than with nails; often it is safer.

American Hardboard Assoc.

Before installing first hardboard panel be sure it is plumb by checking with level. Use of adhesive eliminates nails. If nails are used, select colored annular-thread or ring-grooved ones that will match the panel.

turer's recommendations for these products.

Remove all moldings around doors, windows, and floor. Remove carefully so they may be reused. If pipes or other obstructions are present, which are not to be relocated, box them in with suitable lumber.

POINTERS ON PROCEDURES

Always start the paneling at a corner. You will find that most corners are not plumb or true. Position the panel into the corner using a level to assure that it is plumb vertically. Tack the panel temporarily and scribe the corner with a compass. Trim the scribed line then install the panel. Allow a slight space at top and bottom for expansion. (Moldings will cover these.)

When adhesives are used it's a good idea to drive a few nails at the top and bottom of the panel where they will be hidden by the moldings.

Cutting panels: Here are some tips for cutting panels. Mark the panels with a grease pencil or anything that will wipe clean. Hand or power saws may be used to cut panels. Use a crosscut handsaw to prevent splintering. *Do the cutting only on the down stroke.* Power saws should be fitted with a hollow ground

blade. On table saws, keep the panel face up while cutting. On portable or bayonet type saws, panel face should be down. *A strip of masking tape on the cutting line will keep splintering to a minimum.*

Prefinished moldings to match your paneling are available. These include inside corner, outside corner, base, cove and the necessary door and window trim. Metal moldings are also available for use with hardboard paneling. In addition to the above, metal moldings also include edge, divider and end caps.

UNTRUE OLD WALLS

The following instructions pertain to old walls which are not "true."

Furring strips should be applied so that they run at right angles to the direction of panel application. Furring strips of ⅜" x 1⅞" plywood strips or 1" x 2" lumber should be used. If either plaster, masonry or other type of wall is uneven such that it cannot be trued up by using furring strips and shimming them out where wall bellows; 2" x 3" studs may be necessary.

You can use studs flat against the wall in order to conserve space. Use studs for top and bottom plates and space vertical studs 16" on center. Apply paneling direct to studs or over gypsum or plywood backerboard. Solid backing is required along all four panel edges of each panel.

Add strips wherever needed to insure this support. It is a good idea to place bottom furring strip ½" from floor. Leave a ¼" space between the horizontal strips and the vertical strips to allow for some ventilation.

MASONRY WALLS

Use masonry nails to apply horizontal furring strips every 16" beginning ¼" above floor level. Insert vertical strips to support panel edges. Shim as needed to obtain flush surface (wood shingles make ideal shims). Allow clearance of at least ½" above top furring strip and below bottom furring strip. This space should be provided below horizontal strips between each run of vertical strips.

Attach furring to masonry by drilling holes and inserting wood plugs or expansion shield, then nailing or screwing furring into the plugs or shields. Hardened cut nails, nail or bolt anchors or adhesive anchors can also be used, so can one of the new powder-actuated fastening systems now available.

PLASTER WALLS

Nail strips to studs horizontally starting at the floor line and continuing up wall every 16". Nail vertical strips, also every 4' to support panel edges. Level uneven areas by placing shims (pieces of shingle make excellent shims) behind the furring strips to level.

FURRING

If walls to be paneled are in poor condition, you will have to "fur" out the wall. Furring strips are available in 1" x 2" or 1" x 3" strips. They are inexpensive and they come in various lengths. Install the furring 16" on center horizontally and 48" vertically. The vertical strips will support the panel edges so place them accurately.

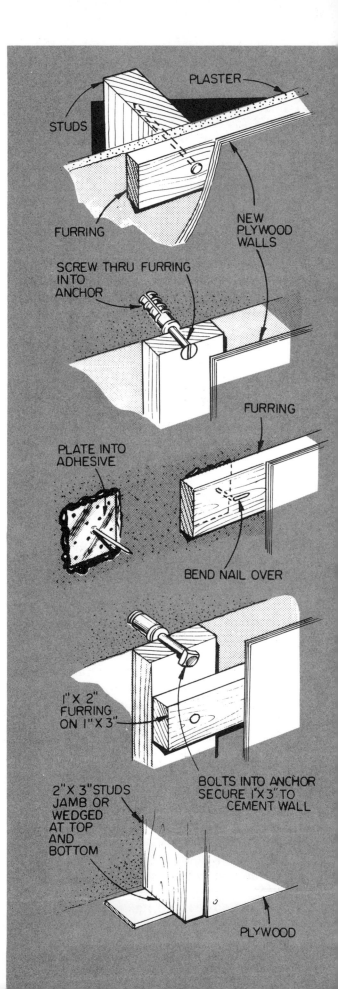

Start the first vertical strip so that its center is exactly 48″ from the corner of the adjacent wall. When applying furring to masonry walls, you can use either masonry nails or adhesive. If nails are used, be sure to wear protective goggles to protect your eyes. Masonry nails are very brittle and if they break while being installed, they can cause considerable damage.

For uneven walls, insert shims to even out the furring. Shingles are ideal for this purpose because of their wedge shape. If paneling is to be installed on exterior masonry walls, the wall must be waterproofed with a waterproofing paint and then a vapor barrier installed. Thin plastic film is available for this purpose.

Most lumber dealers and building supply homes carry the film in several thicknesses. The heavier material costs more, but it is well worth the added cost for it's far more durable than lighter-gauge material. The vapor barrier is installed on the wall before the furring is applied.

THE SECRETS OF WORKING WITH MOLDING

The secret of a good-looking molding job is in making accurate measurements. Ceiling and base moldings will not necessarily be the same length. If the walls are off plumb, these measurements will vary. Measure each piece individually and use a sharp saw blade on your power saw or, if you use a miter box, use a backsaw which is especially designed for cutting moldings.

Most moldings are cut in either a vertical or horizontal position, whichever is convenient. There is an exception, however, and this is when mitering crown or cove moldings. These must be held in the same position when cutting as they will have when mounted.

The best way to position the molding on the saw or in the miter box is to nail a strip of wood to the saw table, or inside the miter box. The strip of wood acts as a stop thus supporting the molding in the proper position while cutting.

While cove moldings are specified for

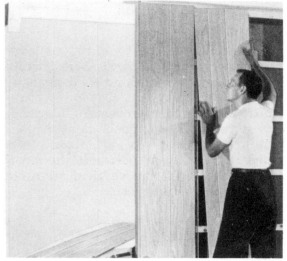

Marlite
Tongue and groove panels 16″ wide and 8′ tall go up fast and easy. These panels are mounted with adhesive and special clips. The clips assure proper spacing in between panels and this will allow for expansion.

use at the joint between wall and ceiling, casing or stop moldings may also be used. These lay flat and are easy to apply.

If a ceiling height is greater than the standard panel, a cap molding may be used to finish off the top of the panels. Cap molding may also be used around doors and windows when remodeling. The cap is rabbeted to allow for the thickness of the panels. Ordinary casing may also be used but it will have to be rabbeted as indicated on the drawing.

The same casing molding used around doors and windows may be used as a base molding. Generally the two are identical in shape with the base being wider of the two.

When necessary to splice a molding, to increase its length along the same wall, it is advisable to make 45° cuts on both pieces.

When nailing moldings use 3-penny finish nails and sink heads then fill with a putty stick in matching color. Colored nails may also be used thus eliminating the sinking and filling operation.

MOLDINGS

Factory-finished moldings simplify an otherwise tedious job. You no longer need to sand, fill, stain and finish them for all of this is taken care of by the manufacturer. Moldings can be installed to match the paneling on a wall, or in a pleasing contrasting color or tone.

While moldings are designed for specific applications, there are no fast hard rules. Casing is generally used to trim doors and windows, but it may also be used in place of base and ceiling moldings.

The factory applied finish is very tough and will resist kicks and bumps, and wipe clean with a damp cloth. Scratches and mars from hard use are easily eliminated by using a matching putty stick.

When measuring a room for paneling, be sure to measure around doors and windows for molding footage. Molding should be purchased when buying the paneling so that it can be compared with the panel for selection of the best harmonizing or contrasting tone.

Here are the most common moldings and their uses: Cove or ceiling molding is used where paneling meets the ceiling. It gives the room a finished appearance and conceals irregular ceiling lines. Cap molding is used to cover ex-

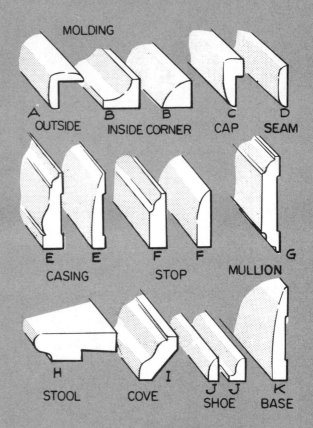

The moldings shown above are standard and are available at most lumber yards and home improvement centers in either raw wood or prefinished. The placement of various shapes is shown in art below.

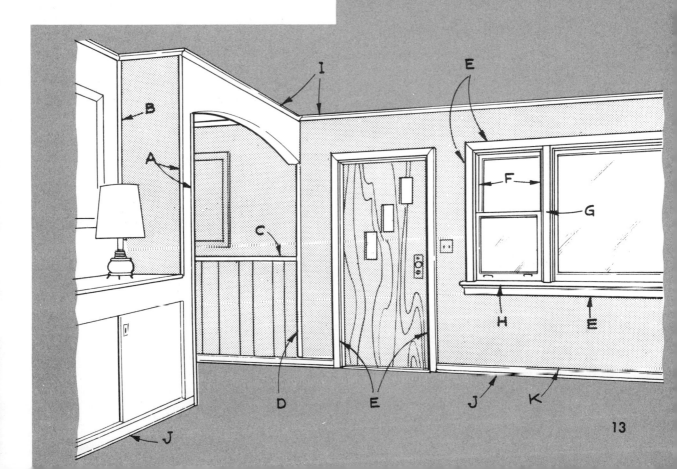

Rough textured wall paneling forms suitable background for primitive artwork over this beautiful fireplace. Modern furniture completes the casual relaxed atmosphere of this spacious and also well-lighted room.

posed panel edges, such as the top of wainscot-height panels. Outside corner guard finishes the outside corners by covering the joints and seams. It lends a finished appearance to a paneled room.

Casing is used to trim doors and windows. It is similar in appearance to base molding but somewhat narrower. Base and shoe moldings are applied around the perimeter of a room at the intersection of the walls and floor. The shoe is somewhat flexible and can be installed to conform to uneven floors.

Seam or batten moldings are used to cover vertical and horizontal joints where two panels butt.

Stop molding is used to finish door and window openings. They keep windows in their tracks and prevent doors from swinging through the door frames.

PREFINISHED MOLDINGS

Prefinished wood moldings "finish" paneling installations. They trim door and window openings to complement paneled walls; cover seams and joints at ceilings, floors, corners and other areas and protect paneling from kicks and bumps. They harmonize with paneling, and have a tough surface finish that resists dirt absorption and is easily cleaned with a damp rag or sponge.

Their factory applied finish eliminates the need for finishing on the job. Scratches and mars from hard use are quickly repaired with a colored putty stick. Easily worked and installed with common woodworking tools, wood moldings are the final step in a paneling installation.

They are available in lengths engineered to reduce installation waste even for novice do-it-yourselfers.

When measuring a room for paneling, additional measurements around doors, windows and other areas give molding footage requirements. To insure enough molding for each 45-degree cut measure the width of the molding, round off to the next higher foot and add to the total required footage.

The best time to buy prefinished moldings is when the paneling is pur-

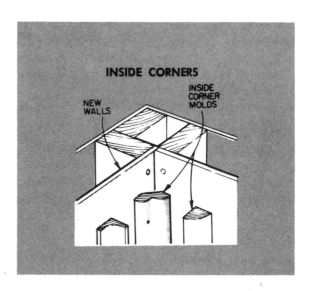

INSIDE CORNERS

NEW WALLS

INSIDE CORNER MOLDS

chased, since the material requirements for both products will already be known. Also, the molding may be compared with paneling for quick selection of the best harmonizing or contrasting color tones.

CORNERS

The following diagrams show the easy way to place moldings in corners, at the ceiling and floor, around windows and doors or for wainscoting. If your walls are over 8′ high you can use a molding at the joint where the additional panel is stacked over your 8′ panel.

POINTERS ON CARE

Walls covered with prefinished paneling, whether it be wood or decorative hardboard, require a minimum of maintenance to keep them looking new. These special finishes resist stain and mars.

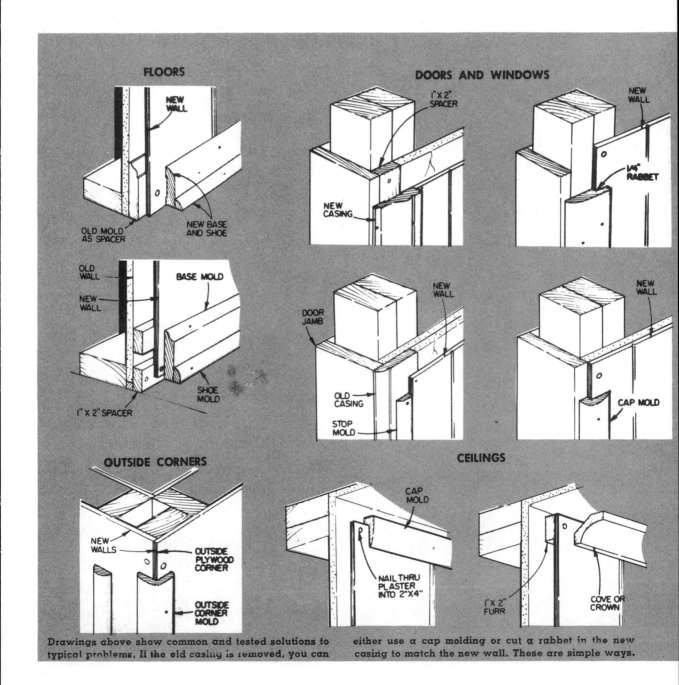

Drawings above show common and tested solutions to typical problems. If the old casing is removed, you can either use a cap molding or cut a rabbet in the new casing to match the new wall. These are simple ways.

Decro-wall Corp.

A SELECTION OF BRICK PATTERNS—

Brick may be laid in a variety of attractive patterns. Here are some of the more commonly used. There are no fast and hard rules that must be followed. Why not try a vertical application? Or how about a diagonal?

Decorating her own room will delight any teenager. These 1' x 2' brick panels are quickly and easily applied with a special adhesive. The bulletin board is of self-sticking natural cork tiles. It's all easy to install.

Plastic-finished, carved-leaf panels used around this fireplace create a striking accent wall. Rectangular panels were first carefully trimmed to the proper size and then cemented to the solid backing; no nails used.

Looks like real brick, feels like real brick, but isn't. It's a decorative brick facing, synthetically made of polyester. Each is ¼" thick, weighs only 4 ounces—for easy use. Economical too! And a snap to decorate.

Brick may be applied to any interior surface that is structurally sound, level, dry and clean. A putty knife is used to spread a thin coat of special mortar over the entire surface to be "bricked." Try to get it all even.

Just before installing the brick, use a putty knife to butter the back cavity of each brick with the special adhesive mortar. Shallow cavity takes little mortar but must be completely filled for best results.

Buttered bricks are pressed into position. Wiggle each one slightly from side to side to make certain they are firmly embedded. The mortar should be allowed to ooze from all 4 sides. Then you can clean off extra.

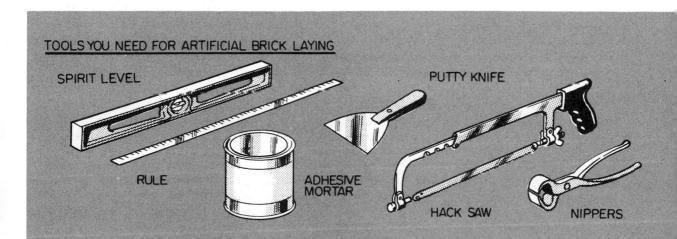

TOOLS YOU NEED FOR ARTIFICIAL BRICK LAYING

SPIRIT LEVEL

PUTTY KNIFE

RULE

ADHESIVE MORTAR

HACK SAW

NIPPERS

Dacor Manufacturing Co., Inc.

A new decorative brick material comes in a can. Material is spread on wall with a trowel. The mortar lines and brick shapes are formed with a special tape (which is later removed), and you have a brick wall.

If the panels must be cleaned, the use of a damp cloth is all that is usually needed. For stubborn pencil and crayon marks, the use of a mild detergent may be required. When soil is removed, rinse and allow to dry thoroughly then apply a clear wax.

Never use a cleanser with a coarse abrasive, it may damage the surface of the panel. Cleansers or waxes which leave a deposit in the pores of the wood must not be used. If the paneling is textured, a heavy cloth should be used so the fibers won't catch in the wood grain.

COVERING UP BLEMISHES

Should a scratch or marring occur on a prefinished panel, it may be necessary to refinish the damaged area. If the damage is severe, it would be best to call in an expert to do the refinishing. Slight scratches can usually be handled with a putty stick. These are available in matching colors and they are simply rubbed over the scratch. The scratch will fill with the special putty and in most cases the repair is invisible.

If only the finish was damaged, use a clear wax, applying it with a damp cloth and rubbing with the grain.

Wood, like most other materials, is sensitive to light to some degree. Fortunately panels mellow with age under the influence of light. However, if pictures are hung flat on the wall, the area behind the picture will not mellow with the rest of the wall, resulting in a lighter area behind the picture.

To minimize this effect, pictures should be hung about ½" away from the wall. This can easily by done by placing nails into the rear of the frame. This will permit light to seep behind the picture eliminating the sharp contrasts.

Artificial stones in various styles are also available. These are applied in the same manner as the bricks. Stones and bricks can be cut with a hacksaw, nippers or table saw. Imitation brick or stone walls are easier to install and maintain, more economical, and much lighter in weight than the genuine materials. They are ideal for fireplace outer walls, and rooms where a rustic or Early American style is desired.

"Instant bricklaying for everyone." That's how the ads read and it's true! Anyone can lay brick using the new high-density polyester bricks. They are only ¼" thick, but they look and feel like the real thing.

That's not all. The adhesive used to apply the bricks looks just like mortar and it has the same texture when dry. Three easy steps are involved. Spread a thin coat of adhesive mortar on the wall, then butter the back of the brick with the same adhesive. Press the brick into place on the wall and when the adhesive dries, it will look like mortar. No "grouting" is necessary.

Another instant brick available to the remodeler is called Brick-In-A-Can. The material is actually troweled onto a wall. A special base coat is first applied, followed by taping which will produce the mortar joint. A finish coat is then applied with a trowel. When the finish coat begins to dry, the tape is peeled away revealing authentic brick and mortar lines.

The material is available in three colors, red, beige, and white.

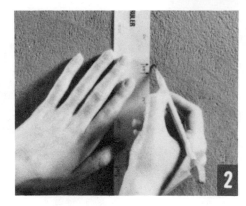

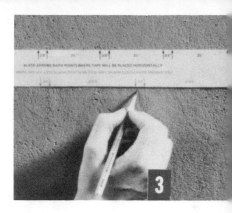

After stirring base coat, use a 3" wide putty knife or trowel with which to spread it out in a thin, even coat.

Using the special ruler furnished, place it against wall and with pencil mark off the mortar lines as indicated.

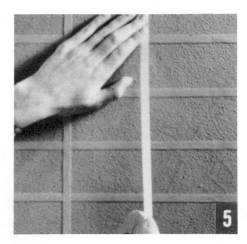

Run stick-on tape between the series of horizontal markings, at ends you may allow overlap of about 2".

With razor blade or matte knife, cut through vertical tape where it crosses over each horizontal tape.

Remove the tape by pulling on overlap left at ends of each row. This is in order to expose the mortar joints.

Remove every other strip of vertical tape to form the brick shapes as shown in this photo. But remove neatly.

NAILS AND SCREWS

Special nails do special chores, but screws look and hold better

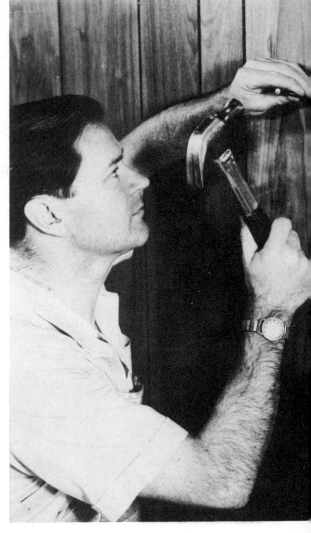

Nail set is always used to drive finishing nails lower than the work surface on paneling and molding, as shown, above. Use the right size nail set, however, to keep hole as small as possible, prevent wood damage.

Of all the nails available there are two types that you will be using for general purpose work. These are the *common nail* and the *finishing nail*. A big difference between the two is in appearance on the project. The common nail has a broad head and is driven flush with the surface of the wood. The finishing nail has a smaller head; really not much bigger than the shank, and it is usually set below the surface of the wood so you can hide it with a putty. So —in general—when choosing the two, decide whether it matters if the nail shows. The common nail is stronger when you think in terms of pulling away the nailed piece. Its head has a bigger grip than the one on a finishing nail.

SPECIAL NAILS

In addition to these there are many special types—items designed to do a better job on a specific material or application. To become familiar with these is quite a task and not really necessary since, more often than not, the name of the nail describes its use. Thus any special job you do will identify the fastener you need.

For example—there are sheetrock nails, siding nails, corrugated roofing nails, asphalt-roofing nails, gutter spikes, flooring brads, metal-lath nails, scaffold nails and so on. When you are puzzled about the right nail to choose simply give it the name of the job you are doing and/or the material you are working with and the dealer will know exactly what you want. The thickness of the materials will decide nail-size. A general rule states that the nail should be three times as long as the thickness of the material you are nailing through. Thus if you are securing ½″ stock the nail should be 1½″ long. Sometimes this can't apply—suppose you nail two pieces of ½″ stock surface-to-surface? The "general rule" nail would be too long. In such a case you would use nails just long enough to do the job without protruding—or use screws.

ACTUAL SIZE OF A 60d 6" COMMON NAIL

OTHER SIZES	
50d	5½"
40d	5"
30d	4½"
20d	3¾"
16d	3½"
12d	3¼"
10d	3"
8d	2½"
6d	2"
4d	1½"
3d	1¼"
2d	1"

APP. NUMBER OF NAILS PER POUND

d SIZE	COMMON	FINISHING	CASING
60	10		
50	13		
40	17		
30	20		
20	30		
16	45		75
12	60		
10	65	125	94
8	100	196	149
6	165	309	245
4	290	600	485
3	540	875	
2	845		

These nails sold in bulk, although you can buy some in packages.
Brads are sold by length and gauge—usually in packages.

Special threaded nails are very good when you want to nail down underlayment and be sure it is secure. They hold much better than the regular smooth-shank nail, and they will guard well against future popping.

COATED NAILS

Nails are also coated or tempered or made of special materials. Case-hardened nails are used to attach materials to masonry—you drive them as if you were going through wood. Coated nails (dipped in cement or maybe etched or barbed) are used where there is a possibility the nail might pop. Typical applications are securing under-layment or sheetrock.

RUST-PROOF NAILS

Copper, aluminum, cad-plated or galvanized nails are available for places where rust and discoloration can occur. Aluminum nails, for example, do a good

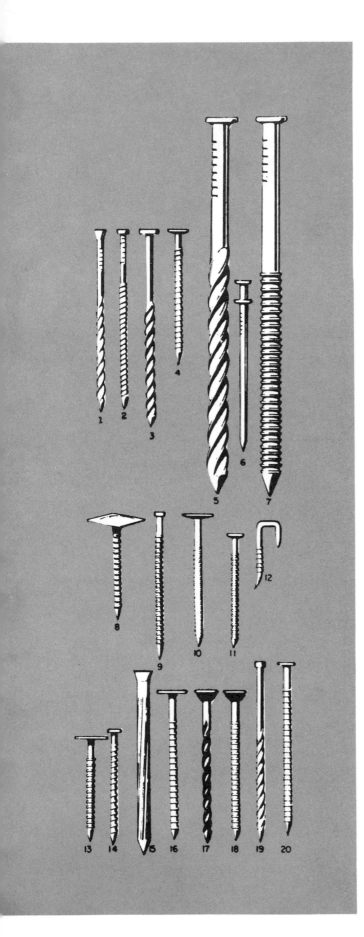

THREADED NAIL GUIDE

NAIL	EXAMPLE USE	NAIL-MATERIAL
1-2	Siding	Depends on Siding
3-4	Sheathing	Steel
5	Framing	Steel
6	Temporary Work	Steel
7	Rafter Anchor	Steel
8	Roll Roofing	Varies
9	Paneling & Trim	Varies
10	Drywall	Steel
11	Flashing, Gutters	Copper
12	Wire Fencing	Steel
13	Asphalt Shingle	Varies
14	Asbestos Shingle	Varies
15	Anchor to Masonry	Steel
16	Wood Shingle	Varies
17-18	Sheet Metal	Varies
19	Flooring	Steel
20	Subfloor Underlay	Steel

job on wood siding since they resist the effects of weather and do not discolor under covering paint. Galvanized nails are available in many styles including the common and the finishing. When doing outdoor projects you use these since they are protected against rust *and* the discoloration that would result.

A very special nail is the scaffold nail we mentioned. This is often called a duplex or a double head. And that describes it exactly; the nail has two heads. You drive it to the first head for securing and use the second head to remove it. Why? It's designed for use on temporary structures.

Threaded nails are becoming more and more popular. These are screw-like in the way they grip and so have greater holding power. As the sketch shows, they are made to fit almost every building need.

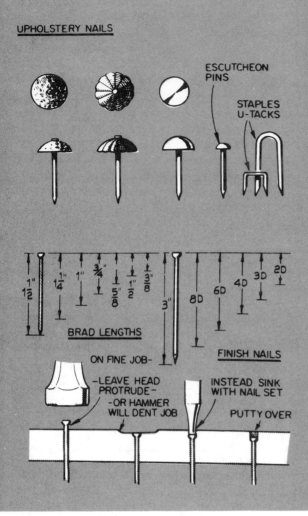

UPHOLSTERY NAILS

ESCUTCHEON PINS

STAPLES U-TACKS

BRAD LENGTHS

FINISH NAILS

ON FINE JOB—
—LEAVE HEAD PROTRUDE—
—OR HAMMER WILL DENT JOB

INSTEAD SINK WITH NAIL SET

PUTTY OVER

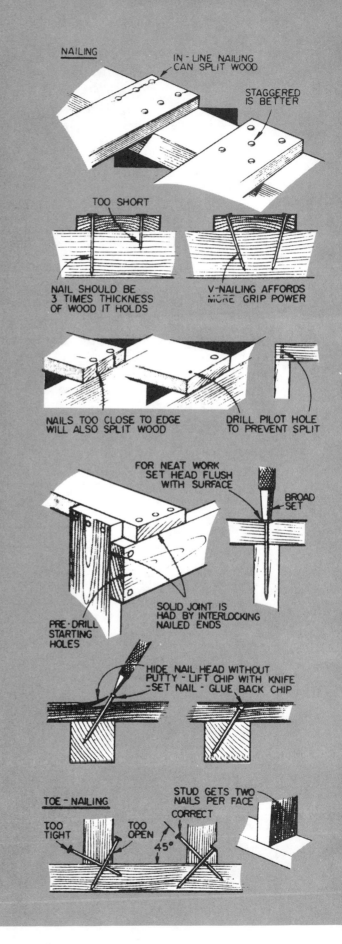

NAILING

IN-LINE NAILING CAN SPLIT WOOD

STAGGERED IS BETTER

TOO SHORT

NAIL SHOULD BE 3 TIMES THICKNESS OF WOOD IT HOLDS

V-NAILING AFFORDS MORE GRIP POWER

NAILS TOO CLOSE TO EDGE WILL ALSO SPLIT WOOD

DRILL PILOT HOLE TO PREVENT SPLIT

FOR NEAT WORK SET HEAD FLUSH WITH SURFACE

BROAD SET

PRE-DRILL STARTING HOLES

SOLID JOINT IS HAD BY INTERLOCKING NAILED ENDS

HIDE NAIL HEAD WITHOUT PUTTY - LIFT CHIP WITH KNIFE - SET NAIL - GLUE BACK CHIP

TOE-NAILING

STUD GETS TWO NAILS PER FACE

CORRECT

TOO TIGHT

TOO OPEN

45°

NAILING TECHNIQUES

Driving a nail should never be a question of showing your power. When wood fibers are torn and distorted as they are by excessively heavy blows, they do not grip the nail as they should. Hit firmly, yes, but not as you would in a carnival where you are trying for a prize. This gives you better control over the hammer anyway, with less chance of slipping off the nail-head and damaging the wood. Also, you feel less arm strain.

AVOID SPLITTING WOOD

Some woods have more tendency to split than others, especially when you are working along an edge or near an end. You can help to avoid this by dulling the point on the nail by tapping it gently with the hammer.

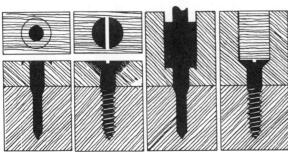

Bits like the one shown above are fine for countersinking, even hiding screws. They first form the pilot hole, then drill the shank hole and then countersink at once. But before you buy, check the charts for sizes.

SCREWS

Screws have great holding power, pull parts together and are easy to remove. They are also more decorative than nails and many times are visually acceptable where nails would not be. Using nails to attach hinges would be a pretty sad touch and the hinge would loosen.

Doing a good job with screws is a

SCREW SIZES AND LENGTHS

Number of Screw	Shank Diameter	Lengths Available
0	.060	¼-⅜
1	.073	¼-½
2	.086	¼-¾
3	.099	¼-1
4	.112	¼-1½
5	.125	⅜-1½
6	.138	⅜-2½
7	.151	⅜-2½
8	.164	⅜-3
9	.177	½-3
10	.190	½-3½
11	.203	⅝-3½
12	.216	⅝-4
14	.242	¾-5
16	.268	1-5
18	.294	1¼-5
20	.320	1½-5
24	.372	3-5

PILOT AND SHANK HOLE SIZES

Screw Size	PILOT HOLE				SHANK HOLE	
	HARDWOOD		SOFTWOOD			
	Fractional Size*	Gauge Size	Fractional Size*	Gauge Size	Fractional Size*	Gauge Size
0	¹⁄₃₂	66	¹⁄₆₄	75	¹⁄₁₆	52
1		57	¹⁄₃₂	71	⁵⁄₆₄	47
2		54	¹⁄₃₂	65	³⁄₃₂	42
3	¹⁄₁₆	53	³⁄₆₄	58	⁷⁄₆₄	37
4	¹⁄₁₆	51	³⁄₆₄	55	⁷⁄₆₄	32
5	⁵⁄₆₄	47	¹⁄₁₆	53	⅛	30
6		44	¹⁄₁₆	52	⁹⁄₆₄	27
7		39	¹⁄₁₆	51	⁵⁄₃₂	22
8	⁷⁄₆₄	35	⁵⁄₆₄	48	¹¹⁄₆₄	18
9	⁷⁄₆₄	33	⁵⁄₆₄	45	³⁄₁₆	14
10	⅛	31	³⁄₃₂	43	³⁄₁₆	10
11		29	³⁄₃₂	40	¹³⁄₆₄	4
12		25	⁷⁄₆₄	38	⁷⁄₃₂	2
14	³⁄₁₆	14	⁷⁄₆₄	32	¼	D
16		10	⁹⁄₆₄	29	¹⁷⁄₆₄	I
18	¹³⁄₆₄	6	⁹⁄₆₄	26	¹⁹⁄₆₄	N
20	⁷⁄₃₂	3	¹¹⁄₆₄	19	²¹⁄₆₄	P
24	¼	D	³⁄₁₆	15	⅜	V

* Fractional size is approximate

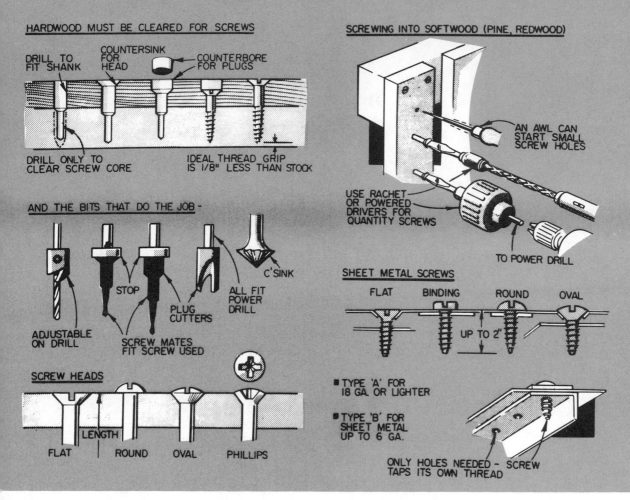

HARDWOOD MUST BE CLEARED FOR SCREWS

DRILL TO FIT SHANK
COUNTERSINK FOR HEAD
COUNTERBORE FOR PLUGS

DRILL ONLY TO CLEAR SCREW CORE
IDEAL THREAD GRIP IS 1/8" LESS THAN STOCK

AND THE BITS THAT DO THE JOB —

ADJUSTABLE ON DRILL
STOP
SCREW MATES FIT SCREW USED
PLUG CUTTERS
ALL FIT POWER DRILL
C'SINK

SCREW HEADS

LENGTH

FLAT   ROUND   OVAL   PHILLIPS

SCREWING INTO SOFTWOOD (PINE, REDWOOD)

AN AWL CAN START SMALL SCREW HOLES

USE RACHET OR POWERED DRIVERS FOR QUANTITY SCREWS

TO POWER DRILL

SHEET METAL SCREWS

FLAT   BINDING   ROUND   OVAL

UP TO 2"

■ TYPE 'A' FOR 18 GA. OR LIGHTER

■ TYPE 'B' FOR SHEET METAL UP TO 6 GA.

ONLY HOLES NEEDED — SCREW TAPS ITS OWN THREAD

question of following simple procedures. When the wood is soft and the screw is small, use an awl to create a starting hole. Doing this with the first screw on the job will tell you if it will work. If you have trouble driving the screw or can't get it down far enough for the head to seat correctly without destroying the threads in the wood, then you have to drill a starting hole and probably even form the countersink. On hardwoods, with large screws, you may even have to provide the shank hole. The size of the pilot hole and of the shank hole is fairly critical if you want the most holding power from the screw. But this is just a question of checking the chart for the size screw you are using. It's pretty bad policy to start a screw by driving it with a hammer.

SPECIAL SCREW BITS

Special bits are available that can be used in a drill press or in a portable drill. These are made for specific size screws and will form the correct pilot hole, shank hole and countersink or counterbore. When you have many similar screws to drive, an item like this will make the job much easier.

Screws, like some nails, can be hidden, but it's not a good idea to use the putty technique. Standard procedure is to drive the screw through a counterbore-hole. This hole is then plugged with a dowel. Using regular dowel for the job may not matter on some projects but suppose you are working on mahogany? Then you buy a plug cutter so you can form the plugs from the same material. These are not expensive and lead to better craftsmanship since, by working carefully, you can cut the plug to match.

Like nails, screws are available in different materials and sizes. You can get them, for example, in brass or aluminum or you can get them coated for use where they might rust or become discolored.

Quality concrete is free from cracks, scaling and other problems plaguing ordinary projects.

ALL ABOUT CONCRETE

by Richard Day

There's no substitute for quality—and you get it using "6666" principle

It's a wonder that concrete is so popular when you look around at the haphazard ways it's used. You see it scaling, cracking, dusting, spalling, crazing, sinking and even disintegrating. It's a shame. Made right, concrete needn't suffer these failures. *Made right* is another way of saying *quality* concrete.

Quality concrete isn't a brand with a trademark to say, "this is quality." Sometimes it doesn't even look different from ordinary concrete. But it is. The advantages of quality concrete over run-of-the-mill concrete are many. And they all add up to lasting satis-

This aggregate sample contains too much silt. Layer in this test should not exceed ⅛ of an inch.

Two-year-old test slabs show that cycles of freezing and thawing have scaled the plain concrete.

But this air-entrained slab was undamaged since it is 100 times more resistant to freeze and thaw.

faction with a sidewalk, driveway, patio, porch slab or whatever you make.

You can make good concrete simply by understanding and following a few easy-to-learn facts.

Quality concrete is really a method for making workable, strong, durable, water-tight, good-looking concrete that will handle easily in the plastic state. In the hardened state is will not develop any of the common faults.

The Portland Cement Association has done considerable research on quality concrete. Moreover, the entire concrete industry, from those who manufacture portland cement—the backbone of concrete—to the ready mix producers who make and deliver the finished product, is engaged in a nationwide quality concrete program. It has been for some time.

Quality begins with the manufacture of cement. *Cement* is short for *portland cement,* the powdery gray stuff in bags that you put into concrete to make it harden. There are a number of brands of portland cement, nearly all of them good.

Concrete, on the other hand, is the mixture of cement, water, sand, stones and perhaps other things. Concrete is used as the building material; cement is an ingredient of concrete. A true cement patio would be so dusty you wouldn't want it around.

Each U.S.-made bag of portland cement holds 1 cubic foot of cement and weighs 94 pounds. You should store cement in as dry a location as possible. When bagged cement is stored for long periods, it sometimes develops what is called a "warehouse pack," a stiffening around the edges. This can usually be corrected by rolling the bag on the floor. To be used, cement should be free-flowing and free of any lumps that

Damp sand contains little water and immediately falls apart after being squeezed in your hand.

Wet sand, when squeezed in your hand, forms a ball, yet leaves little moisture on your fingers.

Very wet sand forms a ball when squeezed in your hand, but does leave moisture on fingers.

can't be broken between your thumb and finger.

Portland cement mixed with water is called *cement paste*. Used as "glue" in concrete, the cement paste sets hard and glues the fine particles of sand and the coarse particles of crushed stones together into a solid mass. Cement comprises from 7 to 14 percent of the volume of a concrete mix. The sand and stone in concrete are called *aggregates*, sand being the *fine aggregate* and crushed stone, gravel or air-cooled slag the *coarse aggregate*. Aggregates make up 66 to 78 percent of the volume of finished concrete.

Concrete made with cement paste but no aggregates would be expensive because it would contain no cheaper materials, like sand and stones, to fill it out. It also would shrink a great deal when it set. While too much cement paste in the mix is not good, there should be enough to surround every particle with paste. A concrete's quality depends largely on the binding qualities of its cement paste. Therefore, nearly every step in making quality concrete is aimed at getting a high quality cement paste.

Because concrete shrinks when it sets, control joints should be made at regular intervals in every large, unreinforced wall or slab so that shrinkage cracks will occur at the joints. There they will not look unsightly. Without control joints the cracks would occur at random. The spacing of control joints is usually a maximum of 10 feet apart. Control joints should be at least one fourth the depth of the wall or slab.

Although making quality concrete may not be as easy as "1, 2, 3," it is as easy as "6666." The four numbers "6666" are the key to concrete quality. They represent cement, water, air (yes, there's air in quality concrete) and curing.

The first "6" is for cement content. Always expressed in bags of cement per cubic yard of concrete, the cement content of good concrete should be 6 bags per cubic yard. This is so that there will be enough cement paste to coat all the particles of aggregate and bind them tightly together. The table of mixes will help you hit the ideal 6-bag mix without sweat.

The second "6" stands for water con-

Start with these proportions when making your trial mix. The purpose of a trial mix is to adjust these figures to make workable concrete using your aggregates. This table was based on average aggregates. If the ones you use are graded similarly to the average, no adjustments will be necessary. These figures give 6 gallons of water per bag of cement, 6 bags of cement per cubic yard of concrete, 6 percent entrained air. Cure six days and you'll have "6666" quality concrete. The weight of sand used depends upon the amount of water held by it. Decide whether your sand is "damp," "wet" or "very wet". The amount of water added to the trial mix also will depend on the amount of water that gets into the mix via the sand. The wetter the sand, the less water you must add to make the equivalent of 6 gallons per bag.

To use the table, first decide on the size of the batch. This will most likely be limited by the capacity of the mixer you are using. Choose the weights of materials in the column for your batch-size as follows:

"6666" CONCRETE TRIAL MIXES

SIZE OF BATCH		1 cu. ft.	2½ cu. ft.	3½ cu. ft.	5 cu. ft.	(Write your trial mix results here.)
CEMENT		21 lb.	52 lb.	73 lb.	105 lb.	
W A T E R	Damp sand	10 lb.	25½ lb.	35½ lb.	51 lb.	
	Wet sand	9 lb.	22 lb.	32½ lb.	46 lb.	
	Very wet sand	7½ lb.	19 lb.	26½ lb.	38 lb.	
S A N D	Damp sand	46 lb.	116 lb.	162 lb.	231 lb.	
	Wet Sand	47 lb.	118 lb.	165 lb.	236 lb.	
	Very wet sand	49 lb.	122 lb.	171 lb.	244 lb.	
STONE		63 lb.	157 lb.	220 lb.	315 lb.	
AIR ENTR. AGENT (Darex)		2 tsp.	1 tb.	1½ tb.	2 tb.	

QUANTITIES TO ORDER
(allows 10 percent for aggregate waste)

CONCRETE NEEDED	CEMENT 1 bag=94 lb.	SAND	STONE	AIR-ENT. AGENT (Darex)
¼ cu. yd.	2 bags	350 lb.	500 lb.	(Get at least a pint and save for future jobs. Need 1 oz. per bag of cement.)
½ cu. yd.	3 bags	700 lb.	1000 lb.	
1 cu. yd.	6 bags	1400 lb.	2000 lb.	

1. Cement—Use the figure given.
2. Water—The amount depends on the wetness of the sand. Select the proper figure.

3. Sand—The amount depends on its wetness. Select the proper figure.
4. Coarse Aggregate—Use the figure given.

5. Air-entraining Agent—Use the figure given (tsp. is teaspoon; tb. is tablespoon).

tent. This is expressed in gallons of water per bag of cement. Quality concrete should contain no more than 6 gallons of water for each bag of cement used in the mix. For instance, if you make a half-bag mix in a small mixer, there should be three gallons of water in it. However, because there is nearly always water in the sand added to a mix, you actually would put somewhat less than 3 gallons of water into a half-bag mix. The table shows just how much water to add with each of three wetnesses of sand.

In reality only three gallons of water per full bag of cement is sufficient to hydrate it fully. But such a mix would be so dry and stiff it wouldn't be practical, so an additional three gallons of water is used. This might be called "water of convenience." More water than this, though, is harmful because, as water is added, the cement paste becomes diluted. The extra water doesn't combine chemically with the cement. Instead it evaporates, leaving pores and capillaries throughout the paste. These weaken it, make it porous and less durable.

The third "6" represents air content. Air is an important ingredient in concrete. Quality concrete should contain 6 percent entrained air. Such concrete is called air-entrained concrete. Air is incorporated into the mix with an air-entraining agent, which causes the formation of billions of microscopic air bubbles throughout the mix. There can be as many as 400-600 billion of these bubbles in a cubic yard of air-entrained concrete. Some cements come with air-entraining agents in them.

Air-entrained concrete has far superior resistance to scaling from freezing and thawing and from salt action. All concrete contains water. When this water freezes, it expands up to 9 percent, producing pressures that can

To get accurate proportions, weigh trial batch materials on scale, using P. 67 table as guide.

Measure out all the materials in similar-sized batch cans and dump them into the mixing drum.

Mark batch cans. Then you can fill them to the line each time, assured of the correct proportions.

rupture the concrete surface and make it scale off. The tiny bubbles of air in air-entrained concrete act as "relief valves" to take up pressures during freezing and thawing cycles without damage to the concrete. Air entrainment is a must for all concrete exposed to freezing and salt action. This includes patios, driveways, garage floors, sidewalks, curbs, walls, planters, etc.

Air-entrained concrete's other benefits make it highly desirable for use even in warm climates. The billions of bubbles act like ball bearings in the mix, lubricating it to increase its workability. Air-entrained concrete also is cohesive. It looks and feels "fatty." The disconnected air bubbles buoy up the pieces of coarse aggregate, keeping them from settling to the bottom and weakening the wall or slab.

If you live in a cold climate, make sure that your concrete is made with air-entraining cement. This is signified by the letter A after the type. You can use either Type IA or Type IIA. Both are air-entraining. Or you can buy a quart of air-entraining agent from a ready-mixed concrete producer. Take him an empty bottle or can. If it's *Darex,* use the quantities shown in the trial mix table. This is figured at the rate of one ounce per bag of cement.

The fourth "6" is for length of curing —at least six days. You can carry quality right up to the last step, but neglect proper curing and you'll end up with weak concrete that lacks durability. Concrete needs six days or more of curing to hold back evaporation of the mixing water until most of its strength has developed. If too much water evaporates, there will not be enough water left to react fully with every particle of cement. Proper curing can develop up to 50 percent more strength in concrete.

While the "6666" principle covers the four most important requirements of quality concrete, a few others are obvious:

Clean Water—Water that you can drink is almost always acceptable for making concrete.

Clean Aggregate—Aggregate should not contain any materials having harmful effects, such as dirt, clay, coal or plant matter. It also should be hard and durable. If you use unwashed aggregate from local pits or creeks, be sure that it has been proved to make good concrete. Most building materials dealers carry aggregates of known performance, but too many don't recognize the difference between concrete sand and mortar sand. The two are not interchangeable. Concrete sand contains particles of ¼ inch and less, while mortar sand has no particles anywhere near as big as ¼ inch. Mortar sand is fine like that you'd want for a sandbox. One good place to get tested aggregates is from your ready mix dealer.

Well-Graded Aggregate—Aggregate particles should have a range of sizes from the largest to the smallest. The big ones fill out the mix; the smaller one fill in spaces between the big ones; and so on down to dust-size particles. It's like a mixture of watermelons, cantaloupes, tomatoes, radishes, beans, peas, grape seeds and radish seeds all surrounded by glue. Not very taste-tempting, but a good range of sizes.

Now you're ready to mix concrete and get quality. A mixer should not be overloaded. The actual mixing size of a drum is about 60 percent of its stated volume. The identification plate attached to the mixer may give its working capacity. Size your batches to stay within this figure.

Prepackaged concrete mixes are a great convenience for small jobs. They are available in two types: one is a regular concrete mix with gravel; the other, a sand mix without gravel. Sand mix is ideal for thin sections, small precast items, etc. The materials for both are selected and carefully proportioned ready for adding water and mixing. Prepackaged mixes are usually available in 1-cubic-foot bags and smaller.

In hand-mixing, the benefits of air-entrained concrete are lost, for the mixing isn't vigorous enough to help the

A "stony mix" is too harsh for easy finishing; too much coarse aggregate and not enough sand.

"Sandy mix" contains too much sand, not enough coarse aggregate; finishes easily but is costly.

"Workable mix" is good. Spaces between particles of the coarse aggregate are all filled with sand.

If the mix is too stiff, add portland cement and water in the same proportions as the trial mix.

This quality concrete is too stiff to be poured into place. However, it is not too stiff to be worked.

air-entraining agent create the billions of air bubbles needed. Prepackaged mixes, therefore, don't contain an air-entraining agent. If you use them in a mixer, you still need to add air-entraining agent.

Small batches of concrete may be hand-mixed in a whelbarrow, on a platform or on a concrete slab. Dump the materials in a pile. Then make a depression in the pile and add some of the water. Mix and add a measured amount of water (at the rate of six gallons per bag of cement) until you get a stiff but workable mix. All the water should be in at this point. If the mix is too dry, reduce the amount of sand and gravel in the next batch. If too wet, add more sand and gravel, but never change the amount of water and cement.

The best way to mix concrete is with a concrete mixer. Any sizable job requires it. Machine-mixing not only saves your energy for placing and finishing, it does a better job of combining the aggregates. One man who's in good shape can handle the mixing, placing and finishing of one to two cubic yards of concrete in a day with a good-sized mixer.

The first step in mixing concrete is to make a trial mix. While a table can give you general proportions of sand and coarse aggregate to use in "6666" concrete, it cannot adjust them to the exact materials you will be using. The trial mix enables you to do this. No adjustments are needed in cement or water because these ingredients don't vary from place to place enough to affect the

concrete. Sand and coarse aggregate gradations vary, depending upon where the materials were obtained and how they were processed. If you select a good source and get the same materials every time you mix concrete, the proportions arrived at by your trial mix should not change.

A trial mix is one batch of concrete placed into the mixer, mixed, inspected and then adjusted, if necessary, for aggregate gradation. Make your first trial mix using the proportions in the "6666" concrete table already shown. The trial mixes in the table are designed around an average sand and gravel. If the one you are using is graded differently from the average, you may need to change the proportions given. Do this by adjusting the quantities of *aggregate*. Consider the cement and water proportions shown in the table constant for obtaining "6666" quality concrete.

Sand used in concrete nearly always contains some free water. When the sand is used in concrete, this excess water combines with the cement and thus must be taken into account in the six gallons of water per bag of cement. The "6666" table makes allowance for the free water in three types of sand that might be encountered. Give your sand the hand-squeeze test before you use the table.

The trial mix should be batched by weight. You'll notice that the table gives all proportions in pounds except the air-entraining agent. This allows you to use a bathroom scale to measure materials. It saves making one-cubic-

You can rent concrete mixer on wheels. It can be hitched to car, easily maneuvered where needed.

For quantities over 1 cubic yard, ready mixed concrete is the answer. Get plenty of assistance.

foot boxes, etc. However, don't forget to "zero" the scale with an empty batch-can on it. Once you get the trial mix adjusted to the aggregates you are using, put marks on your batch-cans and you'll no longer need the scale. From then on, batch to the marks. Galvanized pails or five-gallon buckets make handy batch-cans. Always keep one batch-can dry for cement.

A mixer should be batched as follows: Put about 10 percent of the water into the drum before adding the aggregate and cement. Add the rest of the water uniformly along with your dry materials. Leave about 10 percent to be added after all other materials are in the drum. Add air-entraining agent to the water.

All concrete should be thoroughly mixed and the materials uniformly distributed. This means that quality concrete should mix for at least one minute, and preferably for three minutes, *after* all the materials are in the drum.

When thoroughly mixed, dump out a sample of your trial mix into a wheelbarrow or batch-can and examine it for stiffness and workability. If it is not right, here is how to adjust the trial mix for your aggregate:

Too Wet—The mix contains too little aggregate for the amount of cement paste. Weigh out a little more sand and coarse aggregate. Add them to the mixer. Record the amounts it takes to get the mix the way it should be. Add these amounts to your trial mix totals, weigh out a second batch using these totals, mark your batch-cans and you're ready to go ahead with batch after batch of quality concrete.

Too Stiff—The mix contains too much sand and coarse aggregate. Reduce the

amounts of these added to subsequent batches until you get a workable mix. Never add more water. Instead, adjust the consistency of the mix by adjusting the sand and coarse aggregate.

Too Sandy—Make a second trial batch. Leave out some of the sand and add more stones. Keep weight records so that when you get the mix right, you'll know just how much sand and stones is enough.

Too Stony—Make a second trial batch. In it leave out some of the stones and add more sand. Write down the weights.

With practice, you may get so expert that you can judge consistency and sand-stone proportions while the concrete is mixing.

As long as the sand and coarse aggregate are the same ones as those used in making the adjusted trial batch, the proportions shouldn't need to be varied. The water content of the sand can vary, though, depending on whether the stockpile has been rained on recently. Check the sand before you start work and use proper water quantities from the trial-mix table to account for water changes in the sand.

All of the steps to getting "6666" concrete will make your project that much surer of lasting success.

Complete curing is last step in making quality concrete. Poly sheeting is the simplest method.

PLACING, FINISHING AND CURING

To make a lasting concrete slab

planning and timing are essential

One rule to remember in finishing concrete: work the surface as little as possible to get the finish you desire. Sounds simple and is. But the temptation to overwork concrete is tough to put down. Don't let it hang you up.

Your choice of finish should depend on your skill with a trowel. The very hardest finish to make is the steel-troweled smooth surface you see on most concrete. This finish is fine indoors for basement floors, garages and such. It is hard, takes lots of wear and cleans easily. But it's too slippery for use outdoors. For patios, sidewalks and driveways use a nonslip finish. One of the easiest nonslip surfaces to make is the metal float finish. That's METAL float, not steel trowel. Use an aluminum or magnesium float. A broomed finish is easy to make, too.

You can use a nonslip finish inside and avoid the hard-to-make steel-troweled finish completely. The surface will be harder to sweep and wash down and not as comfortable for roller-skating. Otherwise it will be serviceable.

If you must have the smooth-floor look, it might pay to hire a skilled cement finisher by the hour to produce it for you. You CAN do it yourself, but don't try to do too much in one day. An area of more than 100 square feet can get away from you on a hot, windy day. The part you gave a first-troweling may get past the stage for its second troweling before you finish the first-troweling elsewhere. This can happen to pros too. Watch it.

If you plan a float or broom finish, you can handle much more without danger of "losing it." Cool, damp weather helps too.

SLABS

Most concrete projects you'll build will be slab work. Every slab should be cast on a firm, dry subgrade (in-place soil) or subbase (special material). If your soil is sandy and well drained, you can cast a slab right on the ground. First remove all sod and vegetation. You can also cast on the ground if you live in a nonfreezing climate. Clay and other poorly drained soils call for a compacted 2-inch layer of crushed stones, gravel or sand to keep water away from the bottom of the slab. Sand is easier to shovel and grade but it should not be very wet when concrete-placing begins. Just damp.

"Mucky" soil should be dug out and replaced with gravel or crushed stones in 4-inch lifts. Tamp each one well.

Build forms for 4-inch-thick slabs out of 2x4's. For 6-inch slabs use 2x6's. These give slightly less thickness than the full 4 or 6 inches, of course, but that's the name of the game. Don't worry about it.

Brace forms by driving 1x2 or 2x2 wood stakes into the ground every 4 feet. In nailing through the stakes into the form it helps to back up the form with the head of a sledge hammer or other heavy object. Forms will strip easier later if you use double-headed form nails. Oil the forms with old crankcase oil so they'll strip from the concrete without sticking.

Gently curving forms can be made of doubled-up 1-inch lumber in place of the 2-inch. For sharper curves use ¼- or ⅜-inch plywood or hardboard bent and staked to the desired radius. Build up two or more layers until you have enough thickness to take the pressure of fresh concrete. The sharper your curve the less thickness is needed.

Forms for slabs may be level or sloped for drainage. In order to drain well, you'll need a slope of ⅛ to ¼ inch per foot.

TRANSPORTING CONCRETE

If you use ready mix try to have it dumped directly into the forms. This saves work. Otherwise you'll have to wheel it in and dump from the wheelbarrow. In a pinch you can use a bucket brigade, if you have enough helpers. It's hard on backs and buckets. Mix-your-own concrete will probably have to be transported by wheelbarrow.

Concrete should not be dumped in separate piles and raked together. Nor should it be placed in one pile and pushed or allowed to run into place. This practice makes weak slabs. The less pushing, shoving and raking you do, the better for both you and the concrete. Dump concrete against the forms as near to grade as possible. Start so that each succeeding load can be dumped against the previous one. This tends to compact the mix into place.

Any raking should be with a shovel or hoe. Never with a rake. Don't let water collect at the ends and corners of forms.

Whatever you do, keep your bare hands and feet out of concrete. Concrete not only abrades your skin, it eats through. That hurts.

Never place concrete on wet or frozen ground. On the other hand, in dry weather, dampen the subgrade slightly to keep it from drawing water out of the mix.

The ready-mix truck can be maneuvered to place the concrete mix just where you want it, thus saving work.

If your concrete can't be dumped directly onto the subgrade, then you can transport it with wheelbarrow.

FINISHING

After placing concrete, strike off the surface to the correct elevation. Form tops should be at this elevation so they can be used for supports for the straight-edge. Place the strikeboard across the forms and begin see-sawing along them. Advance an inch or so with each stroke. You'll soon see a roll of excess concrete form ahead of the screed. With air-entrained concrete this roll is typically round and plump, telling you there's air in the mix. The roll of extra concrete fills in any low spots.

If the roll gets too big, shovel some of it away.

Right after strike-off, get going with your bull float or darby. It works mortar to the surface while putting down ridges left by the strikeboard. The leading edge of the bull float should always be raised. This is done by raising or lowering the handle as it is pulled or pushed.

The secret to handling a darby without messing up your newly struck surface is to use a light touch. Hold up some of the weight of the darby if the mix is wet. Bear down a bit if it's stiff. Don't disturb the elevation, just smooth off the ridges. You'll soon get the hang of it.

EDGING AND JOINTING

Soon after bull floating, run all edges and joints with cutting and rounding tools. This is done by moving each tool back and forth on top of the slab. Always use a jointer against a straight-edge as a guide. An edger is run using the form as a guide. You needn't try for a smooth finish on the initial run. If you merely get the big stones out of the way, you've accomplished the purpose.

As you move the tool, keep from pressing hard. The flat portion is supposed to ride over the surface not make a deep impression in it.

Control joints should be placed 10 to 15 feet apart on floor, driveway and

A ½" asphalt-fiber isolation joint must be used between your new pour and your old concrete slab.

For a smooth edge, work the concrete up and down with shovel (or you can use a 2 x 4) next to the forms.

patio slabs, 4 to 5 feet apart on side-walks. If you space them too wide, you'll get intermittent cracks at random throughout the slab. Control joints put these cracks where you want them.

Try to locate joints at weakened planes in the slab. For instance, if there's a planter opening in a patio, joints should be arranged to come at this spot. That's where the slab will want to crack. Help it.

FLOATING

When the jointing is done, take a break. It will be a matter of minutes or hours until the surface is ready for hand-floating, the next step. If your mix was dry, the sun is shining on the slab and the weather hot and dry, you have only a little time. If your mix was wet, the slab is shaded and it's cold and damp, you have a long wait.

The purpose of floating is to compact the surface, remove humps, fill hollows and bring mortar to the surface for subsequent finishing. Swing the float over the surface in overlapping arcs. With air-entrained concrete, a light-weight metal float works best. A wood one may tend to tear the surface. Foat-ing gives a gritty texture to the surface and is great as a final finish for a side-walk, driveway or patio.

The exact timing of hand-floating is puzzling to most of us do-it-yourselfers. The tip-off is how the surface looks. It's different for air-entrained and nonair-entrained concrete.

Air-entrained concrete—Hand-float-ing operation should start before the surface gets too dry and tacky. Finish-ing may begin as soon as the concrete has begun to set. A good guide is to put one of your kneeboards onto the slab and kneel on it. When it sinks only 3/8 inch, start floating. If it sinks more than this, float over the depression to hide it and wait. Make your test in the first-placed section of the slab. This usually begins setting up first. Start your fin-ishing there, too.

Nonair-entrained concrete—Water bleeding out of nonair-entrained con-crete delays finishing. Never float a slab with surface water on it. Wait for the water to evaporate and for the water sheen to disappear. Squeegee it off by dragging a garden hose across, if it persists. The surface should be dull for finishing, not shiny.

STEEL-TROWELING

Where you want a smoother finish, you'll have to follow floating with steel-troweling. Begin troweling only after the concrete has set enough that an ex-cess of cement, water and fine sand isn't brought to the surface. This is nor-mally some time after floating, when the water sheen brought on by floating has disappeared. Too much "soup" at the surface makes a poor-wearing fin-ish.

During the first troweling, hold the trowel as flat against the concrete as

First strike the concrete off with a straightedge (2 x 4) resting it on the 2 x 4 forms on either side of the work.

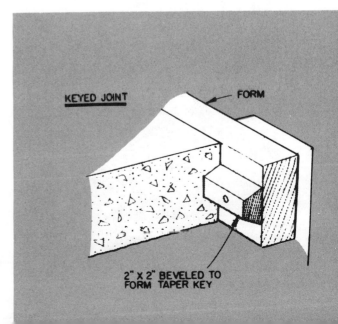

KEYED JOINT   FORM

2" X 2" BEVELED TO FORM TAPER KEY

possible without "digging in." If the trowel blade is tilted much at this stage, you may get a "washboard" finish.

When the water sheen disappears again, follow the first troweling with a second. Tilt the trowel more this time because the concrete is much stiffer and can take added pressure on a smaller blade area. Use a smaller trowel if you have one. It's easier on your wrist.

Kneeboards leave marks on the surface. Work backwards, troweling over the marks as you go. Float and trowel right over your initial grooves and edges, too. Then run them again, leaving everything smooth and finished-looking behind.

You may want more than two trowelings. Allow some time between them to let the concrete gain more strength.

If a really hard finish is needed, re-trowel the slab after it has hardened to

Raise the bull float handle high when pulling toward you, but then lower it when pushing away.

Use an easy stroke with the darby so the slab is smoothed and yet also without changing its elevation.

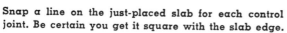

Snap a line on the just-placed slab for each control joint. Be certain you get it square with the slab edge.

Use a straight 1 x 12 board as a guide and platform for yourself when running control joints with a tool.

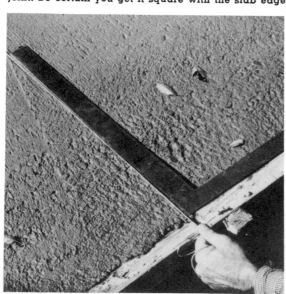

when you build it.

Every slab that meets an existing slab or wall should be separated from it with what is called an *isolation joint*. You can buy strips of ½x4-inch asphalt-impregnated material ready to use. Place them against the existing wall or slab with their tops at or above the level of the new slab. Any excess material can be sliced off after the new slab has hardened. An isolation joint permits independent movement be-

Begin hand-floating when the water sheen has disappeared. Move the float in smooth arcs, also evenly.

Kneeboards of ¾" plywood are moved one at a time. Work backwards to finish over any marks left by them.

Float and trowel right over joints, then run them again with a jointing tool. You can run the edges, too.

To keep the excess concrete from hampering the finishing operations scrape it clean from all the forms.

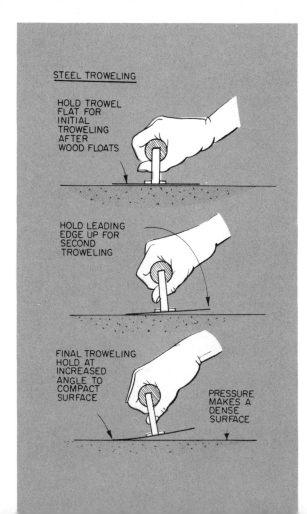

STEEL TROWELING

HOLD TROWEL FLAT FOR INITIAL TROWELING AFTER WOOD FLOATS

HOLD LEADING EDGE UP FOR SECOND TROWELING

FINAL TROWELING HOLD AT INCREASED ANGLE TO COMPACT SURFACE

PRESSURE MAKES A DENSE SURFACE

tween two concrete structures without restraining them.

SPECIAL FINISHES

You have a choice of an unlimited number of textures and designs for your new slab. Many of them are much easier to make than a steel-troweled finish. They all start after the concrete has been struck off and bull-floated.

Broom Finish—For an excellent broom finish, use a soft hair broom for a mild texture, a stiff bristle broom for a coarse texture. Do the brooming soon after the first hand-floating. A push-broom works best. Lay it on the surface and draw it across the slab toward you. If small balls of concrete "pill" up from the surface, it's too early for good brooming. Wait. If you have to bear down on the broom to produce a texture, get going. Time is short.

Swirl—Make a swirl design by moving the float, trowel or other finishing tool in overlapping semicircular arcs. Hold it flat on the surface. The smoother the swirling tool, the finer the texture. Swirling is always the final finishing step.

Stipple—This effect is created with a broom. Pound the hardening floated surface with the bristles of a stiff broom. You may soften the effect if desired, by steel-troweling over the stipples.

Rock salt embedment—This creates a texture looking somewhat like rough marble. To make it, scatter rock salt over the fresh floated surface and press it in with a trowel. Don't start the process too early or your salt will sink out of sight into the slab. It should rest on the surface. Later the salt itself washes out, leaving pockets. Don't use this method in freezing climates.

Leaf impressions—Patterns resembling leaf fossils can be made by troweling real leaves into a fresh concrete surface. The leaves should be embedded after the first steel-troweling. Get them deep enough so you can trowel over their tops without dislodging any, but not so deep that mortar is deposited over them. Remove the leaves after the concrete has set.

Incised patterns—Your ingenuity is

the only limit to the variety of incised (engraved-in) patterns you can apply to a concrete surface. Joints can be troweled to look like flagstones. Star patterns can be created by jabbing the edge of a trowel into the surface in intersecting lines. Different sizes of cans may be used like cookie cutters to make circle patterns. Kitchen utensils you can pirate and use are tablespoons, zig-zag cutters and forks.

CURING

Curing is one of the most important concrete operations, often the most neglected. The newly placed concrete must be protected from drying out by the sun or by a dry wind. Any method that keeps the concrete wet will work —either by adding water, or by preventing evaporation.

Some common curing methods use burlap or canvas coverings kept continuously wet for six days. Polyethylene sheeting also can be used, if the edges are held down with piles of dirt or sand. Place the coverings as soon as the surface has hardened enough that it won't be marred. Other methods of curing are coverings of earth, sand or damp straw.

Another method is to place a lawn sprinkler or soaker hose where it will keep the concrete continuously wet for six-day curing period. Leaving the forms in place will cure a concrete wall.

A great new method is to spray, roll or brush on a curing agent. Some are pigmented. Some clear. Pigmented ones go on more evenly. All soon weather away after they've done the job. One good one I know of is W. R. Meadows' Sealtight *Cure-Hard*. Only one coat is normally needed.

Remember, that the longer concrete is cured—even beyond six days—the better it will be. "6667" or "6668" concrete is even better than "6666."

In both hot- and cold-weather concrete construction, special precautions are necessary. You won't feel like working outdoors when the weather is too cold for normal procedures, but you may place concrete during weather that is hot enough to need special treatment. Plan ahead. Have the necessary

On final troweling, after the concrete is firm, tilt handle as you draw it evenly and firmly over the surface.

Any marks left can be removed by troweling right over them. Support one hand on the float for safety.

For a non-slip broomed texture, pull a hair broom over the just-floated slab, running in straight lines.

equipment and materials on hand. Build sunshades, windbreaks. Consider starting the job after the heat of the day has passed. Sprinkle aggregate piles, use ice in place of some of the mix water. Sprinkle the subgrade and forms before placing cement.

Protect against evaporation by covering the surface until you're ready to finish it. Don't delay placement. Don't let the set get ahead of you. Have plenty of help on hand. Start the cure as soon as the surface will take it with-

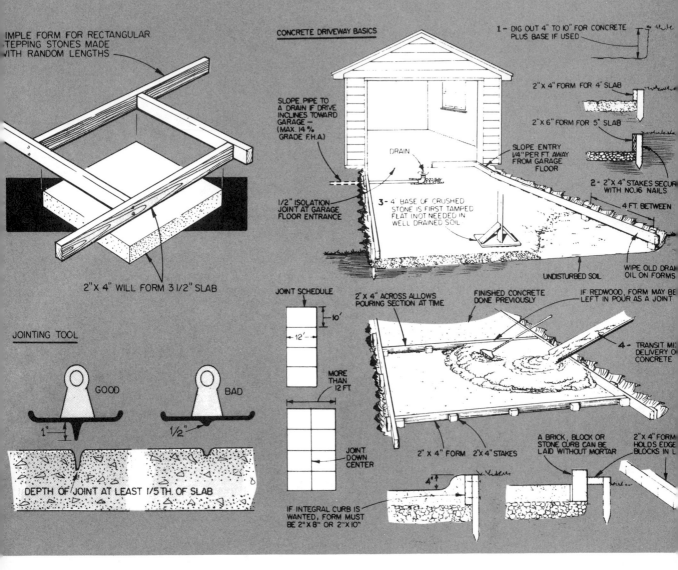

SIMPLE FORM FOR RECTANGULAR STEPPING STONES MADE WITH RANDOM LENGTHS

2"X 4" WILL FORM 3 1/2" SLAB

JOINTING TOOL

GOOD

BAD

1"

1/2"

DEPTH OF JOINT AT LEAST 1/5TH. OF SLAB

CONCRETE DRIVEWAY BASICS

SLOPE PIPE TO A DRAIN IF DRIVE INCLINES TOWARD GARAGE — (MAX. 14% GRADE F.H.A.)

DRAIN

1/2" ISOLATION JOINT AT GARAGE FLOOR ENTRANCE

3-4" BASE OF CRUSHED STONE IS FIRST TAMPED FLAT (NOT NEEDED IN WELL DRAINED SOIL

SLOPE ENTRY 1/4" PER FT. AWAY FROM GARAGE FLOOR

1 - DIG OUT 4" TO 10" FOR CONCRETE PLUS BASE IF USED

2"X 4" FORM FOR 4" SLAB

2"X 6" FORM FOR 5" SLAB

2 - 2"X 4" STAKES SECUR WITH NO.16 NAILS

4 FT. BETWEEN

WIPE OLD DRAIN OIL ON FORMS

UNDISTURBED SOIL

JOINT SCHEDULE

10'

12'

MORE THAN 12 FT.

JOINT DOWN CENTER

IF INTEGRAL CURB IS WANTED, FORM MUST BE 2"X 8" OR 2"X 10"

2"X 4" ACROSS ALLOWS POURING SECTION AT TIME

FINISHED CONCRETE DONE PREVIOUSLY

IF REDWOOD, FORM MAY BE LEFT IN POUR AS A JOINT

4 - TRANSIT MIX DELIVERY OF CONCRETE

2"X 4" FORM   2"X 4" STAKES

A BRICK, BLOCK OR STONE CURB CAN BE LAID WITHOUT MORTAR

2"X 4" FORM HOLDS EDGE BLOCKS IN L

4"

out damage. All of these steps will make your hot-weather job that much surer of success.

CASTING WALLS

Walls are made differently from slabs. Only the top surface may need to be floated, troweled and edged. The rest of the wall will take on whatever finish is provided by the form. For this reason and others, plywood is an excellent material for forms. It produces a smooth wall surface. What's more, it can be bent to form curving walls. They're often more pleasing to the eye and are stronger. Order A-C fir plywood and place the "A" side toward the wall. The face grain should run across the 2x4 supports. If you want the form to be reused many times,

make it of exterior grade plywood. Plywood 5/8 to 3/4-inch thick needs supports every 12 inches. Supports for thicker plywood forms can be placed 16 inches on centers.

A good wall finish free of honeycombs can be produced by tapping the concrete-loaded forms with a hammer. This forces course aggregate away from the form and dislodges trapped air. Consolidate concrete in the forms by spading it with a shovel, especially next to the form. For uniformity, place concrete in layers not more than 12 to 18 inches deep along the wall form. Thoroughly consolidate each layer before placing the next one. Do not drop concrete more than three or four feet into forms. Use a chute instead. Dropping makes the coarse aggregate separate from the rest of the mix. You can make the chute out of a 2-inch-thick plank with 1x4's or 1x6's nailed-on the sides.

All portland cement made in the United States and Canada is designed to meet rigid federal standards for quality. You needn't worry about it being good as long as the bag contains the statement, "Meets ASTM C150." Some imported portland cements may be good, too. See that they contain the ASTM C150 designation.

U.S.-made portland cement comes in 94-pound bags. Each bag contains 1 cubic foot of cement. On the bag the type of cement is designated. There are five types, designated by Roman numerals I through V. Type I is normal portland cement. It's the kind you should use. However, if you want your project to develop strength quickly, say in one to three days, you could use Type III high-early-strength portland cement. It may be tough to buy. Type I or Type II is usually the only kind you can get.

If the designation on the bag shows Type IA or Type IIA, it's air-entraining portland cement. If you use this type, you need not add an air-entraining agent to the mix. Another type of cement is white portland cement. Use it where you want a pure white color or for bright colored concrete using mineral pigments. Still another type of cement is masonry cement. Use it for mixing mortar, but never for making concrete. The lime it contains weakens the mix.

Plastic cements are widely sold in some parts of the country. Plasticizing agents have been added to ordinary Type I cement during manufacture. They're commonly used for making mortar, plaster and stucco, but not concrete. What you want is portland cement, Type I or II, Type IA or IIA for most uses.

Portland cement that has been stored where moisture can get at it sometimes hardens in the bag. This differs from a condition called "warehouse pack," which is a stiffening of cement around the edges of the bag. Warehouse pack can be cured by rolling the bag on the floor. When it's used, cement should be free-flowing and free of lumps that can't be broken between your thumb and finger.

A liquid curing compound may be sprayed, rolled or brushed onto surface after the finishing operation.

Attractive swirl finish is made by swirling a light weight metal float over the surface. It's a final step.

A flagstone effect is cut into concrete with a bent pipe. You should retool after each surface troweling.

Leaf impressions are made with real leaves. Flatten them into the surface and then finish gently over them.

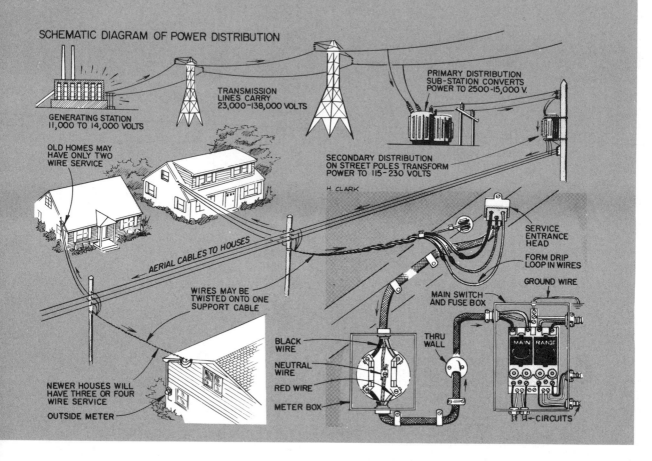

SCHEMATIC DIAGRAM OF POWER DISTRIBUTION

GENERATING STATION 11,000 TO 14,000 VOLTS

TRANSMISSION LINES CARRY 23,000-138,000 VOLTS

PRIMARY DISTRIBUTION SUB-STATION CONVERTS POWER TO 2500-15,000 V.

OLD HOMES MAY HAVE ONLY TWO WIRE SERVICE

SECONDARY DISTRIBUTION ON STREET POLES TRANSFORM POWER TO 115-230 VOLTS

H. CLARK

SERVICE ENTRANCE HEAD

FORM DRIP LOOP IN WIRES

GROUND WIRE

AERIAL CABLES TO HOUSES

WIRES MAY BE TWISTED ONTO ONE SUPPORT CABLE

MAIN SWITCH AND FUSE BOX

THRU WALL

MAIN RANGE

BLACK WIRE

NEUTRAL WIRE

RED WIRE

METER BOX

NEWER HOUSES WILL HAVE THREE OR FOUR WIRE SERVICE

OUTSIDE METER

CIRCUITS

HOW YOUR HOUSE IS WIRED

A well-wired house provides circuits for present and future needs

All house wiring consists of these components: power lines, service entrance, meter, service panel with overcurrent devices (fuses, circuit breakers), and house circuits. Since local electrical codes vary considerably, systems around the nation are not all exactly alike. Basically they are, though.

The beginning of the house wiring system is the point where your house power lines attach to the power company's lines at the top of the pole. From there the lines are run either overhead or underground to a convenient point on your house. The nicest, most modern service enters below ground.

Most house service entrance wiring uses either two or three wires. Having just two wires tells you that your house receives only 120-volt power, way under-wired for today's many needs.

Two wires comprise (1) a neutral wire, which is sometimes uninsulated, and (2) a "hot" wire, which is always insulated. The electric potential across the two is 120 volts, or close to it. The neutral is a current-carrying wire, even though it's grounded at the house entrance and often at the utility pole. Always treat it as such.

THREE WIRES GOOD

If your house has three entrance wires, it's a good sign. They provide 120-140-volt power. One wire is a neutral wire. The others are "hot" wires. The electric potential from either "hot" wire to the neutral wire is 120 volts.

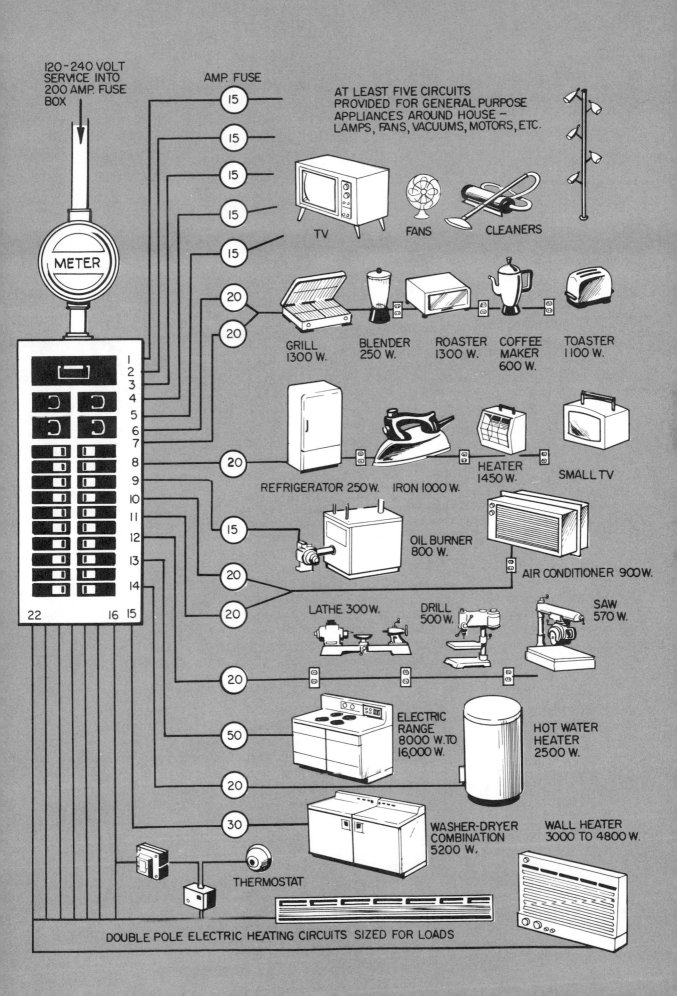

120-240 VOLT
SERVICE INTO
200 AMP. FUSE
BOX

AMP. FUSE

15

15

15

15

15

AT LEAST FIVE CIRCUITS
PROVIDED FOR GENERAL PURPOSE
APPLIANCES AROUND HOUSE —
LAMPS, FANS, VACUUMS, MOTORS, ETC.

TV

FANS

CLEANERS

METER

20

20

GRILL
1300 W.

BLENDER
250 W.

ROASTER
1300 W.

COFFEE
MAKER
600 W.

TOASTER
1100 W.

1
2
3
4
5
6
7
8
9
10
11
12
13
14
22   16 15

20

REFRIGERATOR 250 W.   IRON 1000 W.

HEATER
1450 W.

SMALL TV

15

OIL BURNER
800 W.

20

AIR CONDITIONER 900 W.

20

LATHE 300 W.

DRILL
500 W.

SAW
570 W.

20

50

ELECTRIC
RANGE
8000 W. TO
16,000 W.

HOT WATER
HEATER
2500 W.

20

30

WASHER-DRYER
COMBINATION
5200 W.

WALL HEATER
3000 TO 4800 W.

THERMOSTAT

DOUBLE POLE ELECTRIC HEATING CIRCUITS SIZED FOR LOADS

Modern circuit breaker service panel has main 100-ampere (or larger) breaker, three (or more) 20-amp special appliance breakers, plus twelve circuit breakers for lights and appliances. Keep a chart on box door.

Fused service panel in older home has main fused pull-out block (upper left), and pull-out block for range (upper right), plus six smaller fused circuits for lights and all appliances. Keep a chart on these fuses.

The potential across both hot wires is 240 volts. Depending on which wires are used, motors and appliances can use either voltage. If overhead, the wires are attached firmly to the house around insulators at least 10 feet above the ground. At that point "drip" loops of wire are connected to each wire and run into what is called an *entrance head*. Drip loops keep water from following wires into the entrance head.

From the entrance head wires run down the outside wall with a protective covering to the electric meter. Wires from the meter enter the house and run to a service panel. It is located nearby, to keep costly runs of heavy wires to a minimum. Since the entrance wiring has to carry every ampere of power that will be needed in the whole house, entrance wires must be heavy.

Moreover, they are so closely bunched that any heat formed is slow to dissipate.

HOUSE POWER

The service panel contains one or two large cartridge fuses, one for each hot wire. These may be rated at 30 amperes, 60, 100, 150 or even as much as 200 amperes and more. They indicate the total electric power available in your house. Sometimes, in modern panels, a pair of circuit breakers are used in place of fuses. A house with only 30-amp service, which usually employs two No. 8 wires, is considered inadequately wired. If your house has 30-amp service, you need to start at the pole, renewing everything up to and including the service panel.

Heavier 60-amp service is minimum. This uses three No. 6 wires, usually. It's not bad, unless you have (or want) an electric range, water heater and clothes dryer. It gives ample power for lighting and small portable appliances, but nothing extra for the big power-consuming appliances (see list).

Now considered best for homes with up to 3000 square feet of floor space is 100-ampere service. This makes use of three No. 3 wires (with RHW rubber insulation) or three No. 2 wires, most often. It provides service for lights and for small and major appliances that total up to 10,000 watts in power consumption.

All-electric homes with heating and air-conditioning require 150- and 200-amp service using 1/0 or 3/0 wire, respectively, with RHW rubber insulation.

HOUSE CIRCUITS

An adequately wired house provides circuits for all present and future needs. Each circuit takes off from the service panel. There the black wire of the circuit is fastened to an overcurrent device that protects the wires from being overloaded. This device is either a fuse or a circuit breaker. If the circuit is a 15-amp one, it uses No. 14 copper wire or No. 12 aluminum wire. A 20-amp circuit must use larger No. 12 copper or No. 10 aluminum wire. Aluminum wire is "relaxed" and easy to work. The larger size requirement is a drawback in making splices and in conduit runs where the maximum number of wires is limited according to wire size.

Only the "hot" side of any circuit is fused. The neutral side—the white wire —must never be fused. The white wire is connected to one of the terminals on the neutral strip inside the service panel. These make a direct unfused connection with the neutral entrance wire and with the ground connection.

The service panel itself and its grounding terminals are connected to a metal water pipe in the house. Ordinarily, this connection must be on the

HEAVY CURRENT APPLIANCES (AVERAGE POWER REQUIREMENTS)

Water heater — 2000 to 4500 watts
Range — 8,000 to 16,000 watts
Garbage disposer — 900 watts
Dishwasher (heating-type) — 1800 watts
Freezer, 12 cu. ft. — 600 watts
Electric clothes dryer — 4500 to 8700 watts
Automatic clothes washer — 650 to 900 watts
Fuel-fired heating plant — 100 to 800 watts
Central air conditioning — 5000 watts
Water pump — 300 to 700 watts
Built-in room heater — 1600 watts

MAXIMUM LENGTH OF CIRCUIT (FEET)

WATTS	No. 14	No. 12	No. 10	No. 8
500	100	200	300	400
1000	70	100	175	300
1800*	40	70	100	150
2400**		50	80	125

*15-ampere circuit maximum
**20-ampere circuit maximum

ALLOWABLE CURRENT-CARRYING CAPACITY OF INSULATED CONDUCTORS (LOWEST CURRENT-CARRYING INSULATION TYPES)

WIRE SIZE	Copper	Aluminum
No. 14	15	- -
No. 12	20	15
No. 10	30	25
No. 8	40	30
No. 6	55	40
No. 4	70	55
No. 3	80	65
No. 2	95	75
No. 1	110	85
No. 0	125	100
No. 2/0	145	115
No. 3/0	165	130

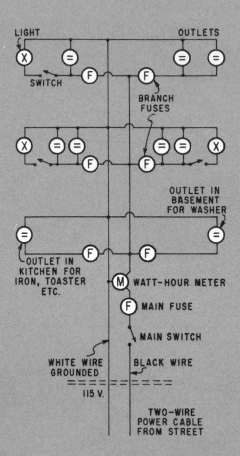

LIGHT   OUTLETS

SWITCH

BRANCH FUSES

OUTLET IN BASEMENT FOR WASHER

OUTLET IN KITCHEN FOR IRON, TOASTER ETC.

M WATT-HOUR METER

F MAIN FUSE

MAIN SWITCH

WHITE WIRE GROUNDED

BLACK WIRE

115 V.

TWO-WIRE POWER CABLE FROM STREET

Top diagram shows basic hookup of two-wire power distribution generally found in older residences. Bottom drawing shows basic three-wire system, which brings both 115 and 230 volts for use in modern homes.

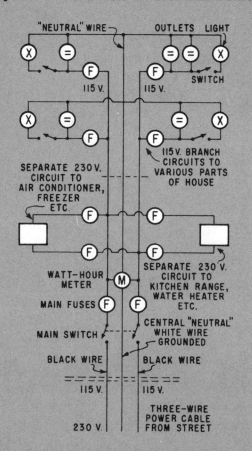

"NEUTRAL" WIRE   OUTLETS LIGHT

115 V.   115 V.

SWITCH

115 V. BRANCH CIRCUITS TO VARIOUS PARTS OF HOUSE

SEPARATE 230 V. CIRCUIT TO AIR CONDITIONER, FREEZER ETC.

WATT-HOUR METER

SEPARATE 230 V. CIRCUIT TO KITCHEN RANGE, WATER HEATER ETC.

MAIN FUSES

CENTRAL "NEUTRAL" WHITE WIRE GROUNDED

MAIN SWITCH

BLACK WIRE   BLACK WIRE

115 V.   115 V.

230 V.

THREE-WIRE POWER CABLE FROM STREET

OVERLOADED

MAX. LOAD 2400 WATTS   1300 WATTS

120 VOLTS

20 AMP.

NO. 12

3000 WATTS OVERLOADED

600 WATTS   1100 WATTS

O.K.

MAX. LOAD NOW 4800 WATTS

20 AMP.   20 AMP.

DOUBLE BREAKER

street side of a water meter, or the water meter must be bypassed with a grounding wire. This, so that a good ground will be intact, if the water meter is removed for repairs. In houses without underground piping the ground connection is made to a long copper rod or galvanized pipe driven into the ground. Bare grounding wires or the metal conduit in every run throughout house circuits carry ground continuity to every outlet. Never ground to a gas pipe or to a plumbing system with a plastic entrance main. The white wire is a *neutral*, not a ground. Only in 3-wire 240-volt circuits is it used as a grounding wire. Good grounding protects house wiring against lightning and shocks caused by barbed wires in circuit or appliances.

SAFETY PLUGS

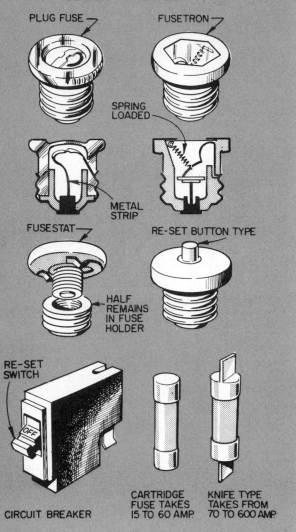

PLUG FUSE

FUSETRON

SPRING LOADED

METAL STRIP

FUSESTAT

RE-SET BUTTON TYPE

HALF REMAINS IN FUSE HOLDER

RE-SET SWITCH

OFF

CIRCUIT BREAKER

CARTRIDGE FUSE TAKES 15 TO 60 AMP.

KNIFE TYPE TAKES FROM 70 TO 600 AMP.

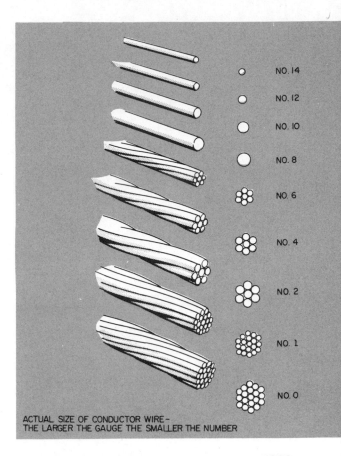

NO. 14
NO. 12
NO. 10
NO. 8
NO. 6
NO. 4
NO. 2
NO. 1
NO. 0

ACTUAL SIZE OF CONDUCTOR WIRE—
THE LARGER THE GAUGE THE SMALLER THE NUMBER

HOLDS MAIN FUSES

A main disconnect inside the service panel holds the main fuses. Pulling this out cuts off all power to the house. If the main protection uses circuit breakers, they can be turned off to cut power to the house.

Fuses or breakers are wired integrally with the service panel, to divide equally both "hot" sides of the circuit.

House circuits are classed as general purpose, appliance or special purpose.

General purpose circuits serve house lights and receptacles for small appliances. Modern ones are 20-amp. One 20-ampere general purpose circuit is recommended for each 500 square feet of floorspace. One 15-amp general purpose circuit should serve only 375 square feet. For instance, a 2000-square-foot house would need at least four general purpose 20-amp circuits. This is minimum. Five such circuits would be better. You can put as many outlets as you want on a circuit, but don't exceed the 500/375 square feet of floorspace served. Also don't wire the circuit to serve more appliances than its capacity will handle. Ordinarily, if you don't exceed the floorspace maximum, the circuit should not be overloaded. A circuit serving a workshop would be an exception. Big motors use lots of amps.

KITCHEN CIRCUITS

The National Code requires at least two 20-amp ground-type circuits for kitchen, laundry and dining room appliances. These must be separate from any lighting circuit. Three such circuits would be better.

General purpose circuits should include enough convenience receptacles —those not allocated for any special appliance— so there is one within every

HOUSE CIRCUIT WIRING

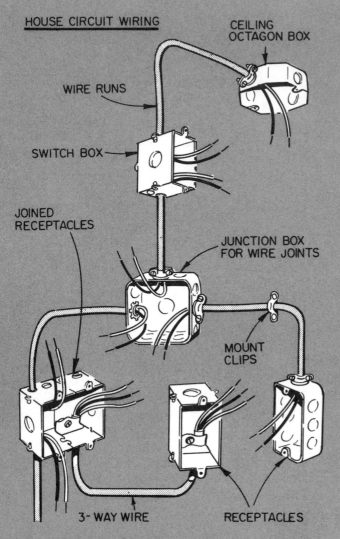

WIRE RUNS

CEILING
OCTAGON BOX

SWITCH BOX

JOINED
RECEPTACLES

JUNCTION BOX
FOR WIRE JOINTS

MOUNT
CLIPS

3- WAY WIRE

RECEPTACLES

LIGHT CIRCUIT WIRING

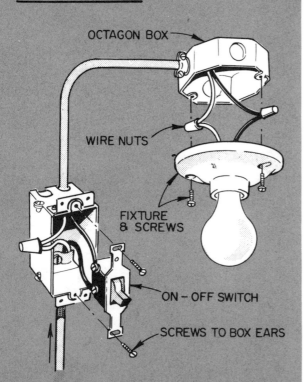

OCTAGON BOX

WIRE NUTS

FIXTURE
& SCREWS

ON - OFF SWITCH

SCREWS TO BOX EARS

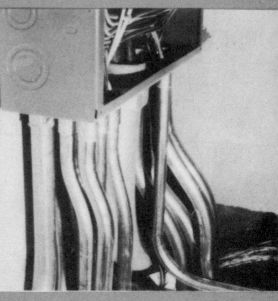

All circuits lead away from service panel, here in thin
wall conduit, and they travel to various parts of house.

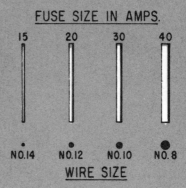

FUSE SIZE IN AMPS.

15	20	30	40
NO.14	NO.12	NO.10	NO.8

WIRE SIZE

12 feet of running wall space. This
gives flexibility to furniture arrangement and does away with the need for
many extension cords. In the kitchen,
you need receptacles every 4 feet along
counter space for plugging in small appliances. You also need outdoor, basement workshop and garage outlets to
make house wiring fully useful.

Special purpose circuits serve heavy
current-using appliances such as a
range, dishwasher, waste disposal, furnace, well pump, electric clothes dryer
and water heater. Some of these are
240-volt circuits wired with three-con-
ductor cable containing the black "hot"
wire, the white neutral wire and another "hot" wire coded red. The circuit
may be wired to a special 240-volt appliance receptacle or directly to the

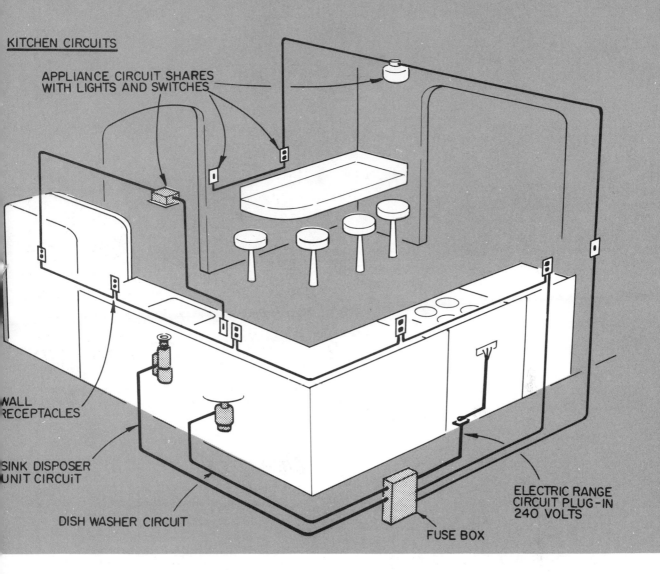

KITCHEN CIRCUITS

APPLIANCE CIRCUIT SHARES
WITH LIGHTS AND SWITCHES

WALL
RECEPTACLES

SINK DISPOSER
UNIT CIRCUIT

DISH WASHER CIRCUIT

FUSE BOX

ELECTRIC RANGE
CIRCUIT PLUG-IN
240 VOLTS

box on the appliance or motor. Any appliance or motor which does not plug in must have some other means of quick disconnect. This usually means that a switch box must be provided within sight of the appliance.

TOOLS GO SLUGGISH

Voltage drop can be a problem in long runs to circuits. For instance, a house that is 70 feet long needs a larger size wire for a run from the service panel at one end to the attic at the other. Voltage drop makes tools and appliances sluggish and slow to do what they're supposed to. Lights dim when heavy-draw appliances are used. See the accompanying chart.

Some houses also contain sub-panels, branches that draw power from power takeoff lugs on the fused side of the main service panel. These sub-panels contain fuses or circuit breakers of their own. Separate house circuits take off from the sub-panels to serve the house, garage or out buildings. In long houses the sub-panel may be used to avoid voltage drop in overly long circuits. Voltage drop is an electrical bad actor. Good wiring is planned to avoid it.

A typical adequately wired house may contain five general purpose circuits, three kitchen-laundry-dining room appliance circuits and 10 special purpose circuits. This is a tremendous difference from the two-circuit houses some of us grew up in.

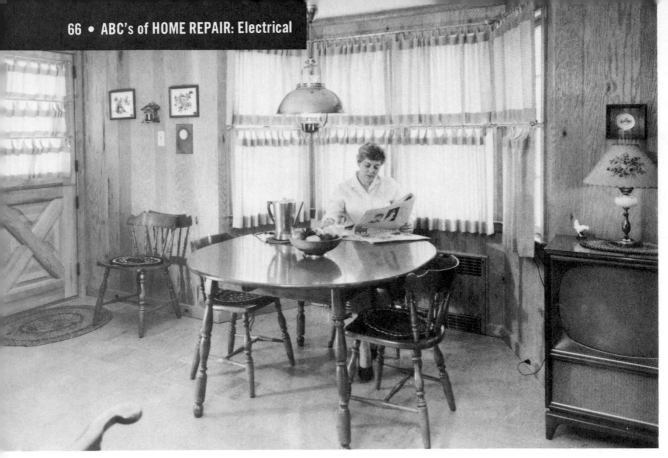

In designing your kitchen, it's possible to get metal plug-mold raceways that look much like an ordinary baseboard, yet allow you to plug into them at intervals around the room. This is a most handy necessity.

HOW TO ADD NEW LIGHTS AND OUTLETS

Updating the electrical system in

your house greatly modernizes it

A home that has too few lights and convenience outlets can be electrically up-dated without too much effort. The Saturday morning electrician can tackle one added outlet, one added light at a time and soon have all the conveniences of modern wiring. New electrical lights and outlets are merely extensions of the present electrical system. The system must, however, be adequate to carry the load (see the chapter on wiring an addition or vacation home). If your electrical system measures up, you can add new receptacles and lights wherever you need them.

Modern convenience dictates that there be a wall receptacle every 12 feet around the room on long walls, plus an outlet on each wall under 12 feet long. Outlets are needed at 4-foot intervals in kitchens. One should be at each work area. You also need at least one outlet by the mirror in the bathroom. Older houses may have only one outlet per wall, or even one per room.

You may add outlets in between or put new outlets on walls that don't already have them. Study your present extension cord system to see where new outlets are most needed. Then put them there.

Outdoors, a weatherproof outlet is needed near the front entrance and two

ENERGY MONEY SAVER IDEA — YARD LIGHTING

While cost of lighting your yard or entrance may seem small, the continued use of many lights adds substantially to your electric bill. As an example, if your electric rate is 5 cents per kilowatt hour (1000 watts burning one hour), a 100 watt incandescent bulb that is on 10 hours a day (as might be the case in a yard light) will cost you 5 cents per day—or $1.50 per month. Not much you may say, but four such yard lights add up to $6 per month, or $72 per year—and more if your rate is higher than 5 cents per KWH. You can save money by placing such a yard light circuit on a timer that can be adjusted to turn your lights on and off automatically at exactly the desired time. Timers such as these consume about as much electricity as an electric clock (about 100 watts per 24 hour day) and at 5 cents per KWH the operating cost would be 15 cents per month. But when properly programmed they can save you in excess of ten times their operating cost and save you the trouble of remembering when to turn a light on or off.

Another popular way to turn lights on and off is to use a photo electric cell. These are sensitive to daylight and will turn a light off as the sun begins to rise and lights on as night approaches. However, for home use the timer has the advantage of being able to be programmed so lights can be turned on at bedtime, long after the sun has set, and in the still dark hours of morning, long before sunrise.

are needed close to any outdoor living area. The garage needs at least one outlet per car.

Light is needed in the modern home for safety and convenience, both indoors and outdoors. For the safety of your family and guests there should be ample light from street and driveway to the entrance, as well as throughout the house interior from attic to basement. Fluorescent lamps can be of a lower wattage than incandescent bulbs because they put out more light per watt.

ARCHITECTURAL LIGHTING

Architectural or built-in lights give the general illumination a room needs if table and floor lamps are not used. Built right into the walls or ceilings and switched from the wall, the lighting units can be made to harmonize

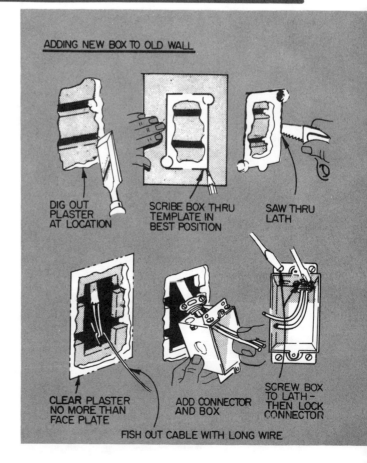

ADDING NEW BOX TO OLD WALL

DIG OUT PLASTER AT LOCATION

SCRIBE BOX THRU TEMPLATE IN BEST POSITION

SAW THRU LATH

CLEAR PLASTER NO MORE THAN FACE PLATE

ADD CONNECTOR AND BOX

SCREW BOX TO LATH — THEN LOCK CONNECTOR

FISH OUT CABLE WITH LONG WIRE

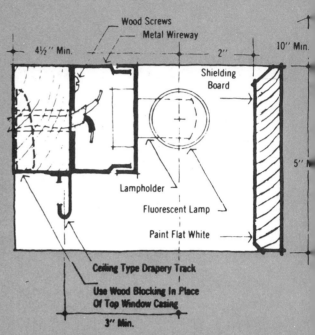

Valances are used at windows to provide uplight that reflects off ceiling for general room lighting, and down-light for drapery accent. There must be at least three inches from lamp center to drapery track to insure that draperies will be uniformly lighted. When the lights are closer to the ceiling than 10 inches, use a closed top to prevent ceiling brightness and glare.

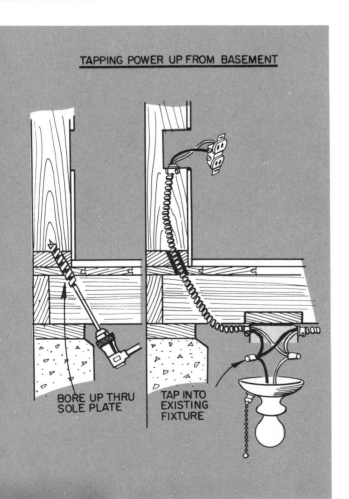

TAPPING POWER UP FROM BASEMENT

BORE UP THRU SOLE PLATE

TAP INTO EXISTING FIXTURE

with the room. Sometimes the unit barely shows behind an opening in the ceiling. Architectural lighting makes a wall or ceiling the main source of light. The basic architectural lighting units for walls—valance, cornices, wall brackets—are formed of three basic parts: Baked white enamel channels, fluorescent tubes to fit the channels, and a faceboard. You can buy the whole unit ready to install, or buy only the channels and tubes and make the faceboard to go with them.

A wall switch at the entrance to each room should control at least one light or fixture in the room. Then you'll never have to walk into a dark room. The light can be a ceiling or wall fixture or a lamp that's plugged into a switched receptacle. Multiple switches are needed at all entrances more than 10 feet apart, as well as at the head and foot of stairways.

ADDING OUTLETS

The installation of new electrical outlets (here *outlets* means lights as well as receptacles) is somewhat different in an older house than in a new

MAXIMUM WIRES IN A BOX				
		No.	No.	No.
Box type	Box size	14	12	10
Junction box	3¼"×1½" oct.	5	4	4
Junction box	4"×1½" oct.	8	7	6
Multi-purpose box	4"×4"×1½"	11	10	9
Switch box	2"×3"×1½"	3	3	3
Switch box	2"×3"×2½"	6	5	5
Handy box	2"×4"×1½"	5	4	4

one. Holes must be cut for the new boxes. Cables have to be pulled through the walls, floors, and ceilings. Often you must cut access holes in walls and ceilings to fish cables through them.

The first step is to locate the new outlets and cut openings for the boxes. Always locate a new outlet between framing members. Find studs or joists by tapping or with a stud-locator. The best box location is a spot 4 to 5 inches from a joist or stud. Put switches 48 inches above the floor, receptacles 12 inches. Wall light fixtures should be 66 to 70 inches above the floor. If you can, use large 2×3-inch boxes that are 2½ inches deep.

If you are cutting into a lath-and-plaster wall, center your box opening over one full oath and parts of two others. This leaves good mounting for the top and bottom of the box. Use the template shown in the drawing, tracing it onto the wall. Drill four half-inch holes as shown. Then saw out the plug with a hacksaw blade. The blade's teeth should point toward you to cut on the *pull* stroke.

GETTING POWER

The next step is to locate a source of electricity. The easiest place to tap power is in the basement or attic, immediately below or above the new outlet. You can also bring power from a wall receptacle or from a light circuit. When tapping into lights and switches you'll have to open the box to tell whether there is a neutral (white) wire. Either the light or the switch will have it.

When you find a convenient box where power can be tapped, make sure

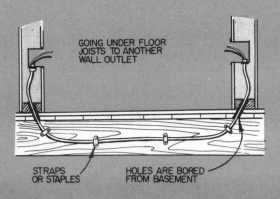

GOING UNDER FLOOR JOISTS TO ANOTHER WALL OUTLET

STRAPS OR STAPLES   HOLES ARE BORED FROM BASEMENT

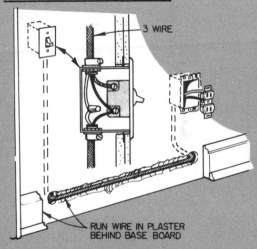

ADDING WALL OUTLET BEYOND A SWITCH

3 WIRE

RUN WIRE IN PLASTER BEHIND BASE BOARD

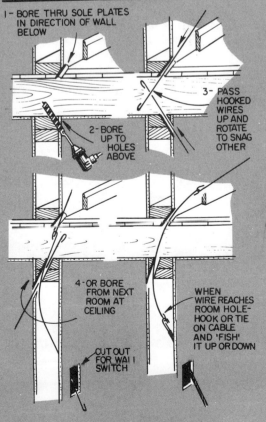

HOW TO 'FISH' A WIRE THROUGH WALLS

1 - BORE THRU SOLE PLATES IN DIRECTION OF WALL BELOW

2 - BORE UP TO HOLES ABOVE

3 - PASS HOOKED WIRES UP AND ROTATE TO SNAG OTHER

4 - OR BORE FROM NEXT ROOM AT CEILING

WHEN WIRE REACHES ROOM HOLE-HOOK OR TIE ON CABLE AND 'FISH' IT UP OR DOWN

CUT OUT FOR WALL SWITCH

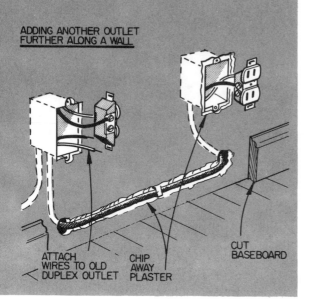

ADDING ANOTHER OUTLET
FURTHER ALONG A WALL

ATTACH
WIRES TO OLD
DUPLEX OUTLET

CHIP
AWAY
PLASTER

CUT
BASEBOARD

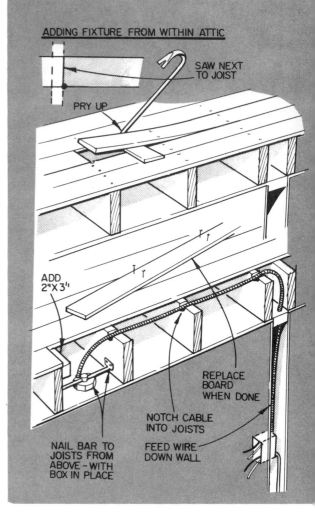

ADDING FIXTURE FROM WITHIN ATTIC

SAW NEXT
TO JOIST

PRY UP

ADD
2"X3"

NAIL BAR TO
JOISTS FROM
ABOVE – WITH
BOX IN PLACE

NOTCH CABLE
INTO JOISTS

FEED WIRE
DOWN WALL

REPLACE
BOARD
WHEN DONE

it doesn't already hold its limit of wires (see Chart). If it does, you'll have to go elsewhere. The last receptacle box in a circuit usually contains only two wires, leaving room for two more. Find it by removing cover plates and peering inside.

Plan your cable route for the easiest fishing. That is the problem in adding new outlets. Cost of cable and other factors take a back seat to easing the cable installation. Do your fishing with baling wire and an electrician's fish tape. Because a fish tape is apt to be quite springy, you may prefer the baling wire method.

You can even bring power from the entrance panel if that is easier. Start a new circuit, if there is one left.

Sometimes the easiest route for a new cable is behind a baseboard or directly across a wall. Chisel holes through the wall to feed the cables and cut a groove along the wall between holes. Fish the cable, lay it in the

ENERGY/MONEY SAVER IDEA — FLUORESCENT LIGHTING

Wider use of fluorescent lighting in the home can keep your lighting cost down while providing the same amount of illumination. As a general rule of thumb, a FLUORESCENT LIGHT provides THREE TIMES the amount of of light as a regular incandescent bulb, using the same number of watts! While many individuals find the type of illumination from fluorescents offensive, some of the newer bulbs provide illumination that is difficult if at all possible to distinguish from the higher operating cost incandescent bulb. While fluorescent fixtures usually cost more than incandescent fixtures, the typical 40 watt bulb has a life span of 8-12 times that of regular incandescent bulbs. Thus, the cost of replacement bulbs can be substantial but the real saving is in the amount of electricity used.

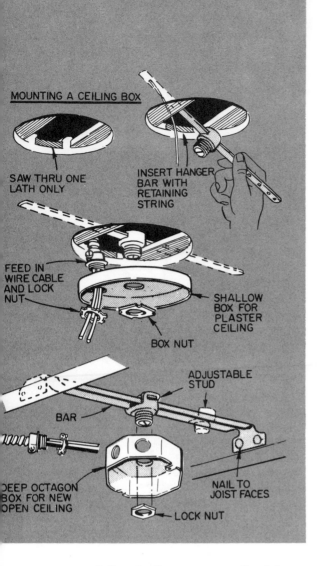

MOUNTING A CEILING BOX

SAW THRU ONE LATH ONLY

INSERT HANGER BAR WITH RETAINING STRING

FEED IN WIRE CABLE AND LOCK NUT

SHALLOW BOX FOR PLASTER CEILING

BOX NUT

ADJUSTABLE STUD

BAR

DEEP OCTAGON BOX FOR NEW OPEN CEILING

NAIL TO JOIST FACES

LOCK NUT

groove and finish the wiring job. Afterward, replaster the wall and repaint or hang new wallpaper. Save the old wallpaper if you can by slitting it with a razor blade and folding a flap of it up out of the way.

Replastering won't be necessary if the cable route goes behind a baseboard. Merely replace the base molding to cover the openings. If the cable interferes with the base molding's fit, chisel it out on the back.

CABLE HOOKUP

Turn off the power. Remove the proper knockout from the existing box and fish one end of your cable into it from behind the wall. The cable connector—either for nonmetallic or armored cable—should be installed on the cable before it is fed behind the wall. You'll have to drill a larger hole than for the cable alone to pass the connector. Fish the cable's lead wires

into the knockout opening. Work the connector through the knockout until you can screw on the locknut and tighten it.

For switches and receptacles, remove the knockout from a box designed for remodeling work. These have side clamps or other means of fastening the box into the wall opening. Insert the cable through the knockout, make up the connection and install the box in the wall according to directions packed with it. Make up all your wires and devices, and the job is ready for try-out.

Back-to-back outlets in the same wall can be wired by drilling matching holes and connecting across them with conduit or a threaded rigid conduit nipple with locknuts and bushings. Every length of rigid conduit needs a bushing screwed on to cover the raw end.

CEILING BOXES

If you have access above the ceiling to mount a box for a light fixture, there's no problem. But if you must work from the room side of the ceiling, use a special, shallow round ceiling box with hanger. Cut away the ceiling surface to the size of the box. Center the opening on a lath if there is one. Cut away only the middle lath. Do it carefully, without breaking up plaster around it. Insert the special hanger (see drawing). Center the hanger in the opening and install the box and locknut after fastening the cable to it with a connector. The new fixture may be hung from the box.

Fixtures mount to boxes in various ways. Some boxes have threaded fixture studs. Others hold with straps. Straps may be held to a stud or to threaded tabs on the box. Still others have threaded nipples. Some boxes make use of a strap with an extension nipple holding the fixture. A cap screws onto the nipple, drawing the fixture's canopy to the wall or ceiling.

Recessed fixtures are installed by sawing out an open space for the fixture between joists. Wood mounting strips are placed above the opening across the lath. Install the fixture box

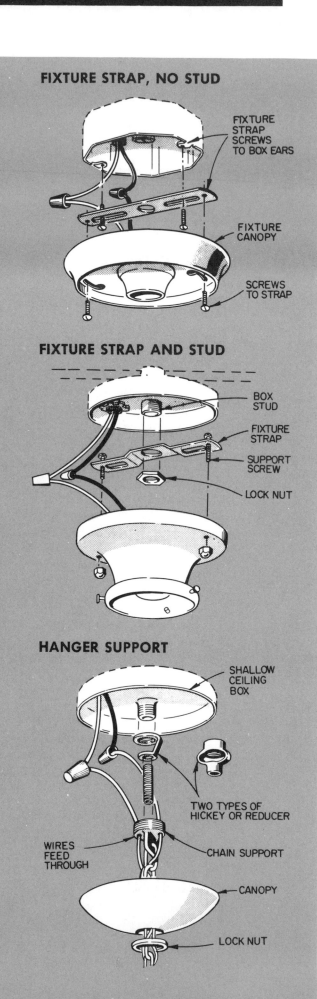

FIXTURE STRAP, NO STUD

FIXTURE STRAP SCREWS TO BOX EARS

FIXTURE CANOPY

SCREWS TO STRAP

FIXTURE STRAP AND STUD

BOX STUD

FIXTURE STRAP

SUPPORT SCREW

LOCK NUT

HANGER SUPPORT

SHALLOW CEILING BOX

TWO TYPES OF HICKEY OR REDUCER

WIRES FEED THROUGH

CHAIN SUPPORT

CANOPY

LOCK NUT

in the opening after making up the cable to it. Some recessed fixtures have mounting straps. Others fasten with screws into the joists or wood strips. Your code may require that a recessed fixture have a separate junction box attached to it. Others don't. Check.

SURFACE WIRING

If fishing wires behind the walls, floors and ceilings of your house scares you, then use surface wiring. If you paint it to match the wall, you'll scarcely notice it after a while. Many different types are available. Local codes may restrict what you may use. You can get surface wiring in plastic or metal. Metal is harder to install but is more permanent. Most codes approve it. What's more, if properly installed, it offers every protection to your wiring that conduit does, including full ground continuity. Metal raceways are designed to go straight as well as around corners in every imaginable direction. They also have end fittings for connecting conduit, non-metallic or armored cable, or to existing outlets. Raceways come in plug- or light-socket moldings, too, if that's what you want. For a full selection see your dealer.

One knd of surface wiring system uses plastic sockets, receptacles and switch components—as many as you like. These are connected to a special dual-purpose plastic cable. This is not "zip" cord or anything like it. The heavy plastic covered cable runs unobtrusively along the baseboard and one end is plugged into the nearest wall outlet. The system is recommended for putting an extra light in the garage, workshop, pantry or closet or other similar locations or for locating an extra receptacle anywhere you need it. Check your Code.

FANCY SWITCHING

When you first look at the wiring diagrams for three- and four-way switching systems, they appear complex. They're not, once you understand

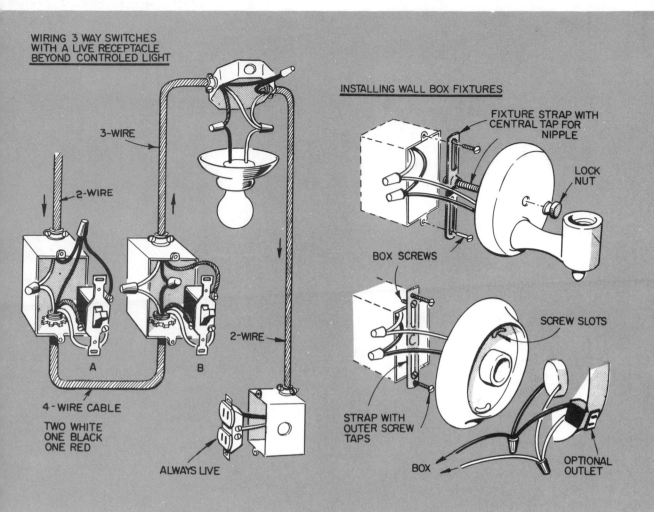

WIRING 3 WAY SWITCHES WITH A LIVE RECEPTACLE BEYOND CONTROLED LIGHT

3-WIRE

2-WIRE

2-WIRE

A

B

4-WIRE CABLE

TWO WHITE
ONE BLACK
ONE RED

ALWAYS LIVE

INSTALLING WALL BOX FIXTURES

FIXTURE STRAP WITH CENTRAL TAP FOR NIPPLE

LOCK NUT

BOX SCREWS

SCREW SLOTS

STRAP WITH OUTER SCREW TAPS

BOX

OPTIONAL OUTLET

them. Three-way switches are used mostly for controlling lights from two different locations—for instance, garage and house. Four-way switches are used when three or more switching locations are desired. Use one four way switch for each switching location more than the first two. The drawing shows hookup. Notice that three-wire cable is used in some runs, two-wire in others. The A and B terminals are the chrome-plated ones. The red and white wires should be connected to these. The C terminals are for black wires. The white wire from the switch must always be painted black at both the switch and the outlet. Switch hookup is the only time a white wire is connected to a black one. Then it has to be painted black. Do it.

Where four-wire cable is shown, use a pair of two-wire cables coming into

the boxes through different knockouts. Be sure you use boxes large enough to hold all the wires.

When using the chart to figure how many wires a box can hold, wires from the fixture to wires in the box are not counted. In conduit work, wires often enter a box and leave it again without being spliced inside. Such a wire is counted only as one wire, not two. If there is a fixture stud, or set of cable clamps inside the box, deduct one wire.

The total deduction from all these sources, however, is only one, no matter how many there are. Cable connectors require no deduction. Subtract also for a switch, receptacle or group of them that fits into the box. Grounding wires are not counted. These are National Electric Code limitations set down for your safety.

YOUR PLUMBING SYSTEM

Basically, it's supplying water to the home and draining all the waste

Every home handyman should know enough about plumbing to: (1) make simple plumbing repairs; (2) know what to do in an emergency; (3) be able to plan plumbing improvements; and (4) know when to call a plumber. If you can actually do your own plumbing around the house, you're one up on many handymen.

Whether you should try to do your own plumbing—the actual installation of pipes, fittings and fixtures—depends on your ability and your local code. Even if you know how, some codes won't let you work on plumbing. Only a licensed plumber may be permitted to work. Such anti-do-it-yourself codes are prevalent in big cities where plumbers' union influence is strong. If you don't understand the principles of plumbing, you're better off hiring a pro anyway.

We're not recommending that everyone try to be his own plumber. It isn't everybody's bag. However, many handymen have done successful plumbing. You probably can, too. Be sure to read up on how to do a job correctly before you tackle it.

By doing your own plumbing, you stand to save up to 50 percent of the cost of having it done. And you can't put a price on the feeling of accomplishment when you turn on the water and watch it flow out of your pipe or your fixture. It works because you made it work. For jobs you don't do yourself, call in a plumbing contractor.

You can do much or all of your plumbing, even for a project as complex as a home remodeling, if you wish.

He is skilled in planning, servicing and installing all your water needs.

Whatever you do, you're bound by your local plumbing codes. Nearly every city has them. If you live outside the city in a rural area, your county plumbing code applies to what you put in. You can get a copy of the code at your municipal building or county courthouse. Some areas have no plumbing codes at all. In this case, for your own protection, follow the National Plumbing Code. Then you'll be sure of ending up with a safe, workable system. Most public libraries have a book outlining the national code.

Codes likely will specify the following: the kind of pipe that's permitted for each use—drainage, water supply, vent, buried underground, etc.; venting requirements; fixture waste connections; trap requirements; and minimum pipe sizes for each use.

Your home plumbing system begins at the water utility's main, usually in front of your house. If yours is a private well, it starts at the well. Plumbing is supposed to bring in all the potable water you need, treat it if necessary, heat some of it and deliver the hot and cold water around to where it's used. Water that isn't consumed must be drained safely out of the house by the plumbing. All of this must be done quietly and without danger to you or others in your community. It's a big job.

The average home has more than 300 feet of plumbing pipes in its walls, floors and buried in the ground around it.

Basically, every home plumbing system comprises three separate parts: water supply system, fixtures and drainage system.

WATER SUPPLY

The water supply system consists of a service entrance line from the water main to the meter (with city water), a main shutoff near the meter, a distribution system, a water heater and perhaps a water softener and other treatment

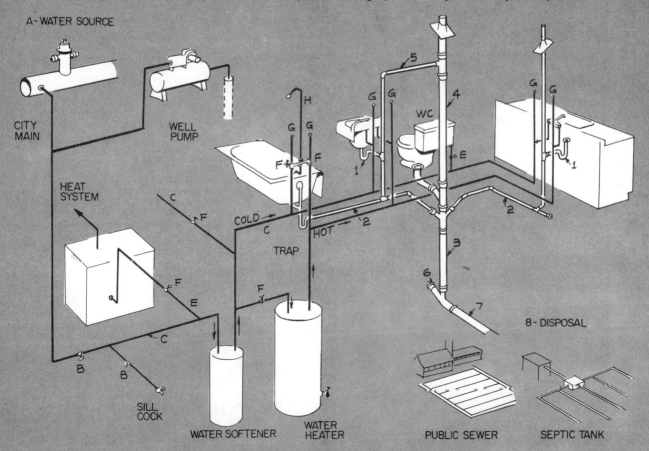

PLUMBING SUPPLY SYSTEM. A. Source of water, public or private, and piping up to house. B. Stop and waste valve should be at the low point of the whole system. C. Cold water main is any line serving two or more fixtures. D. Hot water main is any line serving two or more fixtures. E. Branch is any line serving just one fixture. F. Shut-off valve is needed in every branch line and in mains where cutoff might be needed. G. Use air chambers at every branch line before the fixture to prevent water hammer. H. Fixture supply pipe is part of the branch line that fits it to the fixture. Study the drawing. DRAINAGE SYSTEM. 1. Fixture drain incorporates a trap and leads into the branch waste. 2. Branch waste runs between the fixture and the main drain. 3. Main drain, or soil stack, collects water from the toilet and branch wastes. 4. Vent is the upper portion of the main drain. It reaches up through the roof. 5. Revent is a bypass for air between a branch waste and the vent portion of the main drain. 6. Cleanout opening should be located wherever access to the drainage system may be needed to rod out blockage. 7. Building drain leads from the main drain to the point of final disposal. 8. Final disposal is either a public sewage plant or a private disposal system.

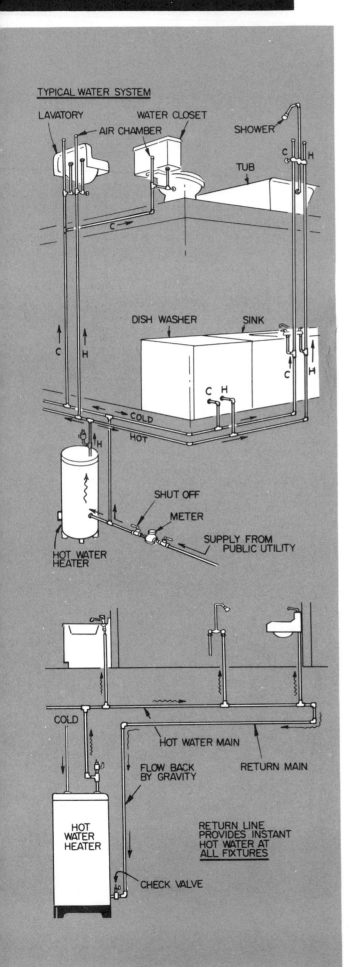

TYPICAL WATER SYSTEM

LAVATORY
AIR CHAMBER
WATER CLOSET
SHOWER
TUB
C H
DISH WASHER
SINK
C
H
C H
C
H
COLD
HOT
SHUT OFF
METER
SUPPLY FROM
PUBLIC UTILITY
HOT WATER
HEATER

COLD
HOT WATER MAIN
RETURN MAIN
FLOW BACK
BY GRAVITY
HOT
WATER
HEATER
RETURN LINE
PROVIDES INSTANT
HOT WATER AT
ALL FIXTURES
CHECK VALVE

To avoid annoying water hammer, water supply lines
must have 12" air chambers near fixtures for relief.

equipment. Room shutoffs and fixture
stop-cocks also are included in the
water supply system. Some fixtures use
only one kind of water, hot or cold. For
instance, most toilets use cold water
only; most dishwashers, hot only. In
that case the untapped main passes that
fixture by. Cold water branches and hot
water branches take off from the mains
and lead to the fixtures. Branches are of
a smaller pipe size than mains because
they normally carry water for only one
fixture. If a branch serves more than
one fixture, it's sized a little larger.
Mains are usually held to the same size
throughout their length. The parts of
mains or branches that go up through
walls are called *risers*.

Cold water mains may be split and
run as double pipes to keep softened and
unsoftened cold water separate. Sometimes hard water is furnished to toilets.
Water should always be furnished hard
to outside hose bibs.

The hot water main may be in the
form of a continuous loop that con-
stantly circulates hot water from the
water heater. Then, no matter how long
the hot water run, you'll have instant
hot water at every tap. A large or long,
rambling house should not be without
this refinement.

A hot water system may be further

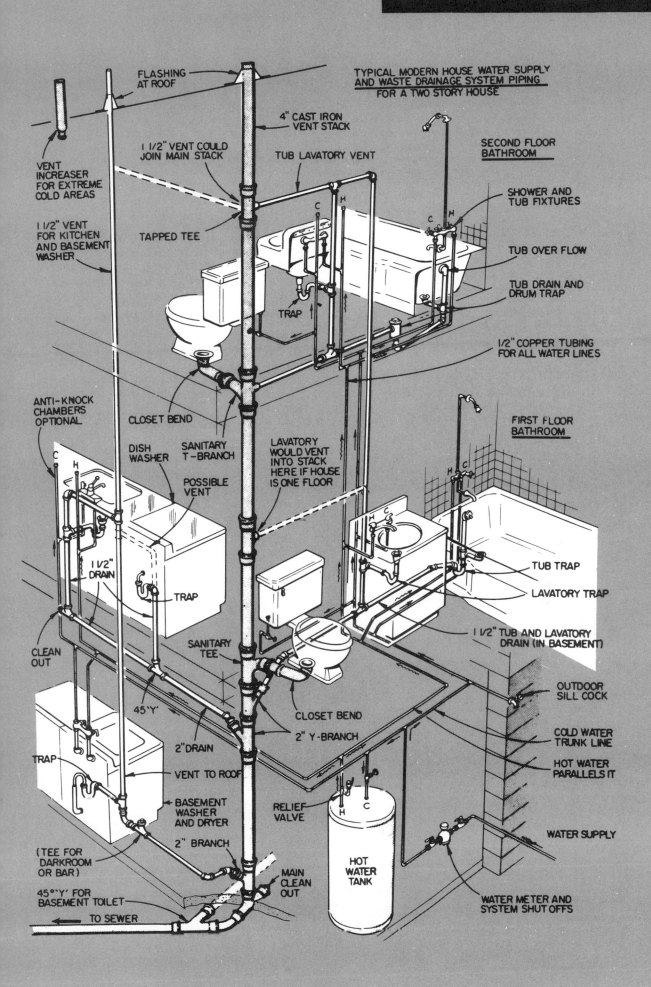

TYPICAL MODERN HOUSE WATER SUPPLY
AND WASTE DRAINAGE SYSTEM PIPING
FOR A TWO STORY HOUSE

FLASHING
AT ROOF

4" CAST IRON
VENT STACK

1 1/2" VENT COULD
JOIN MAIN STACK

TUB LAVATORY VENT

SECOND FLOOR
BATHROOM

VENT
INCREASER
FOR EXTREME
COLD AREAS

SHOWER AND
TUB FIXTURES

1 1/2" VENT
FOR KITCHEN
AND BASEMENT
WASHER

TAPPED TEE

TUB OVER FLOW

TUB DRAIN AND
DRUM TRAP

TRAP

1/2" COPPER TUBING
FOR ALL WATER LINES

ANTI-KNOCK
CHAMBERS
OPTIONAL

CLOSET BEND

DISH
WASHER

SANITARY
T-BRANCH

POSSIBLE
VENT

LAVATORY
WOULD VENT
INTO STACK
HERE IF HOUSE
IS ONE FLOOR

FIRST FLOOR
BATHROOM

1 1/2"
DRAIN

TRAP

TUB TRAP

LAVATORY TRAP

1 1/2" TUB AND LAVATORY
DRAIN (IN BASEMENT)

CLEAN
OUT

SANITARY
TEE

OUTDOOR
SILL COCK

45 'Y'

CLOSET BEND

2" Y-BRANCH

COLD WATER
TRUNK LINE

HOT WATER
PARALLELS IT

TRAP

2" DRAIN

VENT TO ROOF

RELIEF
VALVE

WATER SUPPLY

(TEE FOR
DARKROOM
OR BAR)

BASEMENT
WASHER
AND DRYER

2" BRANCH

H   C

45° 'Y' FOR
BASEMENT TOILET

MAIN
CLEAN
OUT

HOT
WATER
TANK

TO SEWER

WATER METER AND
SYSTEM SHUT OFFS

divided to serve two temperatures of hot water. One is supplied at about 180 degrees for dishwashers and automatic washing machines. The other is a mixture of hot and cold water for hot water taps. This comes out at a safe 120 degrees. The mixing valve is installed on the hot water heater and separate pipes carried from there to the fixture branches.

FIXTURES

Fixtures such as tub, shower, lavatory, sink, toilet, dishwasher, etc., help you use water conveniently. More than anything else in plumbing, fixtures come in varying qualities. A good rule-of-thumb is to buy the best quality you can afford.

Three materials, chiefly, go into most plumbing fixtures: enameled stamped steel, enameled cast iron and vitreous china. Stamped steel tubs, sinks and lavatories are cheap and tinny. Avoid them except where money is the only governing factor. Either cast iron or vitreous china is very serviceable. Both have a solid feel, a "ring" as you tap on

them. Some people rate china as best. It is the most expensive. All toilets are made of china. Other fixtures may be made from any of the three materials. Dishwashers and other appliance-type fixtures, of course, are made in stamped steel only. Nothing wrong with them because of that.

DRAINAGE SYSTEM

Used water that runs out of fixtures has to be carried away and disposed. Gases created by decomposition within the system must be dispelled where you won't have to breathe them. This is the job of the drainage system. It must have pipes of ample capacity, properly pitched to carry wastes away by gravity. The system must be tightly sealed and properly vented. Adequate provision is needed for cleanout, should the drain pipes ever clog. The whole plumbing system is designed around the drainage system, since its pipes are the largest, most costly and most difficult to install.

The large pipe that runs vertically and collects wastes from one or more fixtures is called a *soil stack* or just *stack*. If a toilet empties into the stack, it's called a main soil stack. Every home has at least one main stack. There may be more if required to serve more than one toilet.

If no toilet drains into a stack, it can be of smaller pipe than a main stack. This is called a secondary stack. Each fixture is joined to its stack by a branch drain. The branch drain must slope downward toward the stack. A stack extends from its above-roof vent to below the house. There it connects with a horizontal sloped run that's called a *house drain*. Ordinarily there is only one house drain, although there may be several. The house drain becomes a *house sewer* as it leaves the house and enters the ground outside the foundation. The house sewer connects with the city sewer or with a private sewage disposal system.

Additional pipes serve gas only, no drainage. These are called *vent pipes*. The main vent pipe, of course, is the portion of the soil stack that extends

BASEMENT VENT CAN GO TO ROOF OR JOIN BATH VENT

VENT STACK

BATH VENT STACK

KITCHEN VENT

TRAP

TRAPS

VENT

KITCHEN DRAIN

WASHER DRAIN

4" MAIN SOIL STACK

CLEAN OUT

DRAINAGE SYSTEM FOR TYPICAL RANCH HOUSE

above the highest fixture and up through the roof. Fixtures may be vented into the soil stack through their waste pipes if they are close enough to the stack. This is called *wet venting*. Under the National Plumbing Code, a tub or shower within 3½ feet from trap outlet to soil stack qualifies. So does a lavatory within 2½ feet of the stack. If the fixtures are farther than this from the stack, they need separate pipes running from the fixture, either up through the roof or horizontally and connecting into the soil stack above the highest fixture drain connection. These "vent-only" runs are called *revents*. Horizontal revent pipes are pitched slightly upward from the fixture to make condensation drain back toward the fixture.

Drain and vent pipes are sized according to how much fluid each must carry. More about that in a later chapter. Toilets are hooked up to the soil stack by a large pipe called a *closet bend*.

Every toilet has its own built-in water trap. All other fixtures must be provided with separate traps to keep gases and vermin in drainage pipes from escaping into the house. A trap is a U-shaped pipe that is always filled with water. The water seals off drain piping beyond it.

WATER HEATER

An important part of any plumbing system is the water heater. The most common types are fueled by gas, electricity or oil. They can't heat water as fast as it is used, so some already-hot water must be stored inside the heater's tank.

Another type of heater that is available to those with hot water house heating systems is the instantaneous type. Water to be heated is run through coils that are immersed inside the heating plant's boiler. There the water is warmed to about the same temperature as the boiler water. Sometimes a storage tank is used with this kind of heater, too. One drawback, the boiler must be kept up to full temperature at all times if hot water is wanted. This may not be too practical in any but the coldest

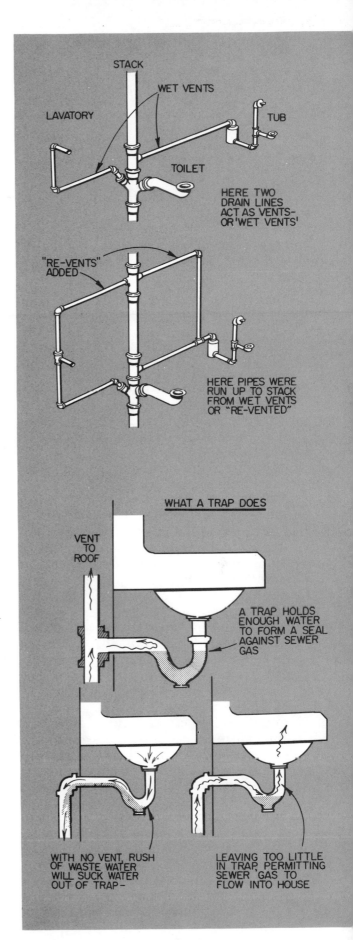

STACK

WET VENTS

LAVATORY

TUB

TOILET

HERE TWO DRAIN LINES ACT AS VENTS— OR 'WET VENTS'

"RE-VENTS" ADDED

HERE PIPES WERE RUN UP TO STACK FROM WET VENTS OR "RE-VENTED"

WHAT A TRAP DOES

VENT TO ROOF

A TRAP HOLDS ENOUGH WATER TO FORM A SEAL AGAINST SEWER GAS

WITH NO VENT, RUSH OF WASTE WATER WILL SUCK WATER OUT OF TRAP—

LEAVING TOO LITTLE IN TRAP, PERMITTING SEWER GAS TO FLOW INTO HOUSE weather.

You can judge the quality of a fueled hot water heater pretty well by the guarantee offered and the reputation of its manufacturer. Since the guarantee represents the manufacturer's confidence (or lack of it) in his product, study it carefully. There are many "10-year guarantees" that give you only five years of full-value guarantee plus five years of pro-rated guarantee. The good guys offer you a full-value guarantee for the whole 10 years. Then if the tank should leak before the 10 year guarantee period is up, you'd get another water heater free.

As for reputation, a number of heater manufacturers have good names in the field.

What size heater? Your family's need for hot water varies from day to day and year to year. However, a 20-gallon tank is the minimum recommended for any heater using gas or oil as a fuel. A family of four should have at least a 30-gallon heater. Larger families and those with automatic laundry equipment or automatic dishwashers need at least a 50-gallon heater in gas or oil.

How much hot water your family uses depends upon how many water-wasters you have. Normally a tub bath takes 10 to 15 gallons, a shower 9 to 12 gallons. An average load of clothes in an automatic washer uses 13 to 20 gallons of hot water, plus what's needed for rinsing. Hand-dishwashing uses 2 to 4 gallons. Automatic-dishwashing takes 7 to 12 gallons. These amounts vary depending on the equipment and the temperature of the water.

The cost to heat water depends on the cost of the fuel used. If you know the fuel prices in your area, you can figure it out. Here is a reasonable estimate of the amounts of each fuel used per year: Natural gas—32,450 cubic feet; manufactured gas—61,800 cubic feet; LP-gas (bottled—1475 pounds; oil—270 gallons; electricity—6658 kilowatt hours; and coal (some still use it)—1.8 tons.

Never forget that a water heater is a potential steam boiler. If the temperature control fails to shut the burner off, the water will heat until it becomes steam. When enough steam pressure builds up, the heater will blow. People

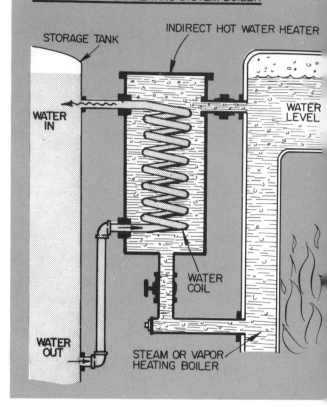

WATER HEATER ON HEATING SYSTEM BOILER

have been injured and killed this way, houses damaged. To be safe, every water heater should be fitted with a temperature-pressure relief valve with its heat-sensing probe reaching down into the tank.

If your temperature pressure relief valve has a pump-like handle (most do), test it to see that it's working by "popping" the valve and squirting off a little water.

Owners of newer water heaters are further protected by devices known as energy cutoffs. If the temperature should get too high, one of these safety controls would shut off the gas or electricity.

WATER TREATMENT

Water pumped out of deep wells is often hard. This means that it contains dissolved calcium and magnesium sulfates or bicarbonates. It may also contain iron and other minerals.

The surest way to tell about your own water hardness is to have it tested for mineral content. The major water softener manufacturing firms will make a

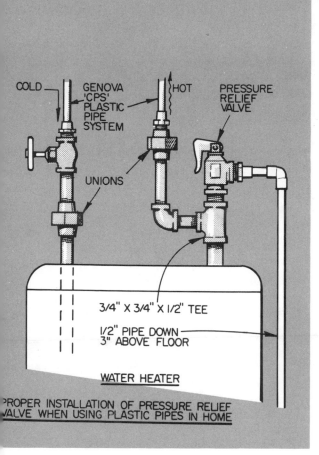

COLD — GENOVA 'CPS' PLASTIC PIPE SYSTEM — HOT — PRESSURE RELIEF VALVE

UNIONS

3/4" X 3/4" X 1/2" TEE

1/2" PIPE DOWN 3" ABOVE FLOOR

WATER HEATER

PROPER INSTALLATION OF PRESSURE RELIEF VALVE WHEN USING PLASTIC PIPES IN HOME

Potassium permanganate is sometimes added to water in iron filter to replace used-up oxygen. Flush unit out thoroughly before using filter as a careful step.

free test of your water. They can then tell you what size of softener you need. Large mail order houses, like Wards and Sears, do this too.

Most softeners remove a small amount of iron and sulfur while softening the water. But when the content of these impurities gets too high, additional water-conditioning equipment may be needed ahead of the softener.

Bad-tasting water can sometimes be improved by running it through a charcoal filter. Small charcoal filters are available for insertion in the line at the faucet where drinking water is usually drawn.

A water softener doesn't actually remove the minerals. Instead it exchanges sodium ions for hard calcium and magnesium ions. When all the sodium ions are used up, they're replaced by running a salt solution through the softener media. Some equipment does this automatically by running water from a brine tank through the softener. In others you dump the salt in and flush it through with water.

Softeners are available for outright purchase or from some firms on a rental basis. Although it's less trouble to rent,

in the long run it's more economical to buy a softener.

Plumbing improvements can be financed through your bank, savings and loan association or other private lender. They also qualify for lower-interest FHA home improvement loans. Time payment plans by those who sell plumbing supplies are available at higher interest. It pays to shop around for the best deal on getting your money.

If you are thinking of buying a house, check out its plumbing system to see that you're not buying trouble.

1. Look at the fixtures closely. Is their style in keeping with the rest of the house? Are they made of enameled stamped metal, enameled cast iron or vitreous china? Are they chipped or scratched?

2. Fill up the lavatory and bathtub with water. Is it clear or murky? Do the stoppers hold water? Do the fixtures drain quickly and quietly?

3. Flush the toilet with a small ball of crumpled-up toilet paper or cigarette butt in it. Is the flush complete? Does the toilet tank refill and shut off fully? How noisy is it?

4. Run the water full blast in the kitchen, then turn it on in the bathroom. Does a good flow come out or just a trickle?

5. Open and close each faucet several times to see whether it leaks.

6. Are there rust stains in the bathtub or lavatory? Lift off the toilet lid and look there for evidence of minerals in the water.

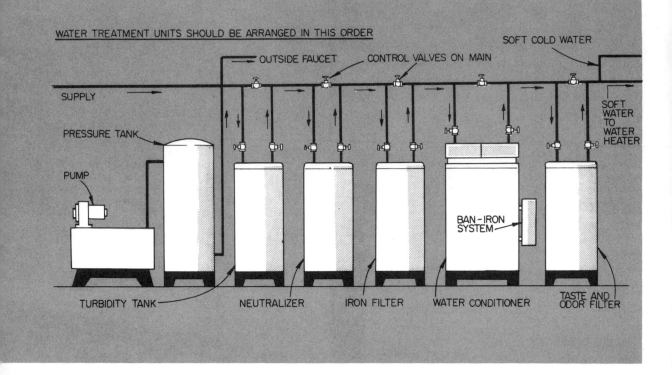

WATER TREATMENT UNITS SHOULD BE ARRANGED IN THIS ORDER

SOFT COLD WATER

OUTSIDE FAUCET   CONTROL VALVES ON MAIN

SUPPLY

SOFT WATER TO WATER HEATER

PRESSURE TANK

PUMP

BAN-IRON SYSTEM

TURBIDITY TANK   NEUTRALIZER   IRON FILTER   WATER CONDITIONER   TASTE AND ODOR FILTER

7. Get a look at the roof above the toilet. See that there is a vent stack and that it's away from windows.

8. Check the size of the water heater to see whether it's ample to supply hot water for your whole family. It should bear the label of the National Board of Fire Underwriters and be fitted with a relief valve.

OUTSIDE YOUR HOUSE

Your municipal water supply and sewage disposal may be considered as extensions of your home plumbing system. Water that has been drawn from a surface or underground source sometimes must be treated to make it fit to drink. Raw water may be precipitated, settled, filtered, softened and chlorinated before it's fit. Water's alkalinity-acidity must be adjusted. *Finished water,* as it is called, is stored in reservoirs until needed, then pumped through underground water mains to your house.

Constant checks are made on city water for health reasons. All this is the responsibility of the governmental agency or utility that furnishes plyour water.

After water leaves your house as sewage, it travels by gravity, usually, through sewer pipes to a sewage treat-

ment plant. There solids are settled and filtered out. Oxygen for bacterial action is provided by aeration. The resulting effluent is chlorinated to kill any remaining bacteria and render it harmless to a river or stream where it is discharged. You've heard the story about the sewage treatment plant operator who drinks a glass of fully treated sewage effluent at the close of a plant tour to show how pure it is. Now *that* takes guts, but it can be done.

CROSS-CONNECTIONS

One thing you should watch out for in any plumbing is a cross-connection. Cross-connections can be murder. You won't believe this, but only one house in thousands is completely free of them. A cross-connection can exist for years without harm. Then, when conditions are right—wrong, actually—it lets pollutants get into your potable water. There is no warning. The first you know, someone is sick. Death can even result.

To keep your family out of all possible danger, make a cross-connection inspection right now.

A cross-connection is a link or channel between a pipe carrying polluted

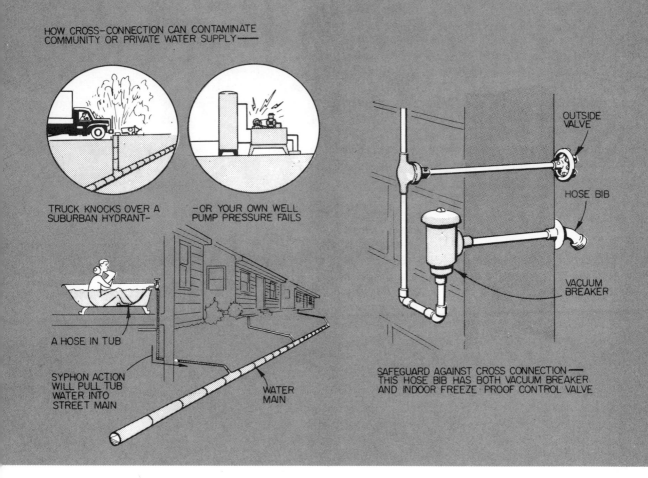

HOW CROSS-CONNECTION CAN CONTAMINATE
COMMUNITY OR PRIVATE WATER SUPPLY——

TRUCK KNOCKS OVER A
SUBURBAN HYDRANT-

—OR YOUR OWN WELL
PUMP PRESSURE FAILS

A HOSE IN TUB

SYPHON ACTION
WILL PULL TUB
WATER INTO
STREET MAIN

WATER
MAIN

OUTSIDE
VALVE

HOSE BIB

VACUUM
BREAKER

SAFEGUARD AGAINST CROSS CONNECTION——
THIS HOSE BIB HAS BOTH VACUUM BREAKER
AND INDOOR FREEZE-PROOF CONTROL VALVE

water and a pipe carrying drinking water. When pressure from the polluted source exceeds pressure on the drinking water, the contaminants enter the potable water system through the link. This action is termed backsiphonage or backflow. It's simply a reversal of water pressure. Backflow can come about in a number of ways. It can happen when water in the house system is turned off, when a car hits a fire hydrant, when emergency use of city water forces a drop in pressure, or in any number of other unusual circumstances. Here's another: In a system where the pipes are poorly sized, a full flow in one pipe, such as might be caused by opening a faucet, can create a vacuum in another pipe. None of these situations is impossible.

Through siphon action, contaminated water can not only flow downhill, it can flow over a "hill" created in house piping. Water can actually be drawn up into your house water pipes. When normal flow is restored, the contaminated water may flow out of any outlet.

Finding cross-connections takes a lit-

tle doing. Correcting them takes real determination. The link may be a lot more subtle and harder to notice than a direct pipe connection. The factors that can produce a reversal of flow may seem remote or even impossible. Yet the siphon principle is always ready to take over any time there's a vacuum in the system.

When making your inspection, look for two types of cross-connections: (1) a solid pipe with a valved connection and (2) a submerged inlet.

The solid connection is installed where necessary to supply an auxiliary piping system from the potable water source. The pipe supplying water to a hot water heating system is a common cross-connection. Most codes permit it. It's a cross-connection that many families live with every day. Whether your family should or not is up to you. A backflow-preventer in the line would head off trouble.

Submerged inlets can be found in old-fashioned lavatories, sinks and bathtubs built before the danger of cross-connections was recognized. Some newer fixtures have them too. It's possible that your toilet tank inlet is submerged. This is another cross-connection most of us live with.

Follow your water pipes from where they leave the water meter or pump to the end of every branch line. Imagine drinking the water in everything they're connected to.

A laundry tub, or pail, with a hose in it is a cross-connection. Disconnect hoses when not in use, or else provide

ENERGY/MONEY SAVER IDEAS — THE BTU

All of us are aware of the energy crisis that exists in this country, which in turn is increasing the cost of electricity, heating oil, gasoline, natural and propane gas, coal and even wood. As homeowners, before we can intelligently cope with the problem of saving energy—and thereby money—we must have some knowledge as to how various fuels relate to each other in dollars and cents. Therefore, in this series of ENERGY/MONEY SAVER IDEAS that will be intermingled throughout this encyclopedia, we will often refer to units of temperature measurement—the BTU. BTU stands for British Thermal Unit , a unit of thermal energy equal to the amount of heat required to raise the temperature of one pound of water one degree Fahrenheit at or near its temperature of maximum density (39.2 degrees). As an example, five pounds of water in a kettle raised 160 degrees requires 5×160 or 800 BTU. How much it costs you to heat, cool or cook depends upon the fuel you are using and the cost of that fuel.

NO. 2 HEATING OIL contains 140,000 BTUs per gallon.
1000 WATTS (kilowatt) of ELECTRICITY is the equivalent to 3413 BTUs.

NATURAL GAS is measured in THERMS, and one THERM is the equivalent to 100,000 BTUs.

PROPANE GAS, like oil, is measured by the gallon and one gallon contains 91,000 BTUs.

Since the cost of these fuels vary considerably the country over, you can easily figure your cost with the simple formula shown below.

$$\frac{\text{BTU value of fuel per unit of sale times overall efficiency}}{\text{cost in cents per unit of sale}} = \text{No. of BTUs for one cent}$$

For these figures, the efficiency of electricity is 100 percent while the efficiency of gas and oil burning equipment is averaged at 80 percent. Some equipment is more efficient than others and therefore the cost of comfort will vary. But to have you understand the BTU and how the cost relates to your fuel at the price you are paying, here are four examples. Substitute your cost of fuel and you will be able to determine how many BTUs your penny will buy.

a vacuum-breaker at every hose connection.

A rain water cistern may have a valved pipe cross-connected to the potable water. Remove the pipe.

See that an in-the-ground lawn sprinkling system is installed with a vacuum-breaker that's at least 12 inches above the highest sprinkler outlet.

The U.S. Public Health Service says that taking *any* chance with family or community health is too much.

Example 1

No. 2 HEATING OIL sells at 35 cents per gallon:

$$\frac{140,000 \text{ BTUs per gallon} \times .80 \text{ (efficiency of burner)}}{35 \text{ (cents per gallon)}} = 3200 \text{ BTUs for one cent}$$

Example 2

NATURAL GAS sells for 15 cents per therm:

$$\frac{100,000 \text{ (BTUs per therm)} \times .80 \text{ (efficiency of burner)}}{15 \text{ (cents per therm)}} = 5333 \text{ BTUs for one cent}$$

Example 3

PROPANE sells for 50 cents per gallon:

$$\frac{91,000 \text{ (BTUs per gallon)} \times .80 \text{ (efficiency of burner)}}{50 \text{ (cents per gallon)}} = 1456 \text{ BTUs for one cent}$$

Example 4

ELECTRICITY sells for 4 cents per kilowatt-hour
(1 kilowatt equals 1000 watts)

$$\frac{3413 \text{ (BTUs per kilowatt} \times 1 \text{ (efficiency)}}{4 \text{ (cents per kilowatt) (abbreviates KWH)}} = 853 \text{ BTUs for one cent}$$

Consult your fuel bills for your cost of your fuel and figure out how many BTUs one cent will buy in your area.

MAINTAINING HOME PLUMBING

Make repairs on faucets and valves; stop leaks in toilet bowl seals

Repairing a leaky faucet is something that every home owner should be able to do. It is easy enough.

The cost of calling a plumber keeps going up. His skill and scarcity demands top dollar in today's market. Consider yourself lucky if you can even get one to come out on short notice. To save some bucks and inconvenience, it may be worthwhile to tackle the simpler of your own plumbing repairs. Jobs that you do with a few inexpensive tools include repairing leaky faucets, clearing clogged drains, fixing leaks in pipes and tanks, thawing frozen pipes, fixing balky toilet tank problems and stopping leaks in toilet bowl seals. Only a few basic tools are needed, including a plumber's force cup and drain-cleaning auger. You should have these tools on hand.

Fixing leaky faucets is probably the most basic home plumbing repair. It's not as easy as it used to be when faucets were built pretty much alike. Several improved designs have gained wide acceptance. However, if you know what you're doing, you can fix them, too. In 10 minutes you can repair a leaky faucet of the ordinary type.

The cure is worth the effort. A faucet that leaks just 60 drops a minute wastes 2300 gallons of water in a year.

Actually, water faucets and globe valves do the same job. The difference, mainly, is that faucets are valves placed at discharge points over sinks, tubs and lavatories. Valves are used to close off portions of the plumbing system. The repairs to a faucet apply also to a globe valve. Mixing faucets found on sinks, laundry tubs and bathtubs are actually two separate faucet units with a common spout. Each faucet is repaired individually.

FIXING A GLOBE FAUCET

When a closed globe faucet drips and "sings" or "flutters" when opened, the trouble is usually a worn washer. Don't force it closed to stop the drip. Replace the faulty washer instead. The faucet washer is located at the lower end of a spindle, the part that turns with the handle. To replace the washer, turn off the water supply to that faucet. Remove the packing nut, then the spindle. Wrap adhesive or other sticky tape around the packing nut to protect the chrome finish. Use a monkey wrench with smooth jaws, not a pipe wrench with toothed jaws. Turn the spindle in the "on" direction to remove it.

Take out the small screw that holds the worn out washer to the spindle. Scrape the old washer parts from the spindle cup and insert a new washer the same size as the old one. Buy washers that will serve both hot and cold water taps.

If you don't have a washer the same size, you can make one by filing down a larger one. Chucking it up on a bolt in an electric drill is an easy way to let power do the work. Never use a faucet washer that's too small.

Look at the seat on the faucet body. If it's nicked or rough, reface it with a seat-dressing tool. Then reassemble the faucet. Don't forget to get the "hot" handle on the "hot" faucet. Don't laugh. It's easy to go wrong.

Sometimes a faucet leaks at the packing. Try tightening the packing nut. If that doesn't work, you'll have to replace the packing. To do it, just remove the handle, packing nut and old packing. Install the new packing or packing washer and reassemble the parts. Other globe faucet or valve parts may be replaced as needed.

Emergency packing can be made by wrapping cotton string tightly around the faucet stem just inside the packing nut. Wrap so that the string follows the same path as the handle's threads.

The final step is to remove and re-align the handle to match the one opposite. Most handles are splined onto the shaft and held with a screw.

FIXING OTHER FAUCETS

The newer faucets don't have washers. Instead they have diaphragms that close off the water supply. They're just as easy to fix. Remove the handle. The screw that holds it usually is under a snap-plate covering the center of the handle. Pry the plate off with a pocket-knife. With the handle off, screw the hex nut around the spindle off, and pull out the spindle assembly. Replace the neoprene diaphragm with a new one and reassemble the faucet. There is no packing on this type of faucet. If it leaks around the shaft, a new diaphragm is the cure.

Other kinds of faucets are designed to eliminate drip and prolong life. Consult the service literature provided for these when repairing them.

Single-lever faucets operate differently from other types. They use spring pressure along with water pressure for shutoff. These are particularly affected by pipe sediment, and so are protected with tiny metal screens to filter out debris. When the screens clog up, they cut down the flow. You have to get at them for cleaning. Other than this, a

Cross-section of a typical globe faucet.

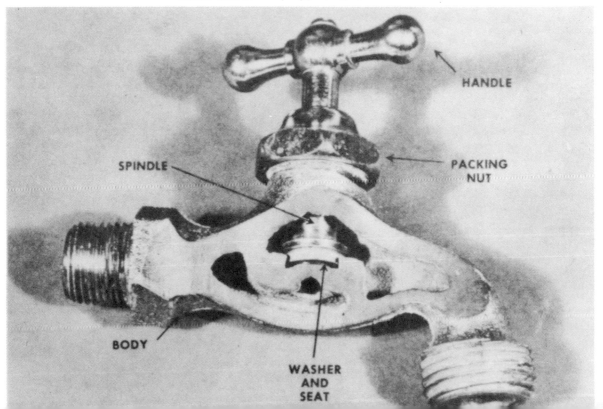

HANDLE

PACKING NUT

SPINDLE

BODY

WASHER AND SEAT

To fix leaky washer, first unscrew the packing nut on globe faucet. But use tape in order to protect nut.

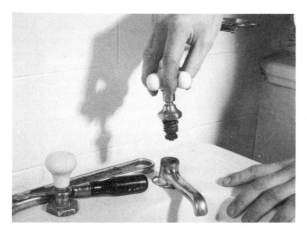

Lift out the spindle, turning it slightly as you do. The water should be turned off first—but of course.

A screw holds the faucet washer to the bottom of spindle. You must remove it to install a new washer.

single-lever doesn't need much attention.

Every make of single-lever faucet is a little different. The best bet is to come by a copy of the manufacturer's literature telling how to service it. Call a plumbing dealer who handles that make and ask him for literature. Or write the factory and get it, along with the name of the dealer where you can buy parts. Send along a snapshot or description of the faucet, so the maker knows which of his models you're talking about.

CLOGGED DRAINS

Drains get clogged by dropping things into them, or by build-ups of grease, dirt and other matter. First try plunging out a stopped-up drain with a plumber's force cup (*plumber's friend*). Fill the bowl about half full of water and roll the plumber's friend into the water so that no air is trapped under it. If the fixture has an overflow opening, plug the opening with a damp rag or hold one hand over it as you plunge. On a double-bowl sink, have someone hold a hand tightly over the opposite drain. Remove the stopper from the drain you are plunging. Give it 20 to 30 good shots, not just a few. Getting the right rhythm can send a powerful shot down the pipes each time you plunge. Every so often, yank the force cup off the drain to give additional plunging action and test whether the drain has been cleared. Plunging action may be increased by coating the bottom lip of the force cup with vaseline. It makes for a tighter seal.

Once the drain has been opened, if only slightly, you can pour liquid drain cleaner down to clear it the rest of the way. Follow directions on the label.

You can make your own drain cleaner by mixing lye with a small amount of aluminum filings. Handle it with care. Pour it into the drain and add cold water. A violent heat- and gas-forming reaction should loosen remaining grease and soap deposits. Then they can be flushed away. Keep your hands out of drain cleaner. It's mean stuff. If any gets into your eyes, flush with cold water and call a doctor. Don't use chemical cleaners in pipes that are completely stopped up. The chemical troops must engage the stoppage in a frontal attack to be effective.

Stubborn deposits that won't come out with a few minutes of vigorous plunging will have to be removed with a clean-out auger or sewer tape. Long flexible steel cables or ribbons, these are commonly called *snakes*. They are run down drainpipes as they're rotated slowly to break up obstructions or hook onto objects and pull them out. They're made in various lengths and sizes and are available at hardware stores and plumbing supply houses. A 10-foot snake is a handy size. It can reach through most drain pipes clear to the main stack. Rarely is the main stack clogged. If the snake hangs up, don't force it. Back it out a few inches and go in again. Try slow. Try fast. Try not turning. Try fast turning. Chances are, you can get it through, if you keep trying.

Water pressure from a hose is a slick way to blow out some stoppages. Insert the hose end well into the pipe. Wrap rags around the hose where it enters the pipe to minimize backflow of water. In case of a stopped-up fixture drain, the overflow opening has to be covered tightly too.

If the stopper in a sink or lavatory leaks, it's probably dirty. Take it out and clean it. Most simply lift out. Some call for cleaning from below with the trap and tailpipe off.

CLOGGED SEWER LINE

A clogged sewer line is cleaned out with a sewer tape, a flat metal band that comes coiled in a carrier. You can rent sewer tapes in lengths of 25 and 50 feet. Work the tape through a clean out opening after draining backed-up water into pails and disposing of it. Uncoil the tape from its rack as you plunge it into the clogged line. When you clear out the stoppage, work the tape back and forth over the area a few times. Then reel it in. Clean the tape and dry it before recoiling and returning.

A clogged toilet usually can be cleared with a plumber's friend used as for a clogged sink drain. Next in line is a plumber's snake. A short model is made specifically for clearing clogged toilet bowls. It's called a *closet auger*.

CLEARING FLOOR DRAINS

Sand, dirt or lint often clogs floor drains. Remove the strainer and scoop out as much sediment as you can. You may have to chip away the concrete around the strainer carefully to free it. Flush the drain with water. If pressure is needed, use a garden hose.

Occasional flushing of floor drains may prevent their clogging. Pour a pail of water down them every few months or so.

Roots growing through cracks or defective joints in outside drains or sewers sometimes clog them. You can clear the stoppage temporarily with a root-cutting tool. To prevent future trouble, the line should be dug up and relaid using sound pipe and making sure all joints are watertight.

LEAKY PIPES, TANKS

Water sometimes corrodes metal pipes. This usually occurs all along the pipe rather than at one point. An exception would be where pipes of dissimilar metals, such as copper and steel, come together. The solution is either water treatment to prevent corrosion or the use of pipe materials that are more compatible with your water. Consult a local plumber.

Pipes split by hard freezing must be replaced.

A leak at a threaded connection often can be stopped by taking apart the fitting and making it up again with a good

Plug the overflow opening with your hand when using a plumber's friend (like this) on stopped-up lavatory.

Turn plumber's "snake" a few inches at a time while feeding it forward into clogged drain. But don't force.

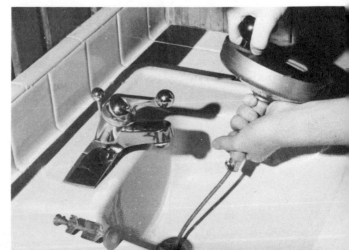

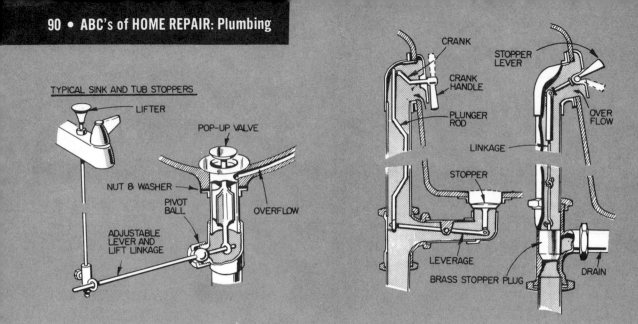

TYPICAL SINK AND TUB STOPPERS

pipe joint material in the threads.

Small leaks can be repaired with special rubber clamp-patches made for that purpose. Treat these as emergency repairs. Later the section of pipe should be replaced.

A large leak in a pipe may call for cutting out the damaged section and installing a new piece of pipe. At least one union will be needed unless the leak is near the end of the pipe.

An emergency pipe repair can be made with plastic or rubber tubing. The tubing must be strong enough to take normal water pressure in the pipe. Slip it over the open ends of the pipe and clamp it with pipe clamps or several turns of wire.

Vibration sometimes breaks a soldered joint in copper pipe causing a leak. If the joint is accessible, clean and resolder it. All water must be removed from the pipe before you can heat it to soldering temperature.

Leaks in tanks are usually caused by corrosion. Sometimes a safety valve may not open and the pressure developed will spring a leak. While a leak may show at only one spot on the tank wall, the wall may be thin in other spots too. For this reason, any repair is temporary. The tank will undoubtedly have to be replaced before very long. Temporary repair lets you replace at the most convenient time, not under duress.

A tank leak can be temporarily repaired with a toggle bolt, rubber gasket and brass washer. You may have to drill out the hole to get the toggle bolt

in. Draw the bolt up tight to compress the rubber gasket against the tank's side (see drawing).

FROZEN PIPES

In cold weather, water may freeze in unheated locations such as crawlspace or along outside walls. When water freezes it expands. Unless the pipe material can expand too, it may split. This is typical of iron and steel pipes. Copper pipe will expand some, but doesn't come back to its original size after freezing. Too many freezings and it will split, too. While flexible plastic pipe will take lots of freezing and thawing, it's wise to keep it from freezing.

You can prevent freezing by insulating the pipe or by installing an electric heating cable to warm it. Wrap the cable around the pipe and cover it with insulation.

The best, safest method of thawing a frozen pipe is with an electric heating cable, because the whole length of pipe is thawed at once. Thawing with a torch can be dangerous. Steam generated can make the pipe blow up in your face. If you must use a torch, never get the pipe hotter than you can hold your hand on.

Thawing with hot water poured over rags wrapped around the pipe is safer than torching.

When flame-thawing a pipe, open a faucet and start thawing at that point, reducing the chance for dangerous pressure build-up.

REMOVING DRUM TRAP COVER

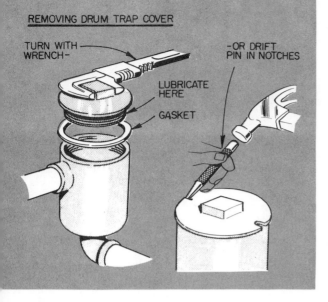

TURN WITH WRENCH–

–OR DRIFT PIN IN NOTCHES

LUBRICATE HERE

GASKET

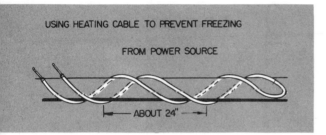

USING HEATING CABLE TO PREVENT FREEZING

FROM POWER SOURCE

ABOUT 24"

TOILET TANK REPAIRS

Toilet tank trouble nearly always spells a leak of some kind. Either the flush valve is failing to seat or the float valve isn't stopping water from entering the tank once it's filled. Hundreds of gallons of water can slip through a toilet tank unnoticed.

Once in a while something else goes wrong with a toilet tank, but a few adjustments can usually fix it. When there's a leak you can usually hear water running, if only slightly.

Here's a quick test that will help you find even a slight toilet tank leak in either the flush valve or float valve system. Touch a piece of paper to the back of the toilet bowl, above the waterline. If the paper gets wet there's a leak.

Take the flush valve system first. There are different types of flush valves in common use. The Douglas-type valve with flush ball is the most common. The newest toilets are equipped with either a brass or plastic Douglas valve and rubber flapper tilt, or bucket stopper. Other combinations are flapper with china seat and flush ball with china seat.

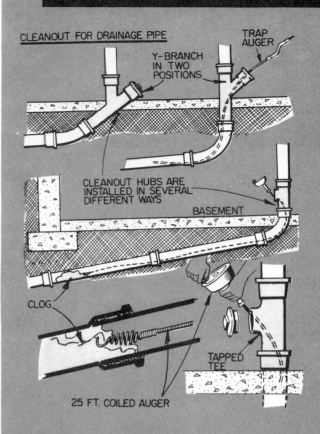

CLEANOUT FOR DRAINAGE PIPE

Y-BRANCH IN TWO POSITIONS

TRAP AUGER

CLEANOUT HUBS ARE INSTALLED IN SEVERAL DIFFERENT WAYS

BASEMENT

CLOG

TAPPED TEE

25 FT. COILED AUGER

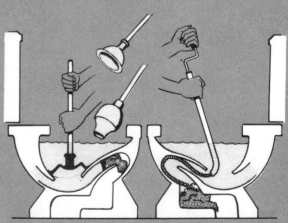

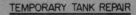

TWO TYPES OF PLUNGERS OR FORCE CUPS

A CLOSET AUGER OR SNAKE FOR DIFFICULT CLOGS

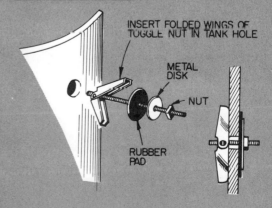

TEMPORARY TANK REPAIR

INSERT FOLDED WINGS OF TOGGLE NUT IN TANK HOLE

METAL DISK

NUT

RUBBER PAD

OPERATION OF TYPICAL TOILET FLUSH TANK

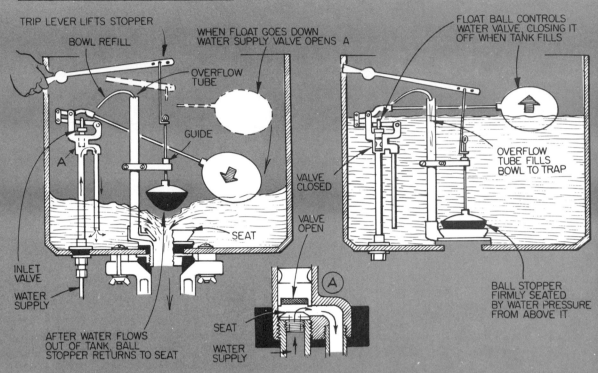

TRIP LEVER LIFTS STOPPER

BOWL REFILL

WHEN FLOAT GOES DOWN
WATER SUPPLY VALVE OPENS A

FLOAT BALL CONTROLS
WATER VALVE, CLOSING IT
OFF WHEN TANK FILLS

OVERFLOW
TUBE

GUIDE

A

VALVE
CLOSED

VALVE
OPEN

SEAT

OVERFLOW
TUBE FILLS
BOWL TO TRAP

INLET
VALVE

WATER
SUPPLY

SEAT

WATER
SUPPLY

A

AFTER WATER FLOWS
OUT OF TANK, BALL
STOPPER RETURNS TO SEAT

BALL STOPPER
FIRMLY SEATED
BY WATER PRESSURE
FROM ABOVE IT

A FEW OTHER TYPES OF FLOAT VALVES (BALL COCKS) ON THE MARKET

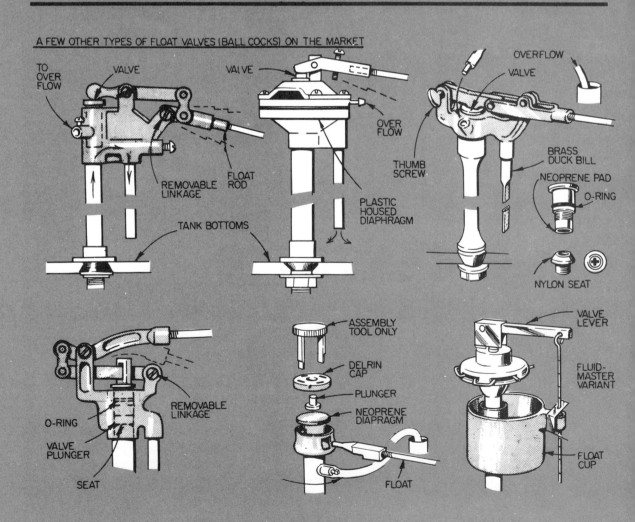

TO
OVER
FLOW

VALVE

VALVE

VALVE

OVERFLOW

VALVE

OVER
FLOW

THUMB
SCREW

BRASS
DUCK BILL

NEOPRENE PAD

O-RING

REMOVABLE
LINKAGE

FLOAT
ROD

PLASTIC
HOUSED
DIAPHRAGM

TANK BOTTOMS

NYLON SEAT

ASSEMBLY
TOOL ONLY

VALVE
LEVER

DELRIN
CAP

PLUNGER

FLUID-
MASTER
VARIANT

O-RING

NEOPRENE
DIAPRAGM

REMOVABLE
LINKAGE

VALVE
PLUNGER

SEAT

FLOAT

FLOAT
CUP

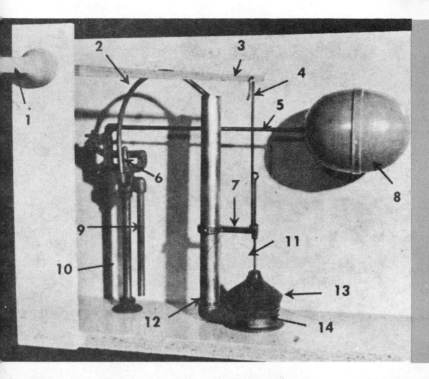

1. Trip handle
2. Refill tube
3. Trip lever
4. Upper lift wire
5. Float arm
6. Ball cock supply valve
7. Guide arm
8. Float
9. Discharge pipe
10. Supply pipe
11. Lower lift wire
12. Overflow pipe
13. Flush ball
14. Flush valve seat

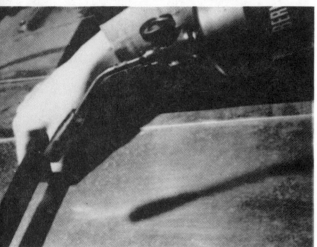

If a propane torch is used to thaw pipe, play flame along the frozen length; don't concentrate in one spot.

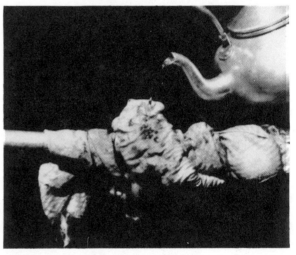

A safer way to thaw is to wrap pipe with rags; then pour hot water over rags. Use catch basin under pipe.

The older flush ball types are operated with upper and lower lift wires guided by arms. The flappers are operated with stainless steel link chains. As long as you keep any type of flush valve clean and well adjusted, you shouldn't have any trouble with it. If a ball or flapper gets coated with minerals or scum, if the rubber parts are defective, if the seat is irregular or if the lift wires are bent, the valve may leak. A ball or flapper that's misshapen, worn out, or one that has lost its elasticity and fails to drop tightly into the hollowed valve seat should be replaced with a new one.

RENEWING A TANK BALL

To replace a tank ball, first turn off the water supply. Usually there's a stop valve for this purpose under the toilet tank. You can also cut the water by propping a stick under the float arm inside the toilet tank. Then unscrew the flush ball from the lower lift wire. Attach a new ball the same diameter as the old one. If the threads are corroded, you may have to snip off the lower lift wire and replace it. No problem. You can buy new wires most anywhere that plumbing supplies are sold. Consider replacing both of the lift wires anyway.

It's cheap insurance. Get brass ones if you can. If you must reuse the old wires, inspect carefully to see that they're not bent. Before you put in the new flush ball, scour the valve seat with fine steel wool or No. 500 wet-or-dry abrasive paper. Get a smooth, uniform bearing for the stopper.

After you install the new tank ball,

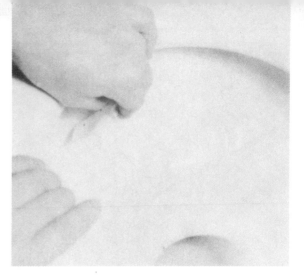

An easy way to tell if toilet tank is leaking is to place a piece of toilet paper to the back of the bowl. There's a leak if you find that the paper gets wet.

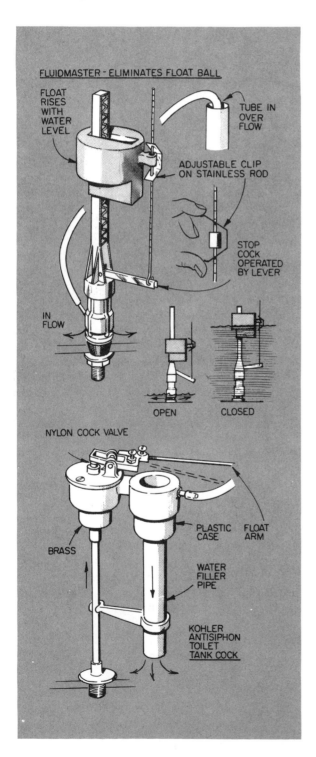

FLUIDMASTER - ELIMINATES FLOAT BALL

FLOAT RISES WITH WATER LEVEL

TUBE IN OVER FLOW

ADJUSTABLE CLIP ON STAINLESS ROD

STOP COCK OPERATED BY LEVER

IN FLOW

OPEN   CLOSED

NYLON COCK VALVE

PLASTIC CASE   FLOAT ARM

BRASS

WATER FILLER PIPE

KOHLER ANTISIPHON TOILET TANK COCK

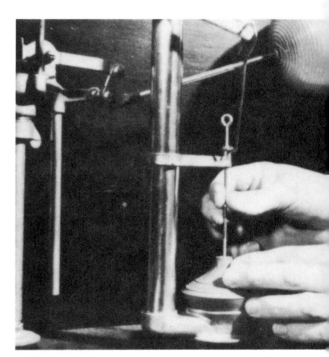

Installing a new flush ball and new lift wires takes care of a leak due to deterioration of the flush ball or bent or broken lift wires. It's a simple enough job.

You can adjust the tank water level by bending the float arm. Bend up to raise, down to lower level to 3/4-in. below the top of overflow pipe. Do not go lower.

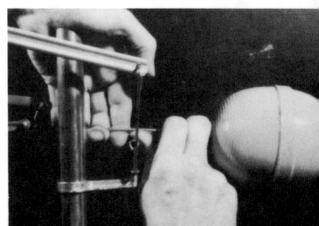

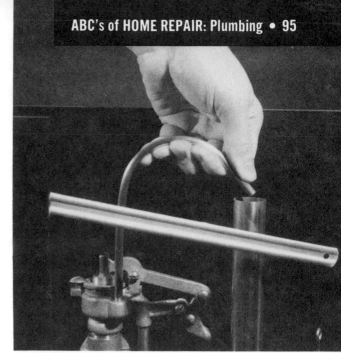

If the float valve still leaks and the float arm is free, remove inlet valve plunger and install a new washer and then you should also place a new packing on it.

Bend the refill tube down so its water spews into the end of overflow pipe. Don't however, get it below the level of water in the tank. Or it won't work.

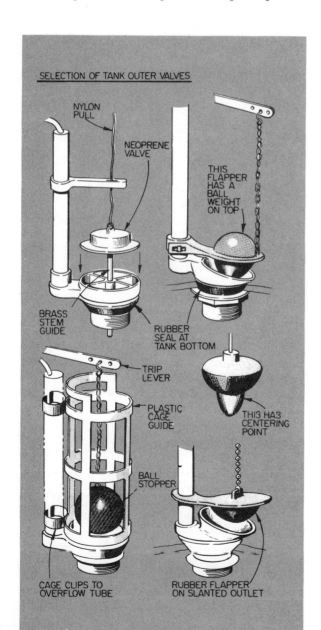

SELECTION OF TANK OUTER VALVES

NYLON PULL

NEOPRENE VALVE

THIS FLAPPER HAS A BALL WEIGHT ON TOP

BRASS STEM GUIDE

RUBBER SEAL AT TANK BOTTOM

TRIP LEVER

PLASTIC CAGE GUIDE

THIS HAS CENTERING POINT

BALL STOPPER

CAGE CLIPS TO OVERFLOW TUBE

RUBBER FLAPPER ON SLANTED OUTLET

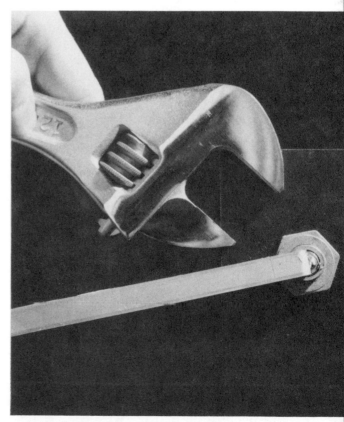

Tightening the nut behind the trip lever is about all the service it needs. Use an adjustable open-end wrench on left hand threaded nut. And tighten gently.

One common way to dry a sweating porcelain toilet tank is simply by cementing insulation to inside of it.

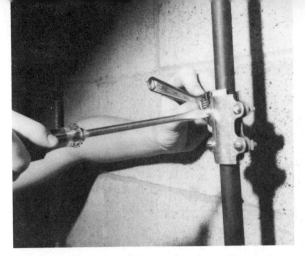

A simple pipe patch can be a big lifesaver. Keep one on hand in case you should develop a leaky pipe.

check to make sure it's centered directly over the seat. Adjust the guide arm if you need to. Some can be made longer or shorter as well as moved sidewise around the overflow pipe.

You can buy a new tank ball guide with a longer slide that reduces the amount of side-play in the flush ball. This may solve your problem. A new stopper with a bottom projection may solve a misalignment problem.

To equip your toilet tank with a rubber flapper flush valve, remove the flush ball, lift wires and ball guide. Slip the flapper onto the overflow pipe. Adjust it to drop neatly into place on the valve seat. Then hook up the trip chain to the right length. If the overflow-to-valve-seat distance on your Douglas valve isn't standard, a flapper may not work right.

Plastic flush valves can be cracked, letting water pass. Brass valves can be scored from past leakage. Replacement of the whole assembly is the only sure cure for these maladies.

FLOAT VALVES

Float valves are the devices that shut off the water to the toilet tank when the level reaches a certain height. They're of two types: vacuum-breaker and non-vacuum-breaker. Vacuum-breaker types have their bonnets and air inlet ports at least an inch above the overflow level of the tank. They're much the preferable of the two because they prevent toilet tank water from being accidentally siphoned back into the house water supply and possibly contaminating it.

Nonvacuum-breaker valves are completely submerged in the tank water.

If your tank leaks at the float valve rather than the flush valve, check to see that the float isn't hanging up against the trip lever or the side of the tank, thus failing to close the intake cock. Bending the float arm will correct this. Unscrew the float and shake it to see whether any water has leaked inside. If it has, replace the float. Some tank floats are plastic, eliminating the corrosion problem of copper floats.

Sometimes a readjustment of the water level in the tank is what's needed to stop the leaking or to provide enough water for a good flush. This is done by bending the metal rod attached to the tank float. When the rod is bent upward, the water will rise higher in the tank. When the rod is bent downward, the water level will be lowered. The water level in most toilet tanks should be ¾ inch below the top of the overflow pipe.

To fix a balky float valve, take it apart. To do this on the common type, turn off the water supply. Remove the screws that hold the float arm levers and lift them out. The stop cock will then lift out. Pull off the old washer with a pair of pliers and install a new one. Usually this is sufficient to stop the leaking. Sometimes the valve seat needs replacing, too. Then it may pay to replace the entire float valve assembly. Most hardware stores carry them in stock. The cost isn't much.

REFILL TUBE

While you're at it, check the refill tube to see that it isn't plugged and that

You will find it much cheaper to repair worn, leaky faucets and also valves than it is to buy new ones.

it's discharging into the overflow pipe. But make sure it isn't bent down into the pipe below the water level. If it is it'll siphon water out of the tank continuously and you won't ever know it.

If you have to hold the trip lever down until the toilet is through flushing, in order to get a complete flush, the trouble is probably in the lift wires. They may not be raising the tank ball high enough so that the force of the outrushing water can't pull it back down again. If you straighten and rebend the upper lift wire to shorten it, that should fix your trouble.

Rarely is the trip-lever the cause of toilet tank problems. There are two types in use on all toilets: single-acting and double-acting. The single-acting kind is more widely used today and seldom needs more than an occasional tightening of the lefthand threaded nut that holds it in the tank opening.

TOILET BOWL LEAKAGE

If a toilet bowl leaks around the bottom, it will have to be removed and resealed with a new bowl gasket. Follow this procedure:

1. Shut off the water and empty the tank and bowl by siphoning or sponging it out.

2. Disconnect the water pipes to the tank.

3. If the toilet and tank are a two-piece unit, disconnect the tank and bowl. Set the tank where it can't be damaged. Always handle the parts carefully. They're made of vitreous china or porcelain which is easily chipped or broken.

4. Remove the seat and cover from the bowl.

5. Carefully pry loose the bolt caps and remove the bolts holding the bowl to the floor flange. Jar the bowl enough to break the seal at the bottom. Lift the bowl off and set it upside down on a thick padding of newspapers.

6. Clean off all of the old sealing material from the bowl and floor flange. Place a new wax or rubber bowl gasket around the bowl horn and press it into place.

7. Set the bowl as described in the chapter on installing fixtures. Install the tank and connect the water pipes to it. It pays to install all new gaskets, after first cleaning the surfaces thoroughly.

8. Test for leaks by flushing a few times. Then bolt on the seat and cover.

ENERGY/MONEY SAVER IDEA — HOT WATER

Hot water for your kitchen and bath can be expensive so make the most of your hot water heating equipment. Set your water temperature control at no more than 140 degrees, which is the "normal" calibration of most water heaters. Remember, the lower the water temperature the less heat is lost from the water heater and the water lines from the heater to the faucet. All water heaters are insulated for heat loss but the lines from the heater to the kitchen and bathroom faucets are usually uninsulated. Therefore, to save on fuel and receive the same amount of hot water, if you have a choice locate the water heater as close to the kitchen and bath as possible and insulate the lines. Easily installed insulation for pipes is readily available from your plumbing supply dealer. As the cost of fuel rises, insulating the hot water pipes can result in a real saving.

A test to determine whether trouble is in outdoor antenna is made with rabbit ears. This is quick and easy.

REMEDYING ANTENNA PROBLEMS

Safety first with rooftop work;

focus attention on lead-in wire

A TV antenna can cause snow, ghosts, overloading, flashing, static, loss of detail, weak color, no color, worms and other troubles closely resembling set troubles. Therefore your first antenna troubleshooting move is to make sure it is really antenna trouble.

A quick test is easy. Take a pair of rabbit ears, indoor antenna, disconnect the outdoor antenna and install the indoor in its place.

Has the trouble disappeared? Are you now getting normal indoor antenna reception? If so the outdoor antenna is really at fault. If the trouble is still as apparent as before, the TV set is causing the symptoms.

Once you have decided it's really the outdoor antenna system that needs work, you are ready to go. Let's go through the various reasons an antenna fails and the techniques required for the repair.

Safety First: Your number one consideration is SAFETY FIRST! Rooftop work should only be performed by people who have experience with a ladder. It's always the novice who gets hurt. There are two main dangers on a roof, falling and bare electrical wires. Be careful!

WEATHER'S TOLL

Commonest Antenna Breakdown: Unlike the TV that sits indoors like one of the family, the antenna system is exposed to the elements day in, day out. Wind, rain, snow and sun takes its toll. Your LEAD-IN WIRE has a limited life. The wire is subject to deterioration and as a result becomes disconnected, loose, waterlogged, touched by metal, frayed and broke.

Each one of these forms of wear causes TV trouble symptoms to appear on your screen. Each form of wear has its own family of symptoms. A good approach is to simply pull out the old wire and install a complete new length. There are new types of lead-in wire being developed all the time. Therefore if your wire is more than two years old, that's what you should do.

However, if your wire is newer, or was a strong type to begin with, maybe you can repair it. Let's go through the lead-in wire troubles.

Loose Wire: From the connection on the antenna head to the TV set

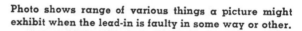

Splice twin lead breaks to make a permanent repair. Trick in TV repair is in locating the site of the break.

Photo shows range of various things a picture might exhibit when the lead-in is faulty in some way or other.

ANTENNA TROUBLES	
TROUBLE	**REMEDY**
Snow, Ghosts, No Color Flashing, Rolling, Bouncing	Replace Wire Check for Poor Connections Snug Down Wire Replace old Standoffs Install More Standoffs Repair or Replace Old Antenna Heads Orient Antenna for Best Heading
Motor Stops or Becomes Erratic	Check connections at Motor and Control box Replace filter capacitor in motor Replace motor Repair or replace control box
Booster Troubles— Snow, Hum Bars, Rolling	Replace Tubes, Transistor or Nuvistors, Replace filter capacitors

If small, antenna doesn't pull good reception. You must choose a more elaborate and maybe expensive rig.

terminals the wire, ideally, should be snug. However, wind over a period of time loosens it. When this happens the wire flaps from even the slightest breeze. The TV picture become erratic. The picture flashes, flops and has color fading in and out. These troubles will have a degree of seriousness in direct relation to the amount of looseness. The remedy: snug down all loose sections of wire.

Disconnected: The wire is vulnerable at connection points—at the antenna head, at any two set couplers, splitters etc., and at the terminals of all the TV's, FM sets or anything else it's connected to. Just one poor connection will cause snow, loss of sound or color, rolling, barberpole effect, worms or ghosts. Check all connections for a complete disconnection, partial disconnection, fraying connection or accidental shorting across terminals by frayed lead-in wire.

It's a good idea to install spade lugs at all connection terminals.

Touched by Metal: If you are using coaxial or shielded cable you can forget about this trouble. With regular twin lead though this is an important consideration. The lead must not touch any rain gutters, drain pipes, TV masts or even lay flat on a roof. Take pains to be sure that the wire is run through enough standoff insulators.

When twin lead touches metal an impedance bump develops at that point. An impedance bump blocks off TV signal like dirt does in a water pipe. The bump not only blocks but bounces the signal back up the wire. These standing waves cancel out some of the incoming signal and combine with some of the signal to cause incorrect impulses to enter the TV set. The metal touching ends up as loss of fine detail, loss of color intensity and ghosts in the TV picture.

NO VISUAL TIPOFF

Broken Wire: If you can see where the lead-in is broken splice it right there. More times than not, though, the wire breaks inside the insulation and there is no visual tipoff. You conclude there might be a break in the wire when snow and flashing appears in your TV picture and the rabbit ears test says the antenna is at fault.

The best approach is replacement of the entire length of wire. Should you want the satisfaction of locating the exact trouble spot, here is how it can be done. You'll need an ohmmeter or other type of continuity device. Disconnect the wire at the set's antenna terminal and short the two ends together. Then working toward the antenna head on the roof, pierce the insulation with the meter probes and shake the wire. As long as the meter reads short you haven't reached the break. As soon as the meter reads open or the needle begins acting erratic you have just passed the break. It lies between that spot and the last one. Zero in on it from there. Then splice in a new section of wire.

Broken or Worn Out Standoffs: These items break, come loose or lose their insulating centers. It is usually obvious when this happens and you can find the bad one by examining them one by one. The bad standoff can cause the lead-in to be loose, break or touch metal. This gives all the snow, flashing, loss of color, etc., symptoms. If in doubt replace the standoffs. They are inexpensive and simple to install.

Worn Out Heads: Antenna heads

become defective because they wear out. The bolts rust, the elements deteriorate, fall off, bend, touch each other and cause the head to swing in the wrong direction.

Another more subtle defect occurs when new high buildings are built nearby or a TV transmitter moves its location. The TV picture symptoms usually occur over a long period of time, little by little, and you hardly realize what bad shape you are in.

When you decide to do work on your antenna head, should you repair or replace? If the head is more than a year old and is an inexpensive type, replace. It will probably fall apart as you take it apart. If it's a fancy rig the repair attempt might be worthwhile, especially if it's anodized.

REPLACE BROKEN ELEMENTS

Bent elements need only be straightened. Broken elements need replacing. Buy some ½-inch aluminum tubing

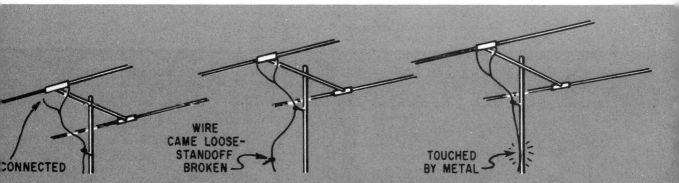

When lead-in loosens it will flap in the slightest breeze. Broken wire's easy to see.

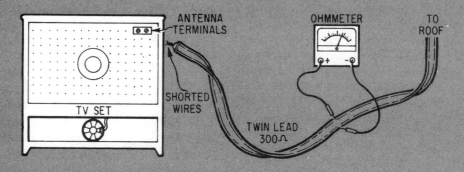

Locate actual break by shorting lead-in at antenna terminals and working your way up.

When a new building is erected it can have bad effect on other sets' reception in area.

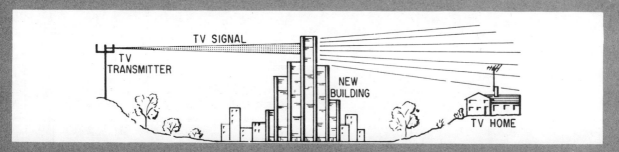

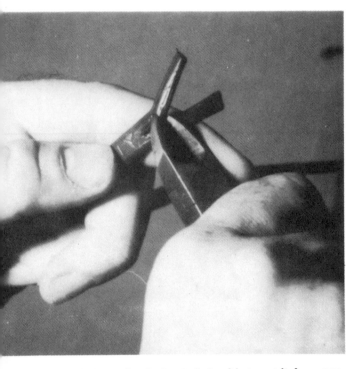

Technique of stripping twin lead is to cut it down center and then take off each side as shown in photo.

If your antenna develops electric charges install a ground rod which should be attached to the main mast.

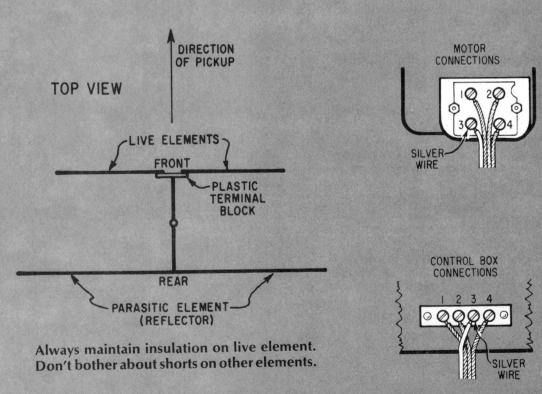

DIRECTION OF PICKUP

TOP VIEW

LIVE ELEMENTS

FRONT

PLASTIC TERMINAL BLOCK

REAR

PARASITIC ELEMENT (REFLECTOR)

Always maintain insulation on live element. Don't bother about shorts on other elements.

MOTOR CONNECTIONS

SILVER WIRE

CONTROL BOX CONNECTIONS

SILVER WIRE

In motor troubleshooting, first check connections. Alliance rotors have this layout.

and a hacksaw. Remove the old element and measure off a new replacement length exactly. Attach the new element.

If it's a parasitic element it's attached directly to the crossbar. You can run screws and bolts through them at will with little concern for insulation. If it's a driven element, one that has lead-in attached to it, be sure you maintain insulation between the elements. Don't short out the spacing between the elements on the insulated element holder.

After you repair the head take a can of plastic spray and put a coat on the antenna, especially around where the lead-in is installed. When you place the new antenna or repaired antenna in place check the orientation. Are you picking up best possible all-around reception? Loosen the mount, rotate the antenna a few degrees at a time and make note of the pictures on your screen. At the heading where best reception is obtained, lock the antenna in.

If you find you need two or three spots for best reception on different channels you can cut a motor in so you can orient your antenna from setside.

Probing the Roof: When your TV picture is a casualty of progress and a new structure has hurt your reception you can probe the roof for a new antenna location and height. This is a two-man walkie-talkie job. One man on the roof walking around with an antenna head on a pole testing different locations on the roof, different angles, and various heights; the second man at setside reporting results. It's time-consuming and dangerous for the rooftop man but often you can get excellent results.

When this produces poor results you can try more expensive rigs and different manufacturers' products.

Servicing Motors: The more complex your antenna system becomes, the more likelihood you'll need service. When you get a motorized antenna in addition to all else, there is a motor, a length of four-wire cable and a control box. These three items are all subject to failure. The symptoms are simple; the motor won't turn.

WIRE NEEDS CHECKING

First check is to make sure all connections are okay. If one of the eight connections, four in the control box and four in the motor, should come off, the motor won't turn. Next check is to look over the wire. It is subject to breakage and fraying due to wind and weather. Be sure to snug it down firmly and replace any standoffs that might have gone bad.

Once you are sure the wire is okay, check out the control box. We prove or eliminate the control box as faulty by installing a new one and see what happens. If performance is restored then we know the box is at fault. Should the trouble persist we know it's not. Perhaps you can borrow a contol box from a neighbor and do the same thing.

Actual servicing of the control box means testing switches, wiring and clock mechanism type equipment. Once

Motor failure is often caused by a defective filter capacitor. The best solution is change before going on.

Hum bars caused by signal booster failure, rolling and overload. You had better check your tubes and filter.

Snow is a problem that can afflict your screen when signal booster has failed. It's an obvious give-away.

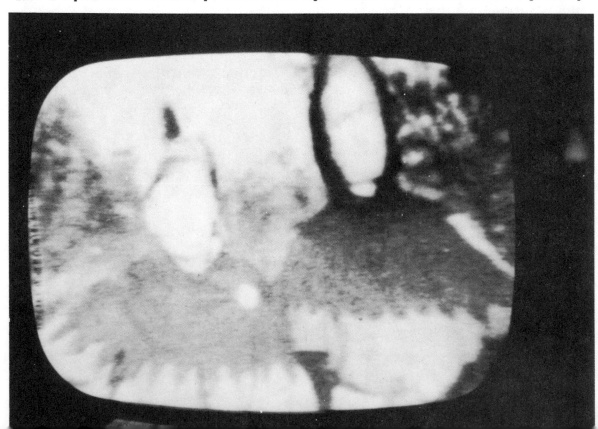

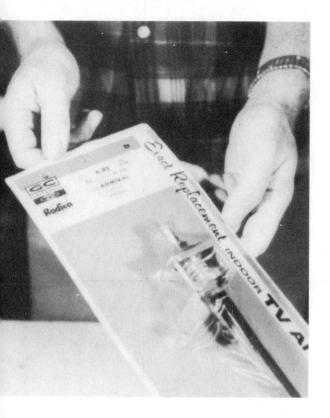

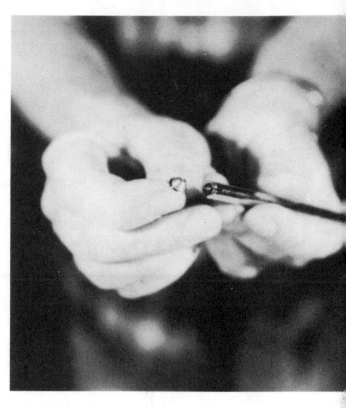

Typical failure is breakage of built-in antenna; replacements are easily available at any TV parts store.

If only the rod of built-in antenna breaks, replace with a cheap, easy-to-install replacement. It's just as good.

you establish that the wire and control box are cleared, the only thing left is the motor. There is a filter condenser in the motor. In a great percentage of motor failures it's that filter that has gone bad. If you can get the motor down, check it first. Everything else in the motor is mechanical, and if you can work on gears and rotation equipment it's all yours. Decide in servicing the motor and control box whether it is worth your while to repair the old equipment or replace it. Unless it's the filter I'd replace the entire motor. It's rough to keep climbing up and down to service it. You can go a little further with the control box since it is convenient. However, too much servicing on it indicates replacement.

Servicing Boosters: Repairing boosters is just like repairing any other circuit. It's electronic work and you need

circuit repair technique. There are two troubles a bad booster can cause: Snow in the picture to a more or less degree, and visible hum in the picture to a more or less degree.

The rabbit ears test will pinpoint the trouble as being either in the booster or in the TV. It's very important to use the test. Since the booster is an auxiliary RF amplifier, it causes exactly the same symptoms as the tuner.

The first approach is to replace the tube, transistor or nuvistor. In boosters ninety-five per cent of the time this will effect the cure. If it doesn't you need a bench repair which you must use your judgment on attempting.

Should you have visible hum trouble, in addition to the tube or equivalent, try replacing the booster's filter condensers. Chances are good you might effect this repair.

BUILD YOUR OWN ULTRASONIC BURGLAR ALARM

It's after midnight. The house is quiet. But trouble is lurking in the shadows. A burglar hiding in the shrubbery approaches a window and starts to open it. He looks carefully for switches, wire strung across the window sill and light beams. Not finding them, he starts to enter. The instant he sticks his hand inside an alarm goes off to alert you of the danger.

Inside a store a shoplifter hides during the day. After the store has closed he leaves his lair and starts for the jewelry counter. As soon as he moves an alarm goes off outside to summon the police.

In your office a prowler intent on cracking the wall safe looks for the usual light beams, switches on the door jamb and wire strung across the room. Not seeing them he heads toward the safe. As he moves towards it an alarm goes off.

What is it that detects the person in each of these situations? It's an invisible spider web of silent sound coming from our ultrasonic burglar alarm system and it fills the room. Our alarm also can be used as a proximity detector or even a fire alarm.

The system consists of a transmitter and a receiver. The transmitter sends out an ultrasonic sound which fills the room. Waves reflected by the walls, ceiling, floor and objects are picked up by the receiver. Any phase or amplitude change in the reflection of the wave appears to the receiver as an amplitude modulation of the signal.

The receiver amplifies the signal and then demodulates it. A Schmitt trigger shapes the demodulated signal and feeds it to a relay driver amplifier, which actuates a small reed relay.

The alarm is sensitive enough to detect the air turbulence that is caused by fire. Connect an oscilloscope to the third-amplifier output (pin 7) of the IC, and you'll be able to see the effect

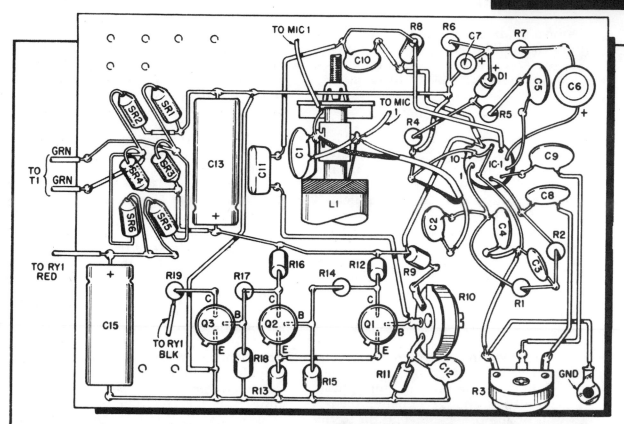

Receiver circuit board is 4 x 5 in. To conserve space, we mounted resistors on end rather than flat. In pictorial we show wiring on top of board; however, as you can see in photo below, wiring in our model is on rear of board.

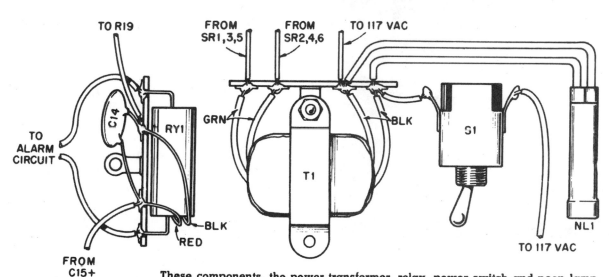

These components, the power transformer, relay, power switch and neon lamp are mounted at the top of the main section of the Minibox as in photo at right.

of normal air currents in a perfectly quiet room. The receiver can cover a 120° arc and is sensitive enough to pick up an intruder at a 20-ft. distance.

How the System Works

The transmitter sends out a 17-kc ultrasonic signal which will saturate a small room. The receiver picks up not only the direct signal from the transmitter, but the waves that are reflected by walls, ceiling and other objects in the room. The many waves which have traveled different distances, have different phase relationships at the receiver. The receiver's microphone algebraically adds the amplitude and phase relationships of all the waves and produces a signal which the receiver sees as a single reflected wave.

If an object in the room moves, its reflected wave, as seen by the receiver, will change in amplitude and phase. The amplitude change depends on the position of the object in relation to the receiver and transmitter. The phase change depends on the speed of the object and the wavelength of the transmitted signal.

mitted signal.

Since the wavelength of a 17-kc signal is about 0.8 in. an object moving at several feet-per-second toward the receiver, will cause phase reversals in its reflected wave at a rate of 30 to 50 cps. These phase reversals will alternately add to and subtract from the total received signal and appear to modulate the signal at a low audio rate.

Crystal mike MIC1 is tuned to 17 kc by L1 and C1. Capacitor C2 feeds the input signal to the first amplifier of IC1. The signal is amplified and the output at pin 3 goes to *sensitivity* pot R3. This pot determines the level of the signal which is sent to the second amplifier input at pin 4.

The output of the second amplifier is demodulated by D1. It is then filtered by C3, which also attenuates the high frequencies and noise in the modulation envelope. The third amplifier in the integrated circuit is used as a straight amplifier for the demodulated signal. The signal is then fed to the Schmitt trigger (Q1, Q2). Capacitors C4 and C10 are RF bypass capacitors. Potentiometer R10 is a trigger-level pot for the Schmitt trigger.

The Schmitt trigger, which is a regenerative switch, converts the demodulated signal into square waves which feed relay-driver Q3 and relay RY1. Relay RY1 is a reed relay which is used to control an external relay. It has a contact rating of 500 ma. An ordinary relay mounted in the same cabinet as MIC1 will, on closing, cause acoustic feedback and send the system into oscillation. The reed relay's contact closing is almost inaudible.

The transmitter is a standard emitter-coupled oscillator which is powered by a 9-V transistor-radio battery. Crystal microphone MIC2 is connected across the tank circuit. The efficiency of the oscillator and the transducer are so high that the battery drain is only 1.5 ma. This enables the battery to operate the transmitter continuously for one week without replacement.

The transmitter can also be powered from the receiver power supply. Connect two wires across C15 and run them to the transmitter. At the transmitter install a decoupling network consisting of a 200-ohm resistor and

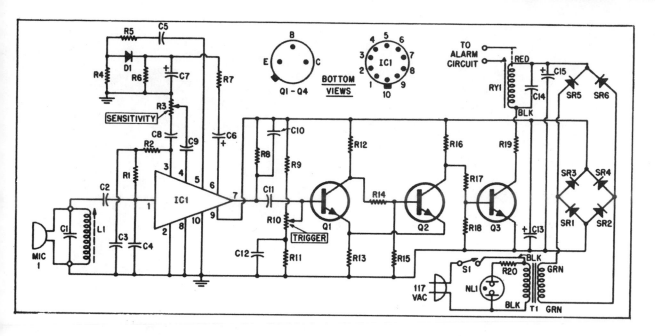

Output of IC1 is fed to Schmitt trigger (Q1,Q2) which converts demodulated signal into square waves that feed relay-driver transistor Q3. Q3 energizes reed relay RY1 which is used to control an external relay.

a 200-μf capacitor.

Construction

The receiver was constructed on perforated circuit board and eyelets were used for mounting parts. This method proved much cheaper and quicker than using a homebrew printed-circuit board.

The CA3035 integrated circuit should be mounted in a 10-pin socket so you don't have to solder directly to the IC's leads. Transistor leads can be pushed through the eyelets and soldered. However, do not push the transistors flush to the board or the eyelets will short to the transistor case. Let the transistors sit about 1/8 in. above the board.

The circuitry layout is not critical, but try to duplicate ours. However, the position of L1 may be a bit touchy. Inductor L1 should be placed well away from the power transformer or it will pick up hum. Mount the microphones in the cabinets in 1⅜-in. dia. punched holes. Epoxy cement can be used to hold the mikes in place. The power-transformer secondary has a center-tap lead which is not used. It should be cut short and taped so it will not touch the cabinet.

Five-lug terminal strips, with center lug mounting, were used for the AC terminals and the relay connections. The relay itself is mounted by its con-

tact leads. This means they should not be slack or the relay will have a tendency to vibrate when the contacts close and cause acoustic feedback.

Adjustments

To start with, turn on the receiver but disconnect the 9-V battery from the transmitter. Turn R3 counterclockwise for minimum sensitivity. Now turn R10 so that the relay closes. Back off on R10 so that the relay opens again. The Schmitt trigger is now set just below its threshold. If RY1 closes unpredictably, back off on R10 a bit until the relay is just into its stable *off* position.

Next, connect a scope from pin 5 of

Transmitter is emitter-coupled oscillator whose ultrasonic frequency is determined by L2. MIC2 is crystal mike. It works well as ultrasonic speaker.

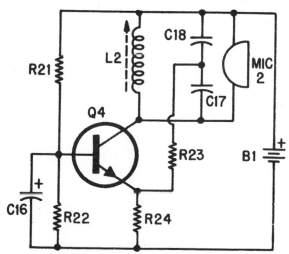

In addition to the ultrasonic burglar system described in this article, moderately priced conventional electric eye alarms are also available to build from kits or purchased complete and ready for installation. Complete unit above with an effective range of 50 feet. Both units available from Allied Radio Shack.

PARTS LIST

B1—9 V battery
Capacitors: 50 V or higher unless otherwise
  indicated
C1,C17—.01 µf, ceramic disc
C2,C3,C5,C8,C9,C10,C14—.04 µf ceramic disc
C4—.005 µf ceramic disc
C6—100 µf, 6-V electrolytic
C7,C16—5 µf, 6-V electrolytic
C11—.25 µf ceramic disc
C12—.002 µf, ceramic disc
C13,C15—1,000 µf, 10-V electrolytic
C18—.1 µf ceramic disc
D1—1N34A diode
IC1—CA3035 integrated circuit (RCA)
L1,L2—1.5-10 mh adjustable width coil (J. W.
  Miller 6322, Lafayette 34 F 88525)
MIC1, MIC2—Crystal-microphone cartridge
  (Lafayette 99 F 45908)
NL1—NE-2 neon lamp and holder
Q1,Q2,Q3—2N696 transistor
Q4—2N2270 transistor
Resistors: ½ watt, 10% unless otherwise
  indicated
R1,R2,R20—100,000 ohms
R3—2,000 ohm linear-taper potentiometer

Mallory Minitrol MTC-23L1, Lafayette
  33 F 16452 or equiv.)
R4,R5—5,600 ohms, 5%
R6,R14,R21—10,000 ohms, 5% R7—680 ohms
R8,R16—3,000 ohms, 5% R9—62,000 ohms, 5%
R10—5,000 ohm, linear-taper potentiometer
  (Mallory Minitrol MTC-53L1, Lafayette
  33 F 16457 or equiv.)
R11—6,800 ohms   R12—5,000 ohms, 5%
R13—330 ohms   R15—2,700 ohms
R17—2,200 ohms, 5%
R18,R22—1,000 ohms, 5%
R19,R24—100 ohms   R23—510 ohms, 5%
RY1—SPST (normally-open contacts) miniature
  reed relay. Coil: 200 ohms, 6V., Magnecraft
  W102 MX-2. Available for $2.25 (plus postage)
  from Allied Radio Corp., 100 N. Western Ave-
  nue, Chicago, Ill. 60680. Stock No. 41 D 4554.
  Not listed in catalogue.
SR1-SR6—Silicon rectifier; minimum ratings: 750
  ma, 50 PIV
T1—Filament transformer, secondary 6.3 V @
  0.6A
Misc.—Perforated circuit board, flea clips, 5 x
  2¼ x 2¼-in. Minibox, 6 x 5 x 4-in. Minibox,
  integrated-circuit socket (Cinch-Jones 10-ICS)

IC1 to ground and slowly turn R3 clockwise toward maximum. If oscillation breaks out connect a 200-ohm resistor across R3. If the 200-ohm resistor does not stop the oscillation, back off on R3 until the oscillation stops. Now connect the scope to the junction of R5/C5 and ground. The transmitter should be about 10 ft. from the receiver. Fire up the transmitter and observe the pattern on the scope. Next, adjust the core of L2 on the transmitter until the pitch of the sound is beyond the range of your hearing. To our ears the frequency was about 17 kc. If the waveform is saturated (flattened at the top and bottom) back off on R3 until the waveform is clean. Now adjust L1 for maximum signal and back off on R3 if

Layout of transmitter's parts on 2 x 3-in. piece of perforated board is not critical. Bracket holding L2 is made from a piece of scrap aluminum.

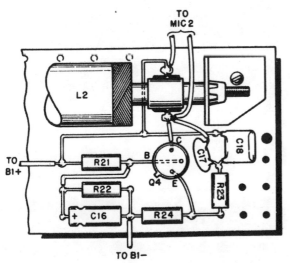

the signal saturates.

A final adjustment should be made with the transmitter in its more-or-less permanent location. If used to detect the opening of a door, the transmitter should face the door and be about 4 ft. from the receiver.

The receiver should also face the door, and all final adjustments should be made from the rear of the receiver, so as not to block the mike. Adjust R3 so that the waveform is saturated. Now back off on R3 until the peak-to-peak signal voltage is half the saturated voltage.

You're now ready for the final test. Stand in front of the receiver about 5-ft. away from it. Now walk toward the receiver. The relay should close. You may have to experiment with the placement of the receiver and the adjustment of R3 and R10 for maximum sensitivity and stability. Relay RY1 should only be used to actuate an external relay, which can operate a bell or any other alarm device.

Keep in mind that spurious responses could be caused by a slowly moving curtain, the movement of a rattling window pane, or the noise of a steam valve.

In any event, you'll get to know the vagaries of the situation, because it's quite clear that whatever can be disturbed by a burglar, an unauthorized person on the premises, can be disturbed by a great many other things.

HOW TO AIR CONDITION AN EXISTING HOUSE

by Arthur M. Watkins

Salvage as much as possible from your present heating system, check insulation, shade, wiring—then find the most suitable cooling unit.

►*How well is your attic insulated?* Biggest cooling problem is almost always from the huge heat load on the roof that builds up furnace-like temperatures in an attic. Engineers find most attics "inadequately insulated." So your first step should be a thorough attic investigation. As much as six inches of bulk insulation laid over the ceiling or the equivalent in aluminum foil insulation will usually pay for itself. Most houses today have less than three inches of insulation, if any at all. The gable ends of the attic should also be opened up with large ventilating louvers.

►*Are large windows shaded from direct sun rays?* If not, they should be protected by outside shading devices. Remember that ten times as much sun heat invades a house through glass as through an equal area of insulated wall.

►*Are the walls insulated?* Although it may be more costly to insulate the finished wall of an existing house, it will still pay when measured against cooling savings. Walls should get three inches of insulation and this can usually be blown in.

►*Can existing heating ducts be salvaged for cooling?* Because cooling generally calls for bigger ducts than those needed just for heating, have a trained dealer measure your existing ducts to see if they are big enough. "Heating ducts almost always work out," says one top engineer, "but some modifications may be needed." You may need a bigger trunk line in the basement or an extra duct run to a big room facing south. ("The easiest room to heat in winter is often the hardest to cool in summer.")

►*Can you keep the existing warm air outlets?* Proper air diffusion is far more important for cooling than heating. Air conditioning usually calls for a double-deflection type of air outlet—one with both vertical and horizontal louvers that can be opened, closed or slanted so the right amount of air is diffused in the right direction for each room. If your warm air outlets are plain metal grilles

Left, basic units for home air conditioning system also include heating and air cleaning equipment. At bottom is outdoor condensing unit supplying refrigerant to cooling coil atop furnace at upper left. Electronic air cleaner is at lower left, central humidifier at lower right, and room air conditioner at center. All products are from Carrier Air Conditioning Co.

Right, individual room cooling units may be as small as this casement window air conditioner by Fedders. It is easily mounted and rarely requires more than removal of a single window pane.

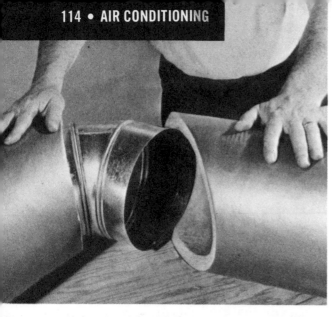

Pre-fabricated ducts are a boon to the home handyman. They include both thermal and acoustical insulation. Lower left, inch-thick duct boards may be formed into varying sizes of rectangular ductwork. Middle, rigid round ducts have inside diameters from 4 to 16 inches. Right, flexible duct is simple to install. Left photo shows 90 degree joint in round duct made by cutting 45 degree angles in two sections and inserting metal elbow. All ductwork shown is from Owens-Corning Fiberglas Corporation.

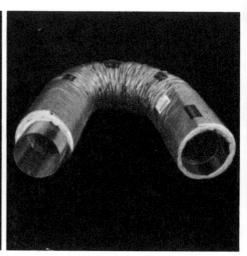

with fixed louvers they probably should be replaced.

►*Is the furnace blower big enough for cooling, too?* In about half of the cases, yes.

►*What can you do if your house has hot-water heat or no central heat?* You can put in a chilled-water system, console units or window units. In many houses, however, engineers say that a ductwork system is still your best bet, furring down the ducts in a central hall, for instance, with short ducts branching out to the rooms around. The hot water boiler remains for heating.

►*Is the present wiring adequate?* Most air-conditioning systems need at least a separate 220-volt, 30-ampere circuit wired straight from the main electric board. The board itself should normally have a capacity of at least 60 amperes for the whole house, preferably 100 amperes. The size of the board is usually marked on the cover. Another solution is a gas-operated air conditioner which only needs a relatively small amount of electricity to run its blower.

►*Which is the best cooling system for a particular house?* There are six principal types, all but one being the same as used in new houses. Here are the advantages and disadvantages of each:

The Add-On Unit

This was designed especially for adding cooling to an existing forced-air heating system.

The add-on unit is the most inexpensive if you start with a good forced-air heating system. For one thing, you usually save the cost of a cooling fan by using the furnace fan. For another, you use the ductwork already installed. And the remote compressor section can be bought with an air-cooled condenser so no water is needed. Total installation costs start at about $1,200 for a 2-ton size, the more complex the installation the higher the cost.

The Attic Cooler

The horizontal attic cooler is good for existing houses where space is at a premium. Actually the unit not only can go in the attic but can also be suspended from a closet or basement ceiling. If a house has heating ducts the unit can be tied into them for distributing cool air. If a house has hot water heat, the unit can be centered in the house and only short supply ducts need be installed to get air to all rooms. Cooling is then independent of the heating.

The Small Duct System

This system gives the advantage in many old houses of using small 3½-inch or four-inch round ducts that can be easily inserted within existing parti-

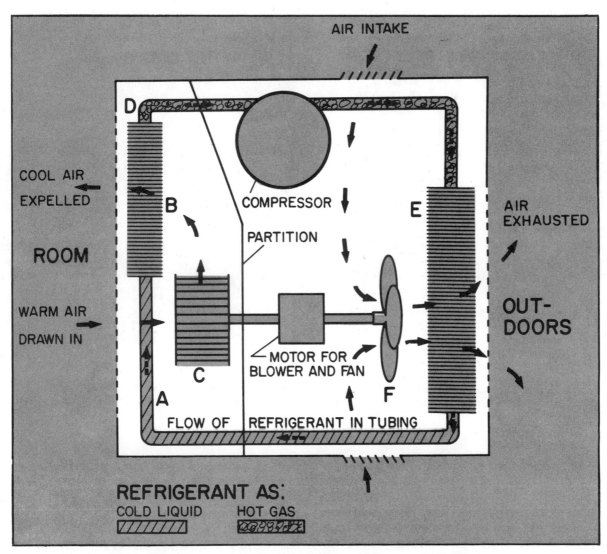

ILLUSTRATION OF THE AIR CONDITIONER IN OPERATION

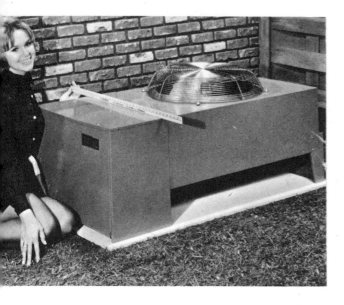

New whole-house cooling systems can be installed as close as 6 inches from house. Unit from York.

Arrangement for a basement installation shows connection between furnace and condensing unit.

Compact unit for apartment and small homes is from Chrysler Air Temp, needs only narrow closet.

Adjustable vanes on this Philco-Ford window air conditioner direct cool air to desired spot in room.

tions. This eliminates much of the cutting and patching in houses where conventional ductwork would normally mean expensive alterations. Thus the small duct system can be a natural in a house without any heating ducts to start.

The basic cooling equipment used is similar in size and cost to conventional equipment except that the air blower may be somewhat larger to deliver air at higher than normal velocities. This is because the smaller ducts require faster air speeds to handle the same overall

Left, air conditioning controls in Lennox system include temperature selector, humidity selector, fan control switch, and the electronic air cleaner lights.

Below, low silhouette and vertical discharge make it much easier to hide this outdoor Lennox condensing installation.

cooling load handled by bigger ducts with relatively low air velocities. But the slightly increased fan horsepower used makes very little difference on overall operating costs.

Room Air Conditioners

Room coolers are the easiest way to add air conditioning, especially in doing it piecemeal. But when a whole house is to be air conditioned the total cost can be much higher than the cost of installing a complete central system at one crack. Furthermore, the operating costs of a battery of room coolers will be higher than for a central system because a number of little compressors all running at one time are less efficient than one large compressor. And an odd array of room coolers sticking out of windows will add little to the appearance of any house.

On the plus side, room coolers can save you money if you only want to air condition part of a house and not all the rooms.

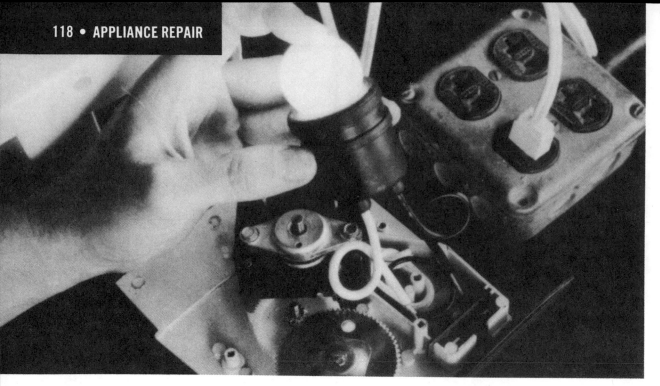

When you have a suspicious appliance cord and plug, the basic test to check its efficiency is to put the probes of a test light across the terminals of the appliance when plugged in. If there is voltage the light shows.

GROUND RULES OF APPLIANCE REPAIR

Repairs can be simple—if you have a VO meter and enjoy the puzzle

Treat your appliances right and they usually will last many years without servicing. But with all the appliances used in homes today the need for service is bound to come up. Mostly it's a simple repair. You can do it yourself if you know what to look for—and how to look.

Before you dive into any appliance repair ask yourself whether you *should* do it yourself. Many small appliances are guaranteed for one year from the date of purchase. If something goes wrong, you have only to take the appliance back where you got it and get another one free. Major appliances also have guarantees. You can void a guarantee by working on the appliance yourself.

Furthermore, don't try to repair appliances unless you know what you're doing and enjoy it. Appliance repair is like working a puzzle or taking apart a clock to see what makes it tick. Often

fixing an appliance is easier than solving a puzzle. More often the biggest problem is getting the appliance apart. For good looks some manufacturers hide the fastenings that hold the body of the appliance together. The fasteners are rarely obvious. Sometimes, once you find them, they're downright discouraging. Some appliances have rivets that must be filed down before the body can be taken apart.

DOES IT NEED TAKE-APART?

Do all the testing you can without taking the appliance apart. Make sure it needs take-apart before you try. Often there is merely an open wire at the plug. Cut the cord, install a new plug, and it works again. Even before you do that, check the receptacle to make sure it has power. Perhaps a fuse is blown.

Other problems that appliances develop are not electrical, but mechanical. The troubleshooting procedures for popular appliances given in another chapter stress electrical troubles, their causes and cures.

Never work on an appliance that is plugged in. You can make certain electrical tests with the plug in, but unplug it again right away. If you plug in a disassembled appliance, remember that the exposed leads, heating elements and other parts are live wires. Treat them that way—always.

VO METER

In line with making it fun to fix home appliances is the VO meter. Great accuracy of meters is not needed in appliance work, so you needn't spend a great deal for a meter. Better to have a low-cost one than do without.

The VO meter is useful for testing AC and DC voltages as well as circuit resistances. If you do much appliance or motor repair, you'll find a VO meter indispensable. It can tell you lots about the appliance without your ever disassembling it.

A VO meter usually has a selector switch to let it be adjusted for measuring different amounts of volts and ohms. For instance, a good meter has voltage settings for measuring as little as 1½ volts and testing voltages to 1½, 5, 15, 50, 150, 500 and sometimes more. It has ohm scales for measuring from 0 to infinite ohms. Each higher ohm class is 10 times the one below it. Where the resistance is high, the meter can be set for the highest ohm scale. Then it can even measure the resistance through your body as you hold the test prods in your hands. Where the resistance is very low, it can be set on the lowest resistance scale. Then the meter can measure resistance through the windings of an electric motor or through the corroded contacts of a switch.

You can use the voltage scale for checking batteries, house voltages, voltage leaks from faulty appliances, voltage drop across the contacts of a switch and house voltage drop when a heavy motor starts up.

SETTING THE SCALE

When testing a known voltage, al-

SAMPLE OHM READINGS	
APPLIANCE	OHMS
Clock	600 to 1200
Toaster (two-slice)	12 to 18
Waffle iron	8 to 10
Deep fat fryer	10
Rotisserie	9
Coffee maker	24
Hand iron	12 to 13
Heating pad	300
Electric blanket (double)	100
Vacuum cleaner	1 to 2
Table fan	20 to 30
Electric knife	40
Electric can opener	8
Shaver	140
Hair dryer	25
¼-inch drill	10 to 20
½-inch drill	4 to 9
Belt sander	3 to 9
Portable circular saw, 7-inch	4
1/20-H.P. split-phase motor	7
¼-H.P. split-phase motor	1 to 4
⅓-H.P. split-phase motor	0.8
⅓-H.P. capacitor motor	1.5
½-H.P. capacitor motor	0.6 to 1.2
¾-H.P. capacitor saw motor	1

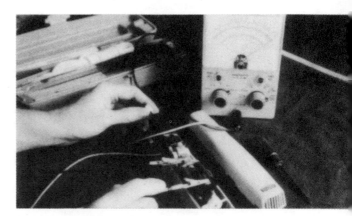

There's nothing like VO meter for making all sorts of electrical checks on appliance circuits. Get one if you make many repairs. It's safer too. And it is a quick way.

ways set the scale for the next higher voltage. For instance, to make a voltage test on a 6-volt lantern battery, set the volt selector at 15 volts. The needle scale will come not quite half-way to the 6-volt mark on the 15-volt scale. If you were to set the voltage selector at 5 volts, and connect it to 110 volts, the needle would jump off the scale. This is not good for the instrument and

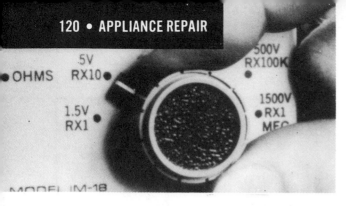

A VO meter should have range of both voltages and resistances. The ranges are made available by a rotating selector switch set for each test, here indicated.

Using a VO meter to check for low voltage at appliance terminals with unit plugged in and selector set for AC volt readings over 1000 volts. Caution: water-holding appliances (coffee pots, etc.) can be damaged by plugging in when empty; so, remember to be careful.

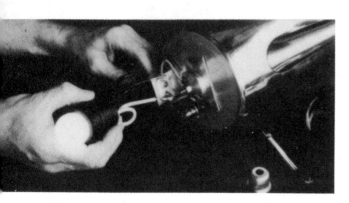

Same test is made without a VO meter by using a simple test light across appliance terminals. Brightness of the light indicates the voltage. It's really that simple.

would probably finish it for good. Think before you make each test.

When testing an unknown voltage, always start with the selector in the highest voltage position and work down one notch at a time until you get a good reading. Follow the specific instructions with the VO meter you are using.

Never take an ohm reading on a "hot" circuit. The VO meter has its own battery that provides power for ohm readings.

On the other hand, voltage readings must be taken on an energized circuit. Otherwise, there would be no voltage to measure.

TEST LIGHT

If you must do without a VO meter, make or buy a test light. The prods can be touched across any two wires to tell if there is voltage between them. If the lamp lights, there is. If it doesn't, there is little if any voltage.

A test light can be used to test receptacles to see if power is available in them. You can use it to test across the terminals of an appliance while it is plugged in. This checks out the cord. You can test between the closed switch or thermostat and the unswitched line at the terminal to see that they are making good electrical contact. If the lamp lights, they probably are. By using a larger wattage test lamp you can test a switch under a heavier load. Bulb size should be matched to the appliance's normal load for the best test of a switch.

One kind of home-made test light, called the series test light, has been widely illustrated in books on electrical repair. It can be dangerous. If you have one be careful with it. Two wires come out from a plug. One lead has a light wired into it. When the leads are touched, the lamp lights. Depending on which way the plug faces when you plug it in, the untapped lead can be a "hot" wire carrying the full 120 volts and 15 amps of the house circuit with no light between to offer resistance. When you touch it to an appliance, the whole appliance body becomes "live." It's best to let the professionals use this kind of light.

You can buy another kind of tester that has some uses a homemade test light can't match. It's a neon tester. Two test prods are wired to a neon lamp. The lamp glows under the slightest voltage. While it won't load a circuit being tested, it will test across the terminals of a switch or thermostat for

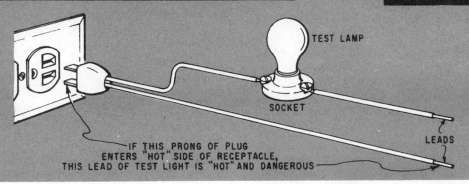

TEST LAMP

SOCKET

LEADS

IF THIS PRONG OF PLUG
ENTERS "HOT" SIDE OF RECEPTACLE,
THIS LEAD OF TEST LIGHT IS "HOT" AND DANGEROUS

voltage drop through it. If with the contacts closed, the neon tube glows, there is voltage drop. Perhaps the contacts need cleaning.

Low-voltage circuit testers come in flashlight form with test probes. You could make one easily enough by soldering a wire to the bulb's center terminal and another to the case.

BASIC TESTS

Familiarize yourself with three basic electrical tests and you'll be able to handle most electrical troubleshooting. There are the *continuity test*, the *resistance test* and the *voltage drop test*. Perhaps the most useful test is for circuit continuity. If electricity will flow through a circuit, it has a continuous path, or continuity.

By setting a VO meter for ohm-testing, the prods are energized with a slight voltage. When you touch them to anything that will carry electricity, the current flows from one test prod through the circuit and back to the other prod. The ohm meter needle moves when the prods are connected to a circuit with continuity. The meter measures the rate of electrical flow and interprets the result as ohms.

If the current flows abundantly, the meter reads low ohms (low resistance). If the current flows only meagerly, the meter reads high ohms (high resistance). Low ohm readings of less than 1 ohm and high ohm readings to infinity are possible with a good ohm meter. If there is current flow, which is shown by readings of less than infinity on the high ohms scale, the circuit has continuity. If there is no current flow, the circuit is open. Never test a "live" circuit for ohms. Take the plug out.

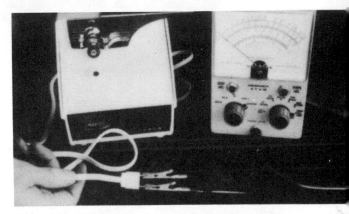

The continuity test is basic to all appliance repairs, small and large alike. Set a VO meter for high ohms and hook its probes across appliance plug. The reading should drop from infinite ohms to zero ohms when the switch is on. This means electricity is continuous.

Your test light will make continuity checks on "live" circuits without telling you much about resistance. If the lamp lights, there is continuity. If the lamp won't light, the circuit is open (see illustrations).

The continuity test is used to look for loose connections, switches that won't carry current, open thermostats, broken wires, and burned-out lamps.

OPEN CIRCUITS

Sometimes an open circuit is desirable. For example, when you throw a switch to *off*, the switch must create an open circuit to stop the flow of electricity and shut off the appliance. You also want an open circuit between the separate windings of an electric motor. If they should become interconnected, the motor would not run right. In testing for an open circuit the VO meter needle should show infinite ohms on the high-ohm scale or the test lamp should not light.

A variation of the continuity test is the ground continuity test. An appli-

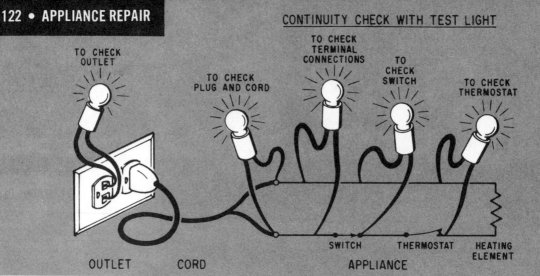

TO CHECK OUTLET

TO CHECK PLUG AND CORD

TO CHECK TERMINAL CONNECTIONS

TO CHECK SWITCH

TO CHECK THERMOSTAT

OUTLET   CORD   APPLIANCE

SWITCH   THERMOSTAT   HEATING ELEMENT

ance can be dangerous if any of the internal wiring is touching the body of the appliance. When a motor winding is grounded to the frame or to the shaft, the motor is in trouble; the user may be, too. In these instances there should be no continuity between the circuit and the body of the motor or appliance.

To test for this kind of ground continuity the VO meter prods are touched across one of the flat plug prongs and the body of the appliance. The selector should be on the highest ohm setting. The appliance should be unplugged but its switch should be on. The meter needle should barely move from the infinity position. Very slight movement is permissible. This indicates a teeny current leakage across insulators and an air gap. It should, however, be many times less than the needle moved when you hold the prods in opposite hands. An indication of continuity from the "live" circuit to the appliance body is bad. Something must be fixed before you use the appliance. Take it apart and find the bad ground.

GROUND TEST

You can't make a reliable ground test with a test light, though it will show up a strong ground. The ground continuity test is made with a test light while the appliance is plugged in. Touch one prod to the appliance body, the other to a water pipe or other good ground. If the lamp even glows, fix the bad ground immediately. You're looking at a dangerous appliance.

Since the amount of current it takes to kill wouldn't light a Christmas tree lamp, also make the test with a volt

meter set on low scale and connected as described for the test light.

After you finish repairing any appliance, make a continuity check for a bad ground. In fact, as soon as you get your VO meter learn how to use it to make a bad ground check on all your appliances. Do the same with every new appliance before using it. During shipping an insulator can get broken or a terminal pulled loose. Without a ground test, you may not know if the item is unsafe until someone gets shocked. Sometimes the leakage is slight, barely more than a slight tingle when you rub lightly across the metal body. That's too much. A tingle today can be lethal tomorrow. Fix it. Also, don't hold the appliance while you plug it in if you're grounded.

A THIRD CIRCUIT

Electric drills, saws and many other small household appliances these days are either double-insulated or grounded. This sort of grounding is different. It isn't the "live" circuit that is grounded to the appliance body, but a third green-wired grounding circuit. The grounding wire is attached to the appliance at one end and wired to the longest prong of a three-prong plug at the other. When plugged into a grounded three-hole outlet, the third wire effectively grounds the body of the appliance to prevent accidental shock while using it.

You can tell the god guys from the bad guys with your VO meter or test light. Using a VO meter, touch one lead to the body of the appliance and the other to the grounding prong of the

With a sensitive VO meter you can even measure your body's resistance to electricity. Set the scale on high ohms, then watch the needle fall as you grasp the test probes with your fingers, and you've an indication.

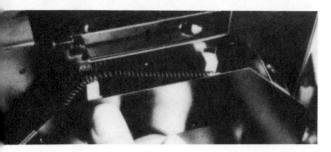

Bad ground could be caused by a heating element wire knocked from its insulator in a shipping accident. Check all new appliances for bad grounds before using. Tighten all grounds. Check rest of equipment.

three-prong plug. There should be complete continuity. The ohm scale should be on its lowest ohm setting and the needle should flick to *0 ohms*. This signifies that there is a complete grounded circuit from the tool to the plug's prong.

The same test can be made with a test light on the plugged-in appliance. The appliance should rest on a nonconductive surface. Put one prod of the light in the "hot" side of a receptacle. This is the one with the shortest hole. Touch the other prod to the body of the appliance. The lamp should light brightly.

BOTH TESTS DESIRABLE

Both the ohm test and the test light check are desirable. The test light (depending on its size) proves the ability of the ground circuit to carry current. Ideally the ground should have enough capacity to blow a fuse. Have serious doubts about any ground system that won't light a 100-watt lamp to full brilliance.

If there is not good ground continuity, part of the grounded circuit is open. The trouble may be in the appliance or in your house wiring. Find it and fix it.

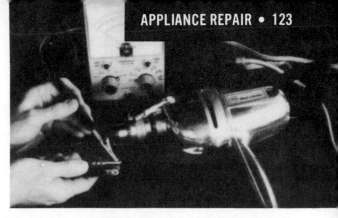

Most home appliances should be grounded to the round prong of a grounding plug. There should be less than half an ohm resistance between the body of the appliance and the plug. Set the VO meter on the low-ohm scale when you are engaged in any checking.

You can check the house circuit ground by taking a voltage reading with your VO meter. Set the volt selector higher than 120 volts. Touch the prods to the "hot" hole of the receptacle and the grounding hole. You should get the same voltage reading as when the prods are touched across the "hot" and neutral holes. (The neutral is the wider of the two parallel holes.) If you don't, either the outlet is not grounded or the black and white leads to it are reversed. Take it out and investigate further with a test light and VO meter.

You can have fun going around to all your receptacles and testing them this way.

HOW TO TEST

The same check can be made with the test light. It's a better check because it proves at least some current-carrying ability, if a 100-watt lamp is used. Plug the test probes in across the "hot" hole and the grounding hole. The lamp should light with full brilliance. No light or a weak light is a tipoff to trouble.

Your VO meter also is useful for making voltage drop readings. These can be helpful in ferreting out a faulty switch or thermostat. With the body off and the appliance plugged in and operating at full load, carefully take a voltage reading across the two terminals of the switch or thermostat contact points. There should not be more than a few volts potential. If the potential is, say, 10 volts across the switch, that means it is stealing 10 volts of electri-

TESTING FOR OUTLET GROUND

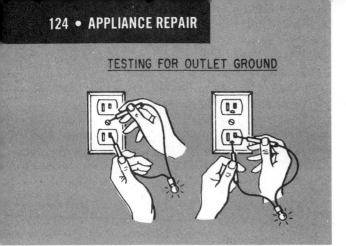

BIMETALLIC THERMOSTAT PRINCIPLE

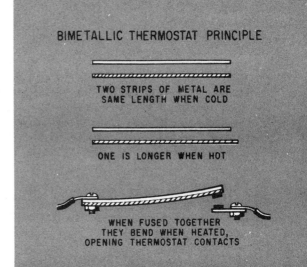

TWO STRIPS OF METAL ARE
SAME LENGTH WHEN COLD

ONE IS LONGER WHEN HOT

WHEN FUSED TOGETHER
THEY BEND WHEN HEATED,
OPENING THERMOSTAT CONTACTS

To measure the voltage drop of a vacuum or extension cord, take a low-volts reading from one end of one wire to the other while the appliance is operating. The voltage drop reading should always be a few volts or less, as in any circuit you may happen to be checking.

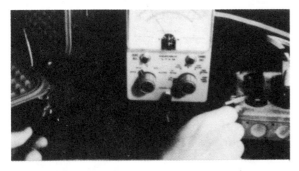

Measure the voltage drop across a suspected circuit—in this case the thermostat of a briefly plugged-in coffee maker. When checking, always set the VO meter on low volts. The voltage drop reading should be a few volts or less. If it isn't, you've located it.

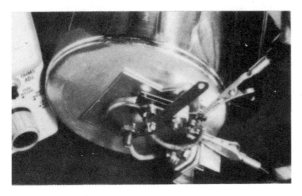

A neon test light is sensitive enough to record minute voltage drops across switches when the appliance is plugged in and the switch closed. The neon indicator light should never glow. This is basic tell-tale sign.

cal pressure from your appliance. Contact cleaning or switch replacement is the cure.

You can likewise test the voltage drop from one end of a power cord to the other. With the appliance under load, test across one plug prong to the same wire at the other end of the power cord. The plug must not be all the way in so the prong is accessible. The appliance body must be partly disassembled to expose the cord end.

THERMOSTATS

Many household appliances use tiny thermostats to switch resistance heating coils on and off and maintain the desired temperature. Irons, toasters, coffee makers, waffle irons and electric cooking utensils all use thermostats. All are basically the same. Two metal contact points make and break the electrical flow. The contacts are often made of silver. One of the contacts is mounted on a bimetallic metal arm. This has two metals fused into one piece. When heated, one of the metals expands much more than the other, making the combination bend. The hotter the arm gets, the more it bends.

In operation, the bimetallic arm bends backward until its contact no longer touches the other contact. The power to the heating element is thus shut off. The appliance cools until the arm straightens out enough for the contacts to touch again. The circuit is closed again, and reheating begins. The cycle is repeated over and over. Temperatures may vary only 5 to 10 de-

Adjustable thermostats have one arm that is moved in and out when dial is turned right or left. This changes the distance that the bimetallic arm must move in order that it can open or close the circuit.

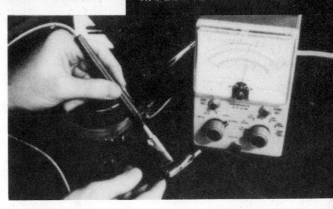

For a resistance test, the appliance is unplugged and then switched on. Take a reading across plug's flat prongs. An infinite resistance means open circuit. No resistance means short-circuit; and you're pinpointed.

grees during an *off-on* cycle.

One contact is adjustable; that is, it can be moved in or out by turning the temperature dial. For higher temperature settings it closes the gap with the other contact making the bimetallic arm bend more to shut off the current. For lower temperature settings, it opens the gap.

USE OF MAGNET

Sometimes one of the contacts is backed with a small magnet to make it cling tightly until the bimetallic force is enough to pull it loose. This makes the contact action rapid and positive. Arcing is reduced and the contacts last longer.

In time the contacts may get corroded or burned. Then they need cleaning or the thermostat needs replacing. You can buy a thermostat from an appliance parts dealer. You'll have to show him the old thermostat or give the make, model and size of your appliance.

OHM TESTING

A VO meter can help you determine whether an appliance has the proper resistance. If a switch or thermostat is making poor contact, the resistance will be too high. So will it be if one of two heating elements is electrically open. An internal short-circuit will make the resistance too low.

An ohm test can be made in a minute without taking the appliance apart. Set the ohm selector on the lowest range. Turn the appliance switch to *on* and connect the prods across the flat prongs of the plug. If the reading is very high, wiggle the thermostat and flick the switch to see if it drops. Suppose the reading on an electric iron comes to 13 ohms. You can tell if that is good or bad by converting it to the amperes the appliance will draw by dividing the ohm reading into the voltage, 115 ($115 \div 13 = 8.8$ amps). Thus, the appliance should draw 8.8 amps when plugged in. If the iron nameplate gives watts instead of amps, you can convert this easily to amps by dividing by the voltage (1000 watts $\div$ 115 volts $= 8.7$ amps).

The less the wattage draw of an appliance the greater the resistance.

Using the simplified formula: watts $= 13,225 \div$ ohms, you can check out any heating appliance with an ohm meter, if you know its wattage. The results cannot be exact, because every heating element increases in resistance when it gets hot. You can only check the cold resistance. Still, it's a way to check out an appliance without much trouble.

The method won't work on electric motors. Their initial resistance is far lower than their power draw would indicate. The reason is that when it is running, the motor's windings create back-voltage. Back-voltage holds current flow back, making it much less than the ohm reading would indicate.

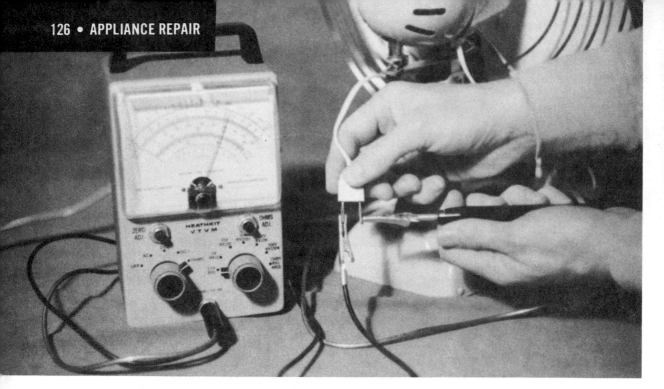

You can often save yourself the trouble of taking apart an appliance by simply checking out its continuity with a volt-ohm meter. It's great aid in troubleshooting. In appliance repair, check simplest things first.

TROUBLESHOOTING SMALL APPLIANCES

Toasters, mixers, irons, clocks and fans pose distinctive problems

nce you know the basics of appliance repair, as outlined in a previous chapter, you are ready to put them to use. Here are descriptions of how a number of popular small appliances work and how to troubleshoot them. In each case if the appliance has a plug and a cord, that is the first place to look for trouble and has been left out of the troubleshooting charts. So has repairing an appliance that shocks. This was covered previously.

See the chapter on ground rules of appliance repair for how to test for continuity, short-circuits, open circuits and bad grounds.

Toaster—toasters last for many years without trouble. Toaster components include a switch, a pop-up control and a pair of heating elements (two-slice). Most toaster troubles are mechanical, power cord or switch. Check these out first.

The mechanical action and timing of toasters varies. Some use a thermostat to end the cycle and pop up the toast. Others use windup clocks. Still others employ an electric timer. If you have pop up troubles the best way to fix it is take the toaster apart and study its action. Then you can usually tell what needs fixing.

Heating elements on both sides are separate circuits hooked so that current can flow through either one or both. Burned out elements can be replaced. Repair of an "open" element is too temporary to bother with. Replace it.

THERMOSTAT CONTROL

Waffle iron—a waffle iron contains upper and lower heating elements strung over ceramic insulators. They are connected so that electricity must flow through one end, then the other. If one burns out, neither will heat. A thermostat controls the heat. An indicator lamp tells when the thermostat

TOASTER TROUBLESHOOTING

Trouble	Cause	Cure
Won't heat	Plug, cord, terminals	Tighten terminals. Replace or repair cord or plug if necessary.
	Faulty switch	Clean contacts with ignition file and fine emery cloth.
	Open coils	Replace coil if defective, or replace toaster.
Blows fuse	Short-circuit	Disassemble and look for wires touching each other.
Won't pop up Burns toast	Mechanical linkage faulty	Disassemble and check catches, levers and latches. Clean and lubricate with silicone grease.
	Timer faulty	Check timer operation. Clean or replace.
Toasts one side	Element burned out	Replace element.

WAFFLE IRON TROUBLESHOOTING

Trouble	Cause	Cure
Won't heat	Terminal loose	Tighten
	Faulty thermostat	Clean contact.
	Open element	Inspect for broken wire. Replace element.
Not enough heat	Low voltage	Check outlet under load for rated voltage. Find cause of low voltage and correct it.
	Terminals loose; thermostat faulty	Tighten loose terminals. Clean contacts on thermostat or replace.
Too much heat	Thermostat stuck or incorrectly adjusted	Sometimes contacts weld together. Replace if defective. Adjust thermostat (see text).
Signal lamp does not light	Burned out filament	Replace with exactly the same lamp.

is calling for heat.

You can get at the works on many waffle irons simply by pulling back clips that hold the griddles in place. The griddles then lift out.

Griddle temperature should run between 360 and 380 degrees F. You can adjust the temperature by pulling off the adjustment knob from its shaft, turning the shaft the way you want it to go, and pushing the knob back on in the desired position.

Coffee maker—various types of coffee makers function slightly differently. All have thermostatically controlled heating coils and often pilot lights to tell when they are heating. Some are automatic; in others you

need to set a lever for brewing coffee or keeping coffee warm.

A high-heat element provides heat for brewing; a low-heat element for warming. On some models a switch controls high heat and a thermostat controls low heat. The opposite is found on other models. On automatic models both heats are controlled by thermostats. The electrical parts are reached by removing the base.

Inside the pot a pump—with a chamber, valve and seat—at the base sends boiling water up and over the spreader plate to brew coffee. Steam created inside the pump does it.

If the unit has ceramic insulators where the heating element leads pass

With the housing off, check the operation of your toaster's trip control. It often goes bad, is easy to fix.

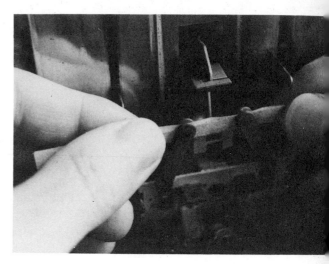

Brightening switch contacts with fine sandpaper can add years of life to your toaster, and save you money.

through holes, make sure they are in place when you complete your repair.

SKILLET, MIXER, BLENDER

Electric skillet—this cooking aid combines a heating element built integrally with the skillet so they can be submerged in water. If the heating element goes bad, the whole skillet may as well be replaced. A separate thermostatic control unit is used. To cook, a temperature sensing probe is inserted into the skillet. The thermostat is located in the control unit. You can easily fix it if something goes wrong. Remove the screws holding the control cover and take it off.

Most troubles with the control result from submerging it in water. It's supposed to be kept dry, dry, dry.

Electric mixer—the electric food mixer has a universal motor to drive a pair of beaters through a system of gears. Several types of speed controls are used; those with centrifugal-governors, tapped-fields and adjustable brushes. All must be clean and free of caked-on food to work properly. Most troubles are due to food deposits on the inner workings. Brush wear comes second.

Blender—a blender works much like a mixer except that the motor is in the base, not the upper portion.

Blenders see so little action that they rarely give trouble. Check the brushes or look for a worn cord.

Electric can opener—this terrific little kitchen addition uses a small shaded-pole motor (see section on motors) and a lot of gearing down to open cans. A momentary-contact switch turns it on when you press the lever. Phillips screws hold the housing together. Take them out and you can expose the opener's workings.

About the only motor problem is caused by lack of lubrication in the bearings. A little oil should fix it. Most other troubles come from dull cutters, worn gears and similar mechanical difficulties. Clean and lubricate the exterior working parts twice a year.

Electric knife—the electric knife is a great supplement to the household. It makes the man of the house an expert meat carver. A small commutator motor runs on low DC voltage made from house current or batteries. Resistors plus a small *rectifier* provide the change in current type and voltage. A rectifier is a device that changes alternating current to direct current.

A press-*on* switch completes the circuit from cord to motor. A set of gears and a drive wheel make side-by-side knife blades reciprocate to cut.

To take apart an electric knife, simply remove the screws holding the halves of the pickle-shaped case together. All the workings will then be exposed.

COFFEE MAKER TROUBLESHOOTING

Trouble	Cause	Cure
Won't heat	Terminals loose	Tighten
	Element burned out	Replace if "open" or get a new appliance. Some elements are tough to replace.
	Thermostat faulty	Too critical to repair. Take to shop or replace thermostat.
Won't perc or boils over	Mechanical or hydraulic faults	Check for defective stem cap, lift disc assembly, pump chamber, valve. Boiling over is often caused by a faulty valve. Replace defective parts.
	Low voltage	Correct
	Faulty thermostat	Have adjusted or replace.
Coffee won't return to power bowl, or improper low-heat temperature	Faulty thermostat	Have adjusted or replace.
Pilot light out	Lamp filament burned out	Replace with a duplicate lamp.

ELECTRIC SKILLET TROUBLESHOOTING

Trouble	Cause	Cure
Won't heat	"Open" heating element	Replace skillet.
	Faulty thermostat	Clean contacts.
Wrong temperature	Thermostat out of adjustment or dirty	Check sensing element and clean. Clean thermostat contacts. If this won't cure trouble, replace the control.

ELECTRIC MIXER, BLENDER TROUBLESHOOTING

Trouble	Cause	Cure
Won't run	Defective speed controls	Clean contacts if necessary. Remove encrusted food. Check connections.
	Switch	Clean controls or replace if defective.
Sparks, sputters	Brushes, commutator	Check brush action, sandpaper commutator. Replace brushes if down to 3/8 inch. Clean inside of machine.
Noisy operation	Gears lack lube	Take gearbox apart and lubricate gears and motor bearings. Follow manufacturer's instructions.
Other motor trouble	Various	(See chapter on electric motor repair.)
Bent blades	Accidents	Straighten or replace blades.
Grease leakage	Worn bearings or thinned-out grease	If cleaning gearbox of old grease and repacking doesn't correct leaking at beater sockets, you need a new mixer.
Vibrates and noisy	Faulty governor	Replace governor if needed.

CORDS WEAR OUT

Electric iron—the major problem with electric irons is cords. The ironing motions eventually wear down the wires or insulation. Replacement is the best cure. Buy a ready-made iron cord set or use heater cord and heavy-duty plugs and iron adapters. Don't forget the strain-relief spring on the iron end of the cord. A retractile cord makes a good iron cord.

An iron consists of a heating element and a thermostat. It couldn't be simpler. Faulty thermostats are more easily replaced than repaired. So are faulty heating elements.

Getting the iron apart may be difficult. Look for hidden screws, hooks or pins, usually in the handle. Try to figure out how the handle is held to the body. Push, pry or turn to see what happens. Don't force. If you can get the handle off, the rest of the repair is easy.

Electric hair dryer—the small household size hair dryer power unit consists of switch, heating element and blower. Tubing carries the stream of hot air created in the power unit to a bonnet worn by the user. The blower draws in cool air and blows it over hot resistance wires in the heating element. Some hair dryers have two elements, one for "low" heat, another for "high." Some have varying fan speeds. A few even have thermostats to control temperature.

The case lifts off the power unit when its attaching screws are removed. Most dryer motors are the simple shaded-pole type. A few more powerful dryers use universal motors.

DUAL CONTROL BEST

Electric blanket—a resistance heating element routed around the blanket is controlled by a thermostat. The thermostat may be in the blanket. If

Glowing test light shows that power is getting through the switch of the blender's power unit okay.

Shaded-pole motors need only an occasional oiling. Follow manufacturer's instructions, and don't overdo.

Remove the screws and hair dryer's plastic cover comes off. Heating element is then cleanly exposed.

Check can opener switch to insure contacts are clean and touching each other when the lever is down.

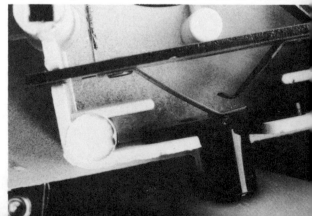

ELECTRIC HAIR DRYER TROUBLESHOOTING

Trouble	Cause	Cure
Won't run or heat	Switch	Replace if "open." Be sure to "tag" wires so you get them back to right terminal.
Heats, but won't run	Fan stuck	Look for fan blade catching.
	Bearing stuck	Clean and oil bearing.
Runs slowly	Bearings dragging	Oil. Align ends of motor if binding.
Won't heat	Element "open"	Replace. Match to old one.
Noisy	Fan hits housing	Loosen set-screw and reposition fan. If fan is bent, straighten it.
Hose collapsed	Mechanical damage	Slip over a broomstick and work wire coils back into place. If vinyl is cut, wrap with plastic electrician's tape or use vinyl patches.

ELECTRIC HEATING PAD, BLANKET TROUBLESHOOTING

Trouble	Cause	Cure
Won't heat	Switch	Clean contacts or replace.
	Loose terminal (blanket only)	Located inside the control box; there may be many. Tighten them all.
	Thermostat	Clean contacts or replace. Thermostats in blanket or pad may be cut out and replaced. Wire carefully.
	Open circuit in heating element	Replace entire pad or blanket.
Too hot (electronically controlled blankets only)	Bypass capacitor burned out and unit won't shut off	Located across thermostat contacts. Replace bypass capacitor.
Wrong temperature	Thermostat	Clean external thermostat or replace internal one.
	Improper use	Blankets with external thermostats must have the controls placed on a night stand or on the floor. Never rest them on or under the blanket.

ELECTRIC HEATER TROUBLESHOOTING

Trouble	Cause	Cure
Won't heat	Element "open"	Install new element of same rating as old one. See nameplate.
	Main switch	Clean contacts or replace switch.
	Tip-over switch	Check operation. Clean contacts or replace switch.
	Terminals	Clean and tighten.
Not enough heat	Low voltage	Correct
	Switch "open" on "high"	Clean contacts or replace switch.
	Thermostat	Clean contacts.
Fan trouble	Various	(See chapter on motor repair.)

so, it's electronic. Other blankets have the thermostat mounted in the external control box. That type measures room temperature and reacts to it. The best blankets for double beds have dual controls. Each half of the blanket is wired separately for individual control.

Blankets have magnetized thermostat contacts. Most problems are found inside the control box. Electric sheets are similar.

Electric heating pad—much like the electric blanket, a heating pad is smaller and wired to get hotter. A selector switch usually lets the user choose among three heats and *off*. A thermostat may be inside the pad wired in series with the resistance wiring. These often are troublemakers.

Electric clock—clocks draw only about 1½ watts of electricity. Powering them is a small, self-contained motor with reduction gear unit. Inside the unit a synchronous motor turns at a set speed in relation to cycles of current. Power companies are careful to control their generator speeds to keep clock time like astronomical time.

Don't try to fix a worn out or defective clock motor unit. Remove it and replace it with an exact duplicate. If a clock develops gear trouble, the whole clock may best be replaced.

Some clocks are powered by shaded-pole motors. Not much goes wrong with them either.

TIP-OVER SWITCH

Electric heater—electric heaters are used for chasing the chill from rooms. Sizes range from 500-watts up. All have resistance heating elements. Some add switch control, thermostatic control, and fans to distribute the heat. Any that might be kicked over and start a

ELECTRIC IRON TROUBLESHOOTING

Trouble	Cause	Cure
Won't heat	Faulty element, thermostat	Clean thermostat contacts. Replace faulty element.
Insufficient heat	Faulty thermostat	Clean or realign contacts. Replace, if defective. Tighten terminals.
	Low voltage	Outlet voltage should match rating of iron. A 15-volt drop lowers heating by one-third.
Improper temperature	Thermostat out of adjustment	A shop job. Take to a qualified repairman.

FAN AND BLOWER TROUBLESHOOTING

Trouble	Cause	Cure
Motor troubles	Various	(See chapter on motor repair.)
Won't run	Switch	Replace or clean contacts.
Vibrates, noisy	Bent blades	Remove fan, lay on table and straighten blades. Check when replaced on shaft.
	Out of balance blades	Replace blades or balance.
	Squirrel cage hits housing.	Straighten squirrel cage.
Oscillating type won't oscillate	Gears worn or stripped	Replace gears or do without this feature.
	Worn clutch	Replace clutch.
Exhaust fan won't move air.	Blocked air passages	Clean out bird's nests, fix automatic doors, clean air filters.
	Dirty fan	Remove blade or squirrel cage and clean off accumulations.

An iron is often difficult to take apart. Rusty screw holding handle to base broke on this one. It's rough.

fire should incorporate a tip-over switch in the base. Whenever the base isn't resting on the floor, a plunger comes out and turns off the juice.

Replacement elements are available in a rating to match that on the heater's nameplate. Fasten the ends, then stretch the new element over the insulators. Leave enough tension in the element to hold it on the supports. The element must not touch the appliance body at any point.

Fans and blowers—fans and blowers come in many types. Both employ small electric motors—usually shaded-pole or split-phase—to turn blades or squirrel cage blowers. A blower can move air along a duct, and is used for kitchen and bathroom ventilating.

Most problems have to do with the motors. Their repairs are covered in another section.

Many fans are equipped with two-speed switches. These sometimes give trouble. So do wires on oscillating fans that get bent so many times that they break. A continuity check will tell.

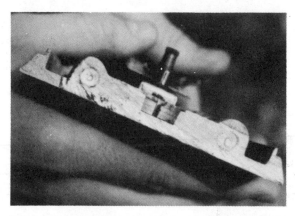

The heating elements of many irons are integral with the shoe, and this is shown in this clear cross-section.

RECHARGING BATTERIES

Cordless appliances—cordless appliances have self-contained batteries. These are usually rechargeable nickel-cadmium cells connected with welded-on straps. Sometimes ordinary flashlight cells are used. Rechargeable appliances come with chargers on which they rest when not in use. The appliance has a switch that connects the batteries to the DC motor.

Disassemble the appliance and take DC voltage readings with the motor running. On a 6-volt battery pack the running voltage should not drop below about 5.8 volts. If it drops to 4 volts, the batteries should be recharged. Test each cell individually under no load and full load. If any reading drops to half voltage or reverses polarity, put in a new set of batteries.

The charger unit can be tested with a DC volt meter, too. It should register 9 volts across a fully charged 6-volt battery pack. The charger module uses a silicon rectifier and resistors to make low-voltage DC out of 120-volt AC.

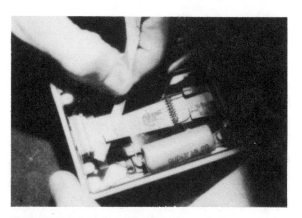

Most electric blanket thermostatic control conacts are easily cleaned with a fine sandpaper and patience.

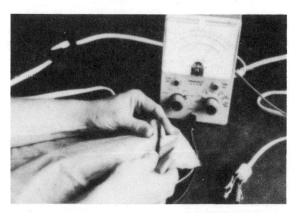

With VO meter reading resistance of heating pad, you can try kneading the pad. Broken wire varies it.

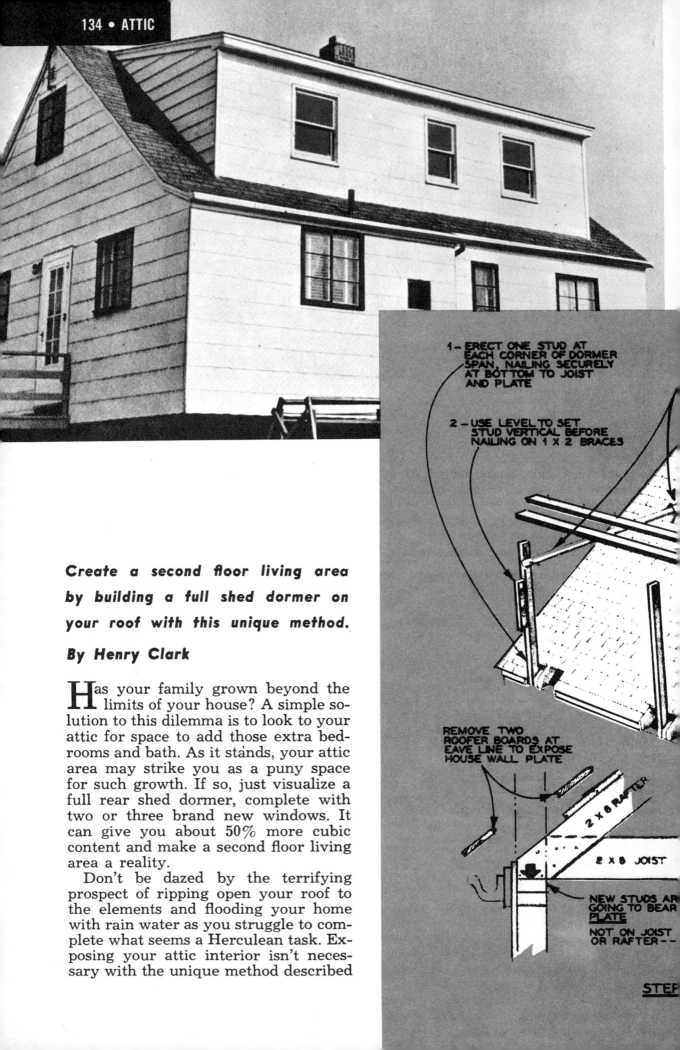

Create a second floor living area by building a full shed dormer on your roof with this unique method.

By Henry Clark

Has your family grown beyond the limits of your house? A simple solution to this dilemma is to look to your attic for space to add those extra bedrooms and bath. As it stands, your attic area may strike you as a puny space for such growth. If so, just visualize a full rear shed dormer, complete with two or three brand new windows. It can give you about 50% more cubic content and make a second floor living area a reality.

Don't be dazed by the terrifying prospect of ripping open your roof to the elements and flooding your home with rain water as you struggle to complete what seems a Herculean task. Exposing your attic interior isn't necessary with the unique method described

1 — ERECT ONE STUD AT EACH CORNER OF DORMER SPAN, NAILING SECURELY AT BOTTOM TO JOIST AND PLATE

2 — USE LEVEL TO SET STUD VERTICAL BEFORE NAILING ON 1 X 2 BRACES

REMOVE TWO ROOFER BOARDS AT EAVE LINE TO EXPOSE HOUSE WALL PLATE

2 X 8 RAFTER

2 X 8 JOIST

NEW STUDS ARE GOING TO BEAR PLATE

NOT ON JOIST OR RAFTER --

STEP

Typical dormer structure begins with erection of studs. Remove or chop hole through eave boards to expose the wall plate upon which studs will bear.

A single 2x4-in. plate is nailed to initial studs. Double plate later. Use 1x2-in. braces to hold studs in true vertical. Check each with a level.

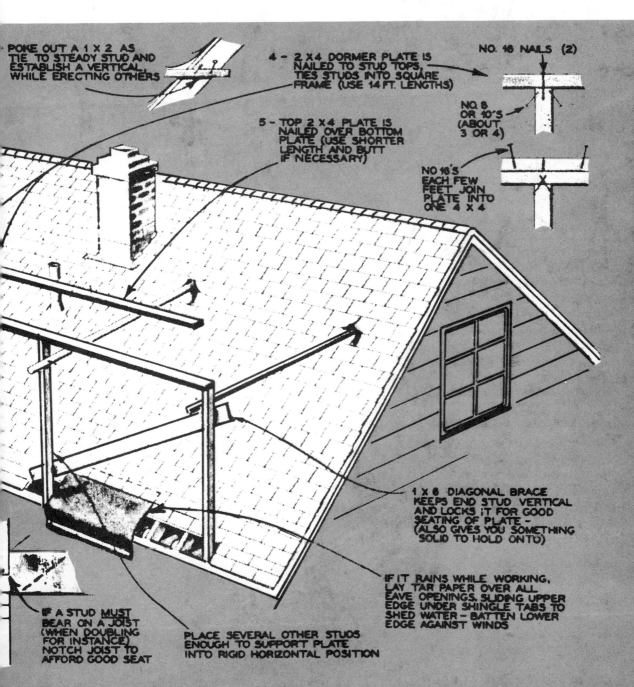

POKE OUT A 1 X 2 AS TIE TO STEADY STUD AND ESTABLISH A VERTICAL, WHILE ERECTING OTHERS

4 - 2 X 4 DORMER PLATE IS NAILED TO STUD TOPS, TIES STUDS INTO SQUARE FRAME (USE 14 FT. LENGTHS)

NO. 16 NAILS (2)

NO. 8 OR 10'S (ABOUT 3 OR 4)

5 - TOP 2 X 4 PLATE IS NAILED OVER BOTTOM PLATE (USE SHORTER LENGTH AND BUTT IF NECESSARY)

NO 16'S EACH FEW FEET JOIN PLATE INTO ONE 4 X 4

1 X 6 DIAGONAL BRACE KEEPS END STUD VERTICAL AND LOCKS IT FOR GOOD SEATING OF PLATE - (ALSO GIVES YOU SOMETHING SOLID TO HOLD ONTO)

IF IT RAINS WHILE WORKING, LAY TAR PAPER OVER ALL EAVE OPENINGS. SLIDING UPPER EDGE UNDER SHINGLE TABS TO SHED WATER - BATTEN LOWER EDGE AGAINST WINDS

IF A STUD MUST BEAR ON A JOIST (WHEN DOUBLING FOR INSTANCE) NOTCH JOIST TO AFFORD GOOD SEAT

PLACE SEVERAL OTHER STUDS ENOUGH TO SUPPORT PLATE INTO RIGID HORIZONTAL POSITION

OPENING EAVE BOARDS FOR LOCATING STUDS TO FORM DORMER GENERAL FRAME

here, and the job itself can be completed by you alone over relatively few weekends of work.

The secret is to build the dormer roof right over your existing roof and rip out the present roof only when the dormer is completely boxed in. Thus you may extend the period of work indefinitely and never subject your home interior to weather damage.

Before plunging into this money-saving project, save yourself the stray chance of a headache by checking your local building codes to see if a building permit is required (the cost is insignificant). Also there may be a few minimum requirements as to spacing between studs, rafters and joists.

Now do a little preliminary commonsense paper work. The photographs and

End rafters and gable plates follow erec initial studs and stud plate. See details

Gable plate is attached at interior end existing rafter and beveled to match roof

Make opening through ridge boards to expo ridge pole to which the end rafters are att

Left, close-up of end rafter spiked to the ridge pole. Bevel ends to seat accurately against pole.

RAFTER IS FLUSH WITH END OF PLATE

END RAFTER IS ONLY ONE NAILED TO OLD RAFTER, OTHERS TO RIDGE ONLY

BOTTOM ANGLE MUST SEAT WE ON PLATE

ADD SUFFICIENT STUDS TO GIVE PLATE GOOD SUPPORT, SINCE ALL RAFTERS WILL NOW BE CUT AND PLACED, AND ROOFED OVER AGAINST WEATHER

NAIL INTO JOIST AND OLD PLATE

LEAVE ROOFER BOARDS IN PLACE WHERE NOT PLACING STUDS, JUST TO AVOID TOO MANY OPENINGS

PLACE STUDS 16" APART ON CENTERS, EXCEPT NEAR WINDOWS — THEN DOUBLE UP

STEP 2 TIEING DORMER WALL TO ROOF AND OPENING RIDGE TO TRY FITTING NEW RAFTERS

sketches in this article illustrate every basic building step you need to know. But exact dimensions for height, width, depth and styling must necessarily depend on the individual home. A number of actual houses are used in the photos to show varieties of procedure and finishing techniques. Plan the size of your dormer, the number of windows you want, the type of finishing to match the present exterior and a dormer roof pitch that will blend architecturally with the house.

To start actual work, remove the first and second eave boards, which will reveal the plate bearing on the wall studs below. At each intersection of a joist and this plate you will spike your new 2x4 dormer studs. At this point be careful to avoid an important pitfall. Do not nail your new studs to existing rafters as these will eventually be torn out from inside. Nail only to the plate and joists.

Put up just a few studs at first to form a support for your new dormer plate. Use 1x2-in. ties to support the studs and establish a vertical. Install the plate atop the studs as illustrated. We might presumably erect all studs at once, but this would form a dangerously heavy structure without ade-

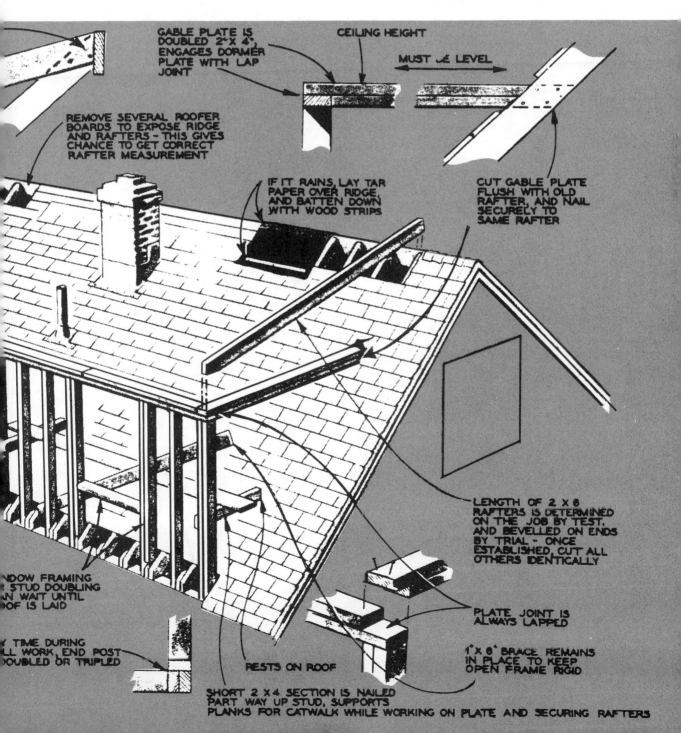

GABLE PLATE IS DOUBLED 2" X 4", ENGAGES DORMER PLATE WITH LAP JOINT

CEILING HEIGHT

MUST BE LEVEL

REMOVE SEVERAL ROOFER BOARDS TO EXPOSE RIDGE AND RAFTERS – THIS GIVES CHANCE TO GET CORRECT RAFTER MEASUREMENT

IF IT RAINS, LAY TAR PAPER OVER RIDGE AND BATTEN DOWN WITH WOOD STRIPS

CUT GABLE PLATE FLUSH WITH OLD RAFTER, AND NAIL SECURELY TO SAME RAFTER

LENGTH OF 2 X 6 RAFTERS IS DETERMINED ON THE JOB BY TEST, AND BEVELLED ON ENDS BY TRIAL – ONCE ESTABLISHED, CUT ALL OTHERS IDENTICALLY

WINDOW FRAMING STUD DOUBLING CAN WAIT UNTIL ROOF IS LAID

PLATE JOINT IS ALWAYS LAPPED

ANY TIME DURING ALL WORK, END POST DOUBLED OR TRIPLED

RESTS ON ROOF

1" X 6" BRACE REMAINS IN PLACE TO KEEP OPEN FRAME RIGID

SHORT 2 X 4 SECTION IS NAILED PART WAY UP STUD, SUPPORTS PLANKS FOR CATWALK WHILE WORKING ON PLATE AND SECURING RAFTERS

quate support. At this point we merely want to form a basic frame of studs, rafters and gable plates.

With stud plates placed, measure, cut and nail in place the two gable plates that form a horizontal directly beneath the end rafters. One end of each gable plate rests on the front dormer plate, while the other end is secured to an existing inside rafter of the house. Note that this is the only instance we will attach a dormer member to an existing rafter, since these particular bearing rafters for the two gable plates will not eventually be removed. See the second photo from the top on this page to note inside attachment of the gable plate.

When the gable plates have been spiked in place, remove the two top ridge boards and install the two end rafters to the ridge pole and dormer plate. First measure properly for span and cut accurate angles at the rafter ends for secure seating on the plate and ridge pole. These will form patterns for all your rafters so cut them carefully. We presume, of course, that the house ridge pole is straight. If not, it will necessitate shortening or lengthening the new rafters accordingly.

You now have a basic frame upon which you may install all remaining studs and rafters. It is perhaps best to cut and place all rafters first since it is desirable to close in a shelter for the old roof as soon as possible. Note that all rafters placed between the two end rafters must be nailed to the plate and ridge pole only. Do *not* nail to existing rafters, as these will be ripped out later.

Installed end rafter and gable plate. Fit end rafters with care as they form pattern for others.

Complete installation of remaining studs by re moving eave boards to reveal wall plate, joists

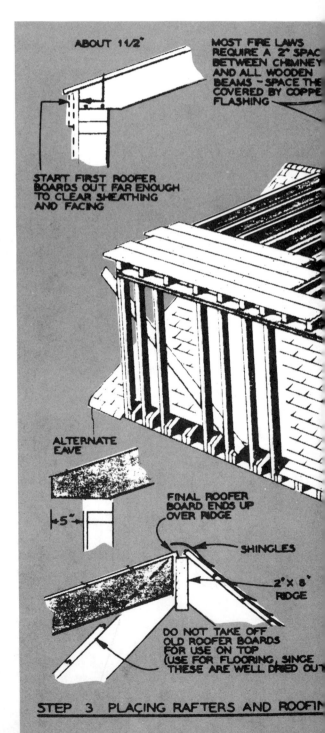

STEP 3 PLACING RAFTERS AND ROOFIN

See the bottom photo on this page to see rafter attachment to the ridge pole.

So far we have our old roof intact but considerably punctured in a number of places. Let us suppose storm clouds are gathering and you don't plan to work on your new dormer for a few days. Merely take some sheets of tar paper and a few battening strips and cover the rafter gaps you've made near the ridge pole and the stud holes made near the eave.

When all rafters are installed, place and nail the roofer boards. These are cut from 1x6-in. tongue-and-groove or ship-lap stock. The amount of overhang you want on the dormer eave will dictate the placement of the first roofer board. It must overhang rafter ends enough to clear sheathing and the facing board. Let the roofer boards lie at odd lengths beyond the end rafters and then trim evenly when all are in place. Secure each board with two No. 8 nails in every rafter. Continue to place and nail boards clear to the ridge.

Upon completion, immediately apply asphalt felt of 15-lb. weight (tar paper) over the entire dormer roof, overlapping generously.

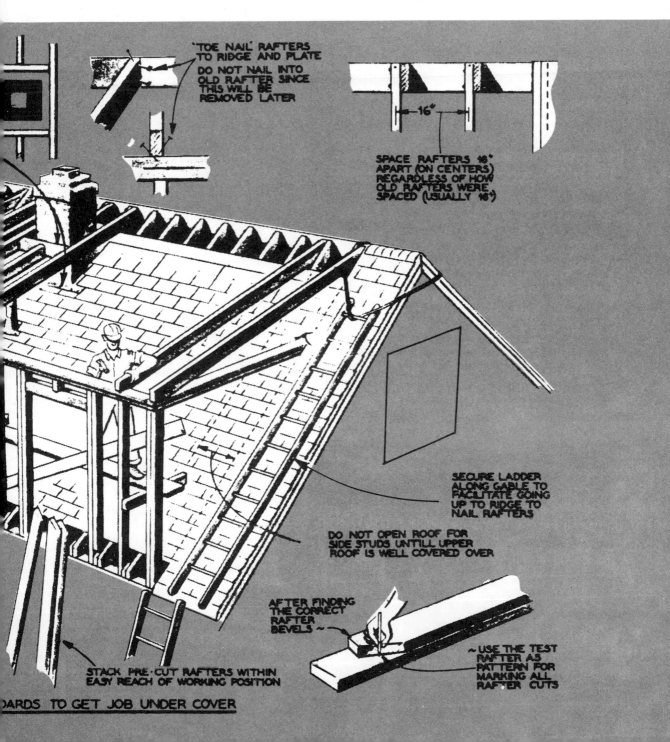

"TOE NAIL" RAFTERS TO RIDGE AND PLATE

DO NOT NAIL INTO OLD RAFTER SINCE THIS WILL BE REMOVED LATER

SPACE RAFTERS 16" APART (ON CENTERS) REGARDLESS OF HOW OLD RAFTERS WERE SPACED (USUALLY 16")

SECURE LADDER ALONG GABLE TO FACILITATE GOING UP TO RIDGE TO NAIL RAFTERS

DO NOT OPEN ROOF FOR SIDE STUDS UNTILL UPPER ROOF IS WELL COVERED OVER

AFTER FINDING THE CORRECT RAFTER BEVELS ~

~ USE THE TEST RAFTER AS PATTERN FOR MARKING ALL RAFTER CUTS

STACK PRE-CUT RAFTERS WITHIN EASY REACH OF WORKING POSITION

...OARDS TO GET JOB UNDER COVER

Shingling can wait till the remainder of the dormer structure is completely sheathed. Also, we do not want too much roof weight until all bearing studs are in place.

Cut and place the rest of the front dormer wall studs, securing as previously mentioned. Double all studs that will bear window assemblies. Be sure you have accurate measurements of proposed window installations at this point and then proceed to place headers and sills. If openings are to be long for large picture windows, use 2x6-in. or 2x8-in. headers to support the rafters bearing on the plate directly above such headers.

Studding for the dormer sides is the next step. Saw away the old roof directly between two rafters where the dormer side wall will enter the attic. Then erect the vertical side studs between the gable plate and a plate installed along a double joist in the floor

of the attic. These studs will butt against the existing rafter holding the gable plate and will be nailed to it. As pointed out previously, this rafter remains permanently in place and forms an untouched natural gable at each end of the house. This completes framing of the dormer "cheeks."

Now sheath the face and sides with ⅜" or ½" plywood sheathing, or 1x6-in. tongue-and-groove boards. Most communities permit ⅜" plywood for roofing but check your building department. Whatever you use, work from

Detail of stud attachment seen from inside. Nail stud to plate and joists, not to existing rafters.

Prepare for rain at any time during construction by battening down tar paper over roof openings.

Stormy weather precautions include covering eave openings well as they receive the most watershed.

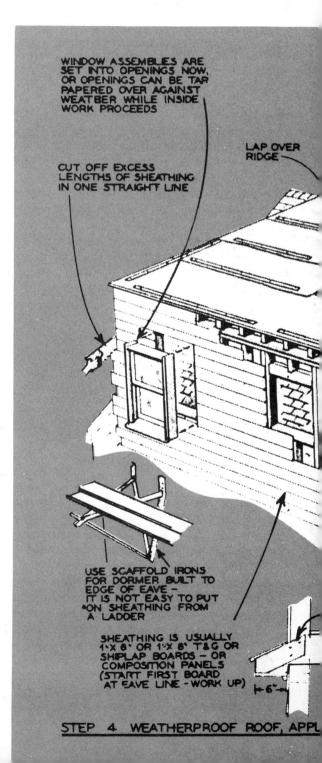

WINDOW ASSEMBLIES ARE SET INTO OPENINGS NOW, OR OPENINGS CAN BE TAR PAPERED OVER AGAINST WEATHER WHILE INSIDE WORK PROCEEDS

CUT OFF EXCESS LENGTHS OF SHEATHING IN ONE STRAIGHT LINE

LAP OVER RIDGE

USE SCAFFOLD IRONS FOR DORMER BUILT TO EDGE OF EAVE — IT IS NOT EASY TO PUT ON SHEATHING FROM A LADDER

SHEATHING IS USUALLY 1"x 6" OR 1"x 8" T&G OR SHIPLAP BOARDS - OR COMPOSITION PANELS (START FIRST BOARD AT EAVE LINE - WORK UP)

STEP 4 WEATHERPROOF ROOF, APPL

Below, framing nears completion. For large window openings use 2x6-in. or 2x8-in. stock for headers to give rigid support to dormer rafters bearing on plate above them.

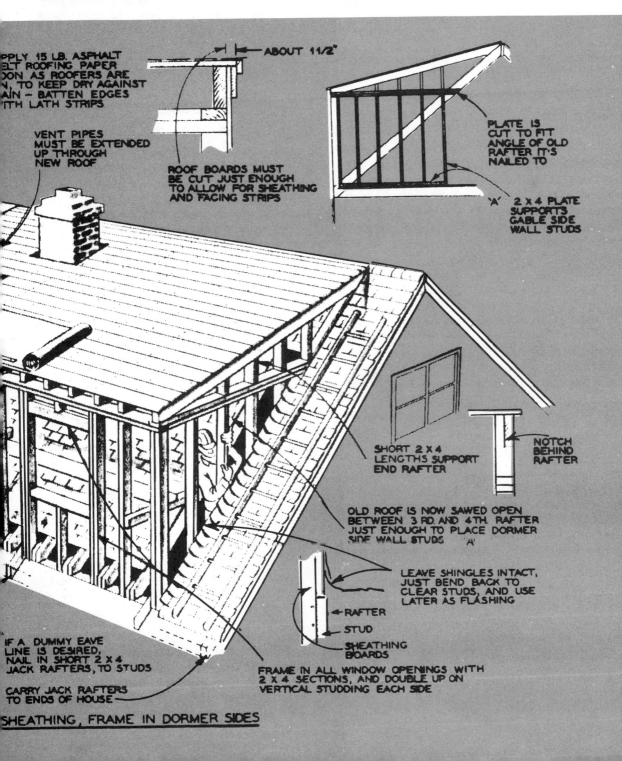

APPLY 15 LB. ASPHALT FELT ROOFING PAPER SOON AS ROOFERS ARE UP, TO KEEP DRY AGAINST RAIN – BATTEN EDGES WITH LATH STRIPS

ABOUT 1 1/2"

ROOF BOARDS MUST BE CUT JUST ENOUGH TO ALLOW FOR SHEATHING AND FACING STRIPS

VENT PIPES MUST BE EXTENDED UP THROUGH NEW ROOF

PLATE IS CUT TO FIT ANGLE OF OLD RAFTER IT'S NAILED TO

'A' 2 X 4 PLATE SUPPORTS GABLE SIDE WALL STUDS

SHORT 2 X 4 LENGTHS SUPPORT END RAFTER

NOTCH BEHIND RAFTER

OLD ROOF IS NOW SAWED OPEN BETWEEN 3 RD. AND 4 TH. RAFTER JUST ENOUGH TO PLACE DORMER SIDE WALL STUDS 'A'

LEAVE SHINGLES INTACT, JUST BEND BACK TO CLEAR STUDS, AND USE LATER AS FLASHING

RAFTER

STUD

SHEATHING BOARDS

IF A DUMMY EAVE LINE IS DESIRED, NAIL IN SHORT 2 X 4 JACK RAFTERS, TO STUDS

CARRY JACK RAFTERS TO ENDS OF HOUSE

FRAME IN ALL WINDOW OPENINGS WITH 2 X 4 SECTIONS, AND DOUBLE UP ON VERTICAL STUDDING EACH SIDE

SHEATHING, FRAME IN DORMER SIDES

the bottom up and secure firmly with 8 penny nails. As with the dormer roof, apply 15-lb. felt over all sheathing.

However, before doing so, note a vitally important precautionary measure. Do *not* remove any rafters until you have erected a group of 4x4-in. temporary supporting studs to hold up the ridge pole in the center of the attic. Space each about ten feet apart. Leave these in place until you have placed attic ceiling joists between the dormer plate and the opposing rafters on the untouched side of the roof. These joists will act as ties or trusses. Still further, leave the supports in place until you have erected one or more bearing partitions inside the attic area to form separate rooms. Be sure these bearing partitions rest on or near a bearing wall on the first floor of the house. Only then is it really safe to remove these temporary studs from beneath the ridge pole.

If you want a wall parallel to the floor joists, double the joist it rests on. Double the top and bottom plates of all bearing wall studs. Try to place a bearing wall as near to the center of the attic as possible to more surely guarantee support for the ridge pole. If you have some spare pieces of 2x4-in. lumber, give the dormer roof added support by installing short lengths of studding between the dormer ceiling joists and the dormer rafters. The pitch of the dormer roof will naturally be shallower than that of the regular house roof and this will be added support against the weight of snow if you are situated in a northern area.

Your dormer is now virtually finished. The installation of electrical outlets, plumbing, etc., is another project.

Shingle the roof and sides to taste. Butt asphalt rectangles are as durable as anything but slate. Work from the eave up, doubling the first course to hide open slits. Flashing around the chimney and extended vents is aluminum, zinc or copper.

With the exterior complete or nearly so, you may plan a period of inside work and get your first glimpse of the added area you have created. Start

knocking out the old roof and you can begin to see the space you've wanted for new bedrooms.

You may have some use for this old lumber, so work carefully in removing the old rafters. Saw as close to the eave as you can and try prying the remainder away from the ridge pole.

If it is necessary to build your dormer around a chimney, remember that most codes specify a 2-in. gap between the chimney and any framing. So box

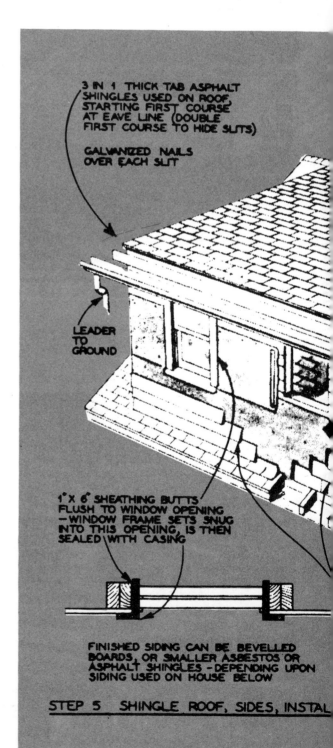

3 IN 1 THICK TAB ASPHALT SHINGLES USED ON ROOF, STARTING FIRST COURSE AT EAVE LINE (DOUBLE FIRST COURSE TO HIDE SLITS)

GALVANIZED NAILS OVER EACH SLIT

LEADER TO GROUND

1" X 6" SHEATHING BUTTS FLUSH TO WINDOW OPENING —WINDOW FRAME SETS SNUG INTO THIS OPENING, IS THEN SEALED WITH CASING

FINISHED SIDING CAN BE BEVELLED BOARDS, OR SMALLER ASBESTOS OR ASPHALT SHINGLES - DEPENDING UPON SIDING USED ON HOUSE BELOW

STEP 5   SHINGLE ROOF, SIDES, INSTAL

Securing remaining rafters which have been pre-cut to match end rafters. Spike firmly to plate.

Fire codes usually require 2-in. gap between a chimney and wood. Cover the gap with flashing.

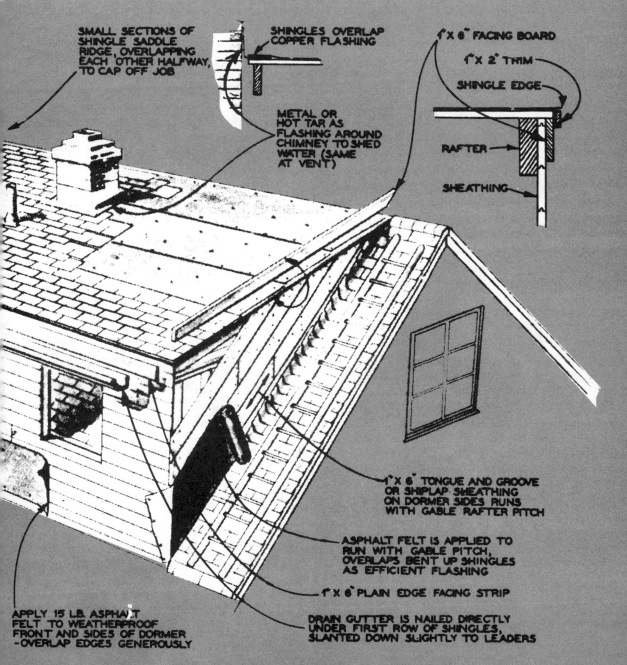

SMALL SECTIONS OF SHINGLE SADDLE RIDGE, OVERLAPPING EACH OTHER HALFWAY TO CAP OFF JOB

SHINGLES OVERLAP COPPER FLASHING

1" X 6" FACING BOARD

1" X 2" TRIM

SHINGLE EDGE

METAL OR HOT TAR AS FLASHING AROUND CHIMNEY TO SHED WATER (SAME AT VENT)

RAFTER

SHEATHING

1" X 6" TONGUE AND GROOVE OR SHIPLAP SHEATHING ON DORMER SIDES RUNS WITH GABLE RAFTER PITCH

ASPHALT FELT IS APPLIED TO RUN WITH GABLE PITCH, OVERLAPS BENT UP SHINGLES AS EFFICIENT FLASHING

1" X 6" PLAIN EDGE FACING STRIP

APPLY 15 LB. ASPHALT FELT TO WEATHERPROOF FRONT AND SIDES OF DORMER -OVERLAP EDGES GENEROUSLY

DRAIN GUTTER IS NAILED DIRECTLY UNDER FIRST ROW OF SHINGLES, SLANTED DOWN SLIGHTLY TO LEADERS

WINDOWS, FLASHINGS, GUTTERS – THEN REMOVE OLD ROOF INSIDE

Close-up of new roofer boards nearing ridge pole. Note old roofers beneath plus old and new rafters.

View from on top of old roof and under new roof shows gable plate and side studding of dormer.

Basic dormer is completed when new dormer joists and bearing wall are installed to suit new layout.

in the chimney with 2x4s, leaving the required space, and then fill the gap with flashing.

Though most front dormers of full length may detract from the architecture of your house, you may add one in addition to the rear dormer and thus nearly double your attic's content. Procedure is basically the same as described here. Build one dormer at a time, however and do not attempt removing all interior rafters simultaneously. In the case of double dormers, the new attic ceiling joists will extend from one new opposing stud plate to another and form a balanced truss. Be sure adequate bearing walls are erected

With roofer boards on, cover entire roof with asphalt felt of 15-lb. weight to avoid wood rot.

Do not rip out old rafters until temporary studs are placed under ridge pole for support. See text.

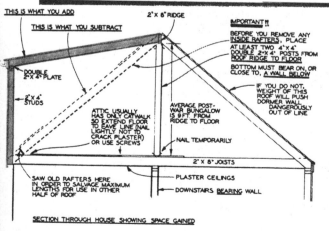

SECTION THROUGH HOUSE SHOWING SPACE GAINED

CEILING JOISTS COMPLETE 'TRUSS' WORK ON ROOF, TIEING IT IN SOLIDLY under these joists.

For space considerations alone, you will find this type of full dormer more advantageous and economical than building twin gable-type domers which, though they add window area and some space, will still leave completely slanting upstairs ceilings and will not appreciably increase the cubic content of your attic area. •

ENERGY/MONEY SAVER IDEA—Insulation

If you're remodeling your attic you will want to do the best job possible of installing the right kind of insulation that will result in the lowest possible heating and cooling costs. When you buy most insulating materials you will note a code letter "R" is printed on the wrapper. This code letter "R" stands for RESISTANCE VALUE and varies with the material, the thickness and the manner in which it is installed. For example, insulating batts or blankets may have one "R" value for use in ceilings and another if the material is used in walls.

MINERAL WOOL AND FIBERGLASS are essentially the same type of material and have an "R" value of 3 for each inch of thickness when installed in a wall and slightly higher when used in a ceiling. Thus, 6 inches of mineral wool or fiberglass in a ceiling will produce an "R" value of 19, which is our recommended minimum.

PARTICLE BOARDS, made of pressed wood fibers in ½" and up thickness have an "R" value of 2.6 per inch of thickness. Common use if for sheathing behind frame or brick veneer construction.

EXPANDED MINERAL materials, such as vermiculite or perlite are available in the form of loose granules and are used to fill wall and ceiling spaces. These granular materials have an "R" value of slightly less than 2 per inch of thickness; Perlite made into a board has an "R" value of 3 per inch of thickness.

FOAMED PLASTICS, commonly polyurethane and polystyrene, are available as rigid boards and also can be sprayed in place as foam. Polystyrene foam has an "R" value of 4, while polyurethane has an "R" value of 6, which is why polyurethane is widely used to insulate freezers and refrigerators.

REFLECTIVE INSULATION, usually an aluminum or foil faced material differs from other types of insulation. The smooth polished surface reflects heat back to the source and also emits less heat to the cold side. A sheet of reflective material, highly polished on both sides, and exposed to an air space of at least ½", is equal to about 2½" of fiberglass when used against downward heat flow as in a floor. Against horizontal heat flow, as in a wall, a polished surface facing an air space has an "R" value of about 2.

CELLULOSE FIBER insulation is made from wood pulp (and often recycled paper) which has been chemically treated to resist moisture and fire. It comes as loose fill, batts and blankets and has an "R" value of 3 per inch of thickness.

We all know insulation saves energy but we rarely can understand just how much is saved. To illustrate the tremendous contribution insulation makes, an uninsulated ceiling of 1000 square feet will lose 23,000 BTUs per hour to a well-ventilated attic if the room temperature is 75 degrees and the outdoor temperature is zero. Install 6 inches of fiberglass, mineral wool or its equivalent and the heat loss will be only 2900 BTUs per hour!

ENGINE TUNE-UPS

Here's how to handle the most important phase of auto maintenance

A few years ago a major spark plug manufacturer conducted an advertising campaign with the slogan "An Untuned Car Is Trouble." Alas, truer words were never spoken. If every car on the highway received a complete tune-up each 10,000 miles there would be a virtual end to cars that refuse to start, millions of dollars worth of gasoline saved and a very worthwhile reduction in air pollution levels.

SPARK PLUGS

Because they have the roughest job in an engine, spark plugs are the heart of every tune-up. Their electrodes begin eroding due to high voltages and combustion heat from the moment they are placed in service. This causes the center and side electrodes to assume a worn, rounded appearance and the gap between to grow by about .001" every 1,000 miles.

Very high voltages are needed to ionize the air in a plug gap so that a spark may arc across it. Ionization is promoted by sharp-cornered electrodes and fairly narrow gaps. Several thou-

sand additional volts are needed to fire a plug with worn electrodes and, after 5,000 or 6,000 miles of service, plugs often begin to operate unreliably when the available voltage is low or when cylinder pressures are exceptionally high. Starting may therefore become difficult and the engine often "misses" during hard acceleration.

After 5,000 or 6,000 miles of service, spark plugs should be removed from the engine and re-gapped to their original specifications. A round wire gauge is best for this purpose since it conforms better to worn electrodes than does a flat feeler gauge. After 10,000 or 12,000 miles of service the plugs should be replaced with new ones.

Badly worn engines and high-performance engines which are seldom used at full power often accumulate a considerable load of deposits on the firing ends of their spark plugs. Sandblast cleaning, as practiced in most service stations, is of questionable value since it increases the voltage required to fire the plugs by further rounding the electrodes. Also, mechanics will sometimes "pre-clean" the plugs with a wire brush which may leave conductive "pencil lines" on the insulator that will later cause the plug to short and misfire. If you have your plugs sand blasted take time to file the end of the center electrode flat so that its edges are sharp and square. This is a good practice whether the plug has been cleaned or not and is a worthwhile addition to your re-gapping operation. Plugs can also be cleaned at home using solvent and a sharp wooden stick.

Different engines require different plugs. Every major spark plug manufacturer has developed plugs designed particularly for the engine in your car, but steer clear of re-manufactured and off-brand replacements. Tell the parts man the year, make, model and engine type for your car and he will locate the correct plug for your engine in his specification book.

Make sure that the plug holes are clean and lubricate the threads of the new spark plugs lightly before installing them. New plugs are gapped at the factory, but check them anyway to make sure that they match the specifications given in your owner's manual. Torque plugs to 20 or 25 foot-pounds, or about one-half turn after they are finger-tight. Over-tightening may ruin the gaskets.

THE DISTRIBUTOR

"Tune-up kits" consisting of a new distributor rotor, condenser and point set are sold by practically every store with an automotive department. This along with a new set of plugs is what most car owners call a "tune-up." Actually, factory-quality condensers seldom go bad and distributor rotors are usually good for at least 50,000 miles. These items are often replaced quite needlessly. Unless the rotor is conspicuously worn or a test at the local auto store shows your condenser to be faulty, there's no reason why they should be replaced.

Distributor points need to be checked at least once every 10,000 miles to make sure that they are not seriously burned and that their gap hasn't narrowed due to rubbing block wear. Narrow point

Gapping spark plugs is one of the vital little tasks that go into a tune-up. New plugs are generally needed every 10,000 to 12,000 miles and these should be gapped also (to make sure). Be wise—play it safe.

These diagrams explain the relationship of dwell to distributor point gap. A dwell meter will check the gap quickly and with ease, but a feeler gauge is just as accurate. And it is accuracy that you'll want.

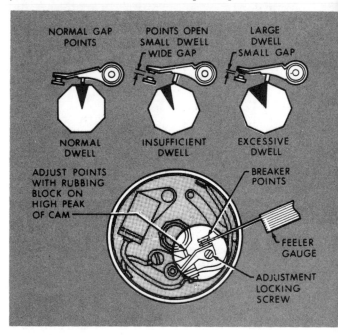

The first step when adjusting the distributor point gap is to loosen the screw locking the breaker assembly to the distributor's advance plate. Locations vary slightly with different cars, but are essentially alike.

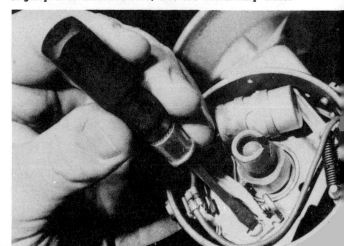

Select the feeler gauge thickness which meets the car's specifications and turn the engine to open points. Move points to obtain the correct gap, tighten the lock screw. You may have to make a further adjustment.

LATERAL MISALIGNMENT

PROPER LATERAL ALIGNMENT

CORRECT LATERAL MISALIGNMENT BY BENDING FIXED CONTACT SUPPORT
NEVER BEND BREAKER LEVER

Even brand new point assemblies may not be in perfect alignment. If not they will wear prematurely. Check and bend the stationary contact to correct any misalignment which exists. Take time; work carefully.

gaps are responsible for a great deal of hard starting, stalling, and cars that suddenly cease running in traffic. A flat feeler gauge should be used to adjust the point gap after first turning the engine with the starter so that the rubbing block of the movable contact arm is atop one of the "bumps" on the distributor cam.

Gapping the points with a feeler gauge can be a genuine pain in the neck on some engines. Dwell meters have therefore come into wide use for checking distributor point adjustment. Although they cost between $10 and $25, depending on quality, they are easy to use. The red lead on the meter should be clipped onto the ignition coil terminal which receives a small wire coming from the side of the distributor. Connect the black lead to "ground" somewhere on the engine and turn the meter's selector to the number of cylinders.

Operate the engine at an idle. The needle should indicate a reading that is within the specifications listed for your car. New points must still be given a preliminary feeler gauge gapping before they can be tested with a dwell meter. Nevertheless, a meter makes it a lot easier to keep track of points that are already in service.

Most cars must have their engines switched off and the distributor cap removed so that the point adjustment can be altered. The cap must then be replaced and the engine started for another dwell test. However, GM and AM cars with Delco ignition are fitted with what is known as a "window" distribu-

tor. This unit permits dwell adjustments to be made while the engine is running. The meter's needle can therefore be "tuned in" 'til it's right on the money.

When installing new points or a condenser, make certain that the floor of the distributor and the part of the condenser or point assembly that comes into contact with it are clean and free of oil. Good electrical contact is a "must." In fact, most burned and pitted points are not caused by faulty condensers, but by poor contact between the condenser's case and the distributor.

The distributor cam should be lubricated with white lithium or special cam grease. These lubricants are not so likely to splash onto the points and cause burning. Lubricate the advance mechanism sparingly with motor oil and inspect the distributor cap to make sure it's clean and free of cracks or carbon tracks.

IGNITION WIRES

Faulty plug cables can cause more trouble than a jar of lightning bugs let loose in a planatarium, yet they're probably the most frequently overlooked part of a tune-up. All new cars are equipped with non-metallic radio resistance cables. These bits of glamourized spaghetti won't carry enough current to light a flashlight bulb, but their carbon-impregnated core is conductive enough to provide a path for high-voltage spark impulses to travel along.

In recent years all car manufacturers have begun using point assemblies rather than point sets that must be installed piece by piece in the distributor. Note good alignment. This is a boon to car owners.

The high tension and spark plug cables are often overlooked at tune-up time and can cause many "mysterious" misses later on. An ohmmeter is needed so that you can easily check modern resistance cable.

There are good resistance cables and bad resistance cables. Unfortunately, about 90% of the world's car makers have stuck with the bad stuff even though several types are available which are impossible to fault. Belden IRS cable is the best. It has a continuous conductive rubber-like extruded tube through its center which cannot be damaged by rough handling or deliberate abuse. It also offers a fool-proof terminal system. Packard Radio TV Suppression cable ranks very close to it, but most other resistance cables on the market are strictly also-rans.

Check the plugs and cables with a spark plug tester or check the cables with an ohmmeter at each tune-up or at the first sign of misfiring. If a cable is not firing regularly, or if it tests above 4,000 ohms per foot or over 20,000 ohms for any individual cable, it's time for a new set of cables. Don't switch to metallic core cables. They'll not only cause enough radio interference to get you into a "fix" with the "fuzz," but will probably cause added spark plug erosion as well.

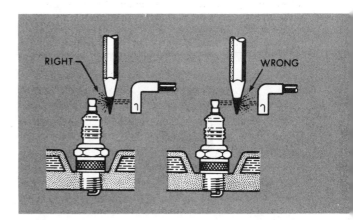

Whenever the ignition coil is removed for testing or replacement there is a chance that its small wires will be reversed when replaced. Spark should flare between pencil and the plug. It should be a bright blue.

THE COIL

Don't forget the ignition coil when you do a tune-up. Make sure its nose is clean and that the nipple over the high tension cable fits tightly. You can test the coil by removing the high tension cable from the center of the distributor cap and holding it about ¼-inch from a grounded place on the engine. Grip it with a wooden or plastic clothes pin to avoid electrical shocks.

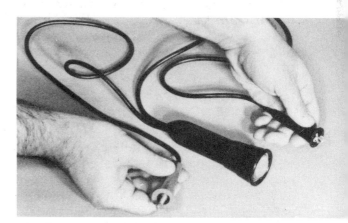

Inexpensive neon timing lights like this are very practical for home service, but require a darkened room for their weak flash. No. 1 plug fires through unit to produce light. Disconnect vac hose from distributor.

Have somebody run the starter and observe the spark that jumps between the cable to "ground." If it's bright blue and snaps loudly, your coil is in good

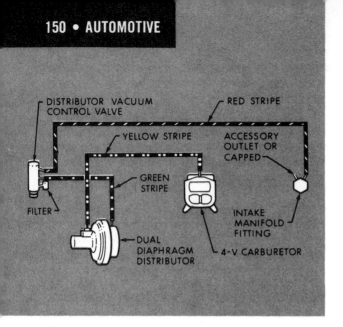

When timing the engine, all vacuum hoses to the distributor must be removed and securely plugged. This includes BOTH hoses on all Ford Motor cars with pollution control, engines with dual vacuum distributors.

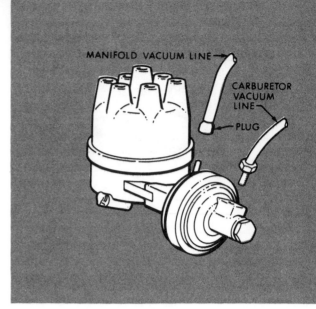

The vacuum lines controlling spark advance on all Ford Motor Company cars with IMCO are shown here. Unless all are in perfectly sound condition, a faulty advance usually results. And so, keep a careful watch.

shape. A yellow spark indicates low voltage and a coil that's getting weak. If the spark won't jump ¼-inch, you'd better start walking toward the parts store for a new coil, 'cause the one you have might not even start the engine!

TIMING

Hook your timing light up to the #1 cylinder's spark plug lead as described in the instructions packaged with the light. The vacuum hose should be disconnected from the distributor. Late Chrysler Corporation engines may be fitted with a solenoid distributor having a plastic box beside the vacuum diaphragm. The small wire leading to this box should be disconnected along with the vacuum hose. Do this when checking dwell also. Remove both hoses on late Ford engines with dual vacuum distributors. Always plug vacuum hoses which are removed during timing operations on any engine.

Loosen the distributor hold-down bolt slightly so that the distributor body can just barely be turned by hand. Let the engine idle and aim the timing light at the timing marks on the engine. These are usually located on the crankshaft pulley, so be careful of the spinning fan. Move the distributor from side to side until the timing marks line

up in the correct position. Tighten the distributor hold-down, and you're ready to re-connect the vacuum lines and move on to the next phase of your tune-up.

VALVE ADJUSTMENT

If your engine has hydraulic lifters you can usually forget about valve adjustments during a tune-up. Adjustments are a "must" on engines with mechanical lifters, and on Volkswagens they're a matter of life or death. Remove the valve cover(s) and distributor cap. The engine must be turned by hand or with the starter until the distributor cam is just about to open the points. Check the position of the rotor against the wires on the distributor cap to determine which cylinder is about to fire. Adjust that cylinder's valves, then turn the engine until the rotor is aligned with the next cylinder in the firing order and the points are about to open. Adjust the valves of that cylinder and continue until all cylinders have been done. Many car owners prefer to adjust the valves while the spark plugs are out for re-gapping since it makes the engine easier to turn and stop in the right position.

Valve adjustments must be made according to the specifications listed in your car owner's manual. Some engines should have their valves adjusted while the engine is hot, others with the engine completely cold. Exhaust valves normally require a wider gap than intakes. You can tell one from the other by looking at the intake and exhaust manifolds to see which parts the individual valve lines up with. Usually there's an exhaust valve at the end of the head, then two intakes, and then two exhausts, two intakes *etc.*, until you reach a final single exhaust valve at the other end of the head.

Select the two blades on your feeler gauge which match the engine's specifications. Insert the correct gauge between the valve stem and the rocker arm. If it slides in easily and can be moved around with just noticeable drag, the valve is in proper adjustment. If the gauge will not go in, or if it fits loosely within the gap, the valve needs adjusting.

A majority of engines have a lock nut holding the adjustment screw in place. This must be loosened slightly so that the screw can be turned and re-tightened when the correct gap has been achieved. The job can be a bit tricky the first time you try it, so *always* re-check the gap after the lock nut has been tightened. Many domestic cars now have self-locking adjusting screws which make the job much easier.

FUEL SYSTEM

Inspect the fuel pump and lines at each tune-up to detect any leaks which may have developed. If the fuel pump has a built-in filter now's the time to clean it. In-line filters should be serviced as required. Look for leaks around the carburetor hold-down nuts and check the screws that hold the top onto the carburetor for tightness.

EMISSION CONTROL

Air injection systems should have their filter replaced or cleaned as required. All engines now have positive crankcase ventilation systems, so clean the valve in solvent at each tune-up and install a new one at the interval recommended by the car manufacturer.

Cars built since 1968 have closed PCV systems. Here's a quick check that will tell you if they are working right: (1) With the engine idling, remove the hose from the rocker arm cover and place your thumb over the end. There should be definite suction and loss of engine speed. (2) If no suction is felt, remove the oil filler cap and replace the hose. Hold a piece of stiff paper loosely over the oil filler pipe. After a few seconds, the tag should be drawn against the filler pipe with noticeable force. If it is, the flame arrester screen in the hose leading the air cleaner is probably clogged. If it is not drawn against the pipe, the PCV valve is probably clogged.

CARBURETOR ADJUSTMENT

Turning the idle adjustment(s) on the carburetor should produce a noticeable change in engine speed and opera-

Here's what the FoMoCo IMCO advance system looks like in real life. Valve in the engine block advances spark if the engine overheats. Extra hose is used with air conditioning. It's not really as rough as it may look.

Beginning with the 1970 models, Chrysler Corporation cars with big engine options got this solenoid-controlled spark advance unit. Remove wire and hose when checking the timing. And when checking dwell.

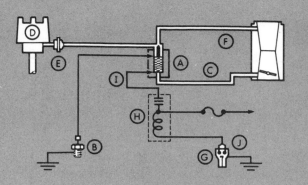
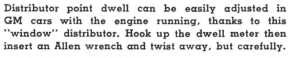

Late model General Motors cars with automatic transmission have had this transmission-controlled spark circuit. "B" is switch in transmission that limits advance in low gears. "A" is the solenoid, "F" and "C" are the vacuum lines to the carburetor. Only hose "E" needs to be removed and plugged while the car's distributor ("D") is being re-timed. It's simple.

Here's the solenoid in General Motor's TCS (Transmission Controlled Spark) setup. A check of its wires and the hoses is in order at tune-up time lest something be adrift. It is sensible to check on everything.

Distributor point dwell can be easily adjusted in GM cars with the engine running, thanks to this "window" distributor. Hook up the dwell meter then insert an Allen wrench and twist away, but carefully.

Thanks to hydraulic valve lifters, valve lash adjustments at tune-up time are virtually a thing of the past. First step in making necessary adjustments is to loosen the rocker arm nut, and using the proper wrench.

The cylinder must be in the right position to fire, so check the distributor rotor's position. Turn the adjusting screw until the correct size feeler gauge moves about with slight drag. It's really a matter of feel.

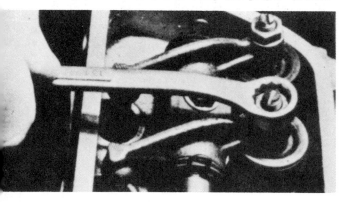

Hold the adjuster in position and tighten the lock nut. This may take some practice until you get it right. Do not overdo the tightening operation or you might strip the threads. Be firm but never force work.

After tightening the lock nut, test the gap with a feeler gauge that's .002" oversize. If the gauge will enter the gap it is too wide and the space adjustment should be done over. Trial and error is the best way.

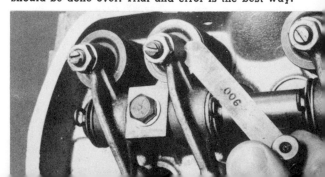

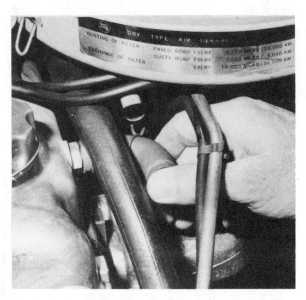

Check the crankcase ventilation system by removing the hose leading from valve cover to the air cleaner. There should be suction. If not, replace the hose and take off oil filler cap. Hold paper over pipe.

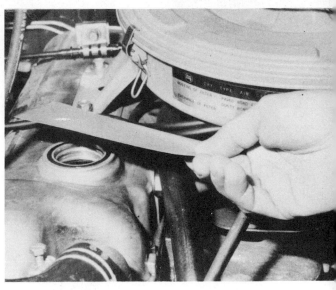

If vacuum draws paper against filler, the flame arresting screen in the air cleaner or hose is clogged. If not, the positive crankcase ventilation valve is at fault, that is to say, it is probably clogged.

tion. If it doesn't, the carburetor is undoubtedly due for a cleaning or rebuild. The classic method for adjusting the idle is to turn the mixture screw in until the engine begins to falter. Note the position of the screw, then turn it counterclockwise until the engine again "rolls" or loses speed. The correct setting is usually about midway between these two positions.

A vacuum gauge makes the job more precise. Connect the gauge to the engine's manifold vacuum port and adjust the idle screws until the maximum vacuum reading is obtained. Adjust one screw at a time on V-8 engines, going back and forth between the two adjustments. Multiple carburetors should be set with the help of a Uni-Syn, or other multiple carburetor synchronizing tool.

On engines with exhaust emission controls there may be plastic stops on the idle needles to limit their travel or, in some cases, no adjustment at all. Most emission controlled engines should not be set for maximum vacuum or "best idle." Check the service manual for your car to find the correct vacuum specifications and stick to them. Some car makers give such idle adjustment specifications as 1.5% to 2.5% CO (carbon monoxide). It requires an expensive exhaust gas analyzer to check this accurately. What it means, however, is to set the adjustment near its lean limit. Smog laws or not, there are relatively few service departments that use, or even have analyzing equipment.

If the idle speed of the engine is too fast or too slow after adjustment, the throttle stop screw must be adjusted to bring the idle into the correct speed range. Cars with automatic transmissions should be in "drive" with the parking brake set during carb adjustments. After the correct speed is obtained, the idle mixture adjusting screws must once again be adjusted.

That's it for the tune-up. Certain other operations should take place at this time such as a compression check, battery test, and cooling system inspected. Many service stations offer a "bargain" tune-up which is really just a plug cleaning and point adjustment job. If you want the kind of tune-up outlined here you can count on at least a $25 bill. For that kind of money it's probably worth taking all of Saturday morning to do it yourself!

Installing brake linings isn't really hard, but if your car has drum brakes and the drums need to be re-ground, fitting the new linings should probably be left to a professional, because then it could be rough.

YOUR CAR'S BRAKES

Why wait for the brakes to fail before doing anything about them?

Driving a car with a slipping clutch may never get you into trouble but taking to the highway with sick brakes is asking for an instant case of "the deads." There's rarely such a thing as a "sudden" brake failure. There are always plenty of warnings for those who are willing to heed them. Every car owner should make certain that the maintenance operations required to keep his car's brakes functioning safely are carried out according to schedule.

BRAKE FLUID

When the brake pedal is depressed it operates a pump called the *master cylinder*. This pump forces hydraulic fluid through a system of pipes and hoses to the four wheels of the car. At each wheel there are "slave" cylinders which fill with fluid as pressure from the "master" cylinder is increased. The influx of fluid forces the pistons in the wheel cylinders to move outward and press the brake linings against the wheel's rotating brake surfaces. When the driver raises his foot from the pedal ing the wheel cylinders ETAO SHR springs retract the brake linings causing the wheel cylinders to force the additional fluid back into the master cylinder's reservoir.

Brake fluid tends to attract moisture from the air. This in turn causes corrosion in the brake system and sludging

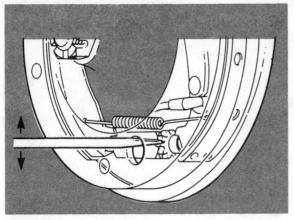

Band brakes are adjusted by inserting a special tool or screwdriver and advancing a star wheel inside the brake drum. These may have to be backed off slightly to remove the brake drums, but that is simple.

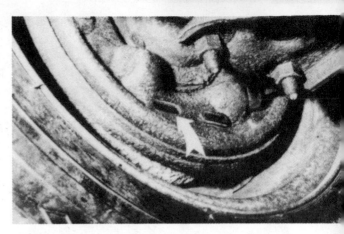

Most cars have the brake adjusting slots in the brake backing plate. Remove the rubber plug as shown and then insert the adjusting tool. Replace all plugs which are missing. This seems simple, but is important.

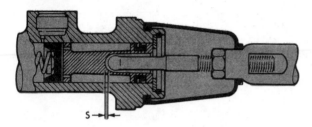

Cross section drawing of a typical brake master cylinder shows how the piston must uncover a tiny port in the cylinder wall. Freeplay (S) must be about 1/10-inch to guarantee that piston can move to retracted position. It's a simple operation but needs checking.

of the fluid. In extreme cases the water may form a concentration that significantly lowers the fluid's boiling point. If heat from the linings causes the fluid to boil there will be an almost complete loss of braking power. Air in the fluid has a similar effect. It usually enters the system through worn wheel cylinders with leaking piston seals. Swollen seals or a sludged return valve in the master cylinder will often cause the brakes to stay on even after the pedal has been released. This can wreck the entire braking system if not taken care of immediately.

All these problems can be largely prevented merely by changing the brake fluid annually or every 20,000 miles, yet no domestic car maker makes this recommendation. Builders of expensive imported cars do. Apparently their customers are more interested in keeping their cars in top-notch shape than in owning "maintenance free" transportation. A word to the wise should be sufficient!

CHANGING FLUID

Don't mix types and brands of brake fluid. When you change fluid be sure that the new juice meets the specifica-

tions established for your car.

Cars having disc brakes must be serviced with a fluid designed especially for disc brake systems.

Near where the hose enters the back of each brake assembly you'll find what appears to be a sort of grease fitting. *It's not.* It is the brake bleeding valve. To change the fluid, park the car in a location where spilled fluid will not be harmful. Open all four bleeding valves about two turns. Pump the brake pedal to the floor slowly several times or until most of the fluid is gone from the master cylinder reservoir. Fill the reservoir with fresh fluid and pump this out also. Repeat the process one more time, then close the bleeders and refill the reservoir. The brakes must now be bled.

BLEEDING BRAKES

Brake bleeding is a job which must be done any time the hydraulic system has been opened either for repairs or to replace fluid. You'll need a helper to work the brake pedal, a length of 7/32-in inside diameter transparent fuel tubing, and a small cup or jar to catch the fluid.

Start with the brake that is furthest

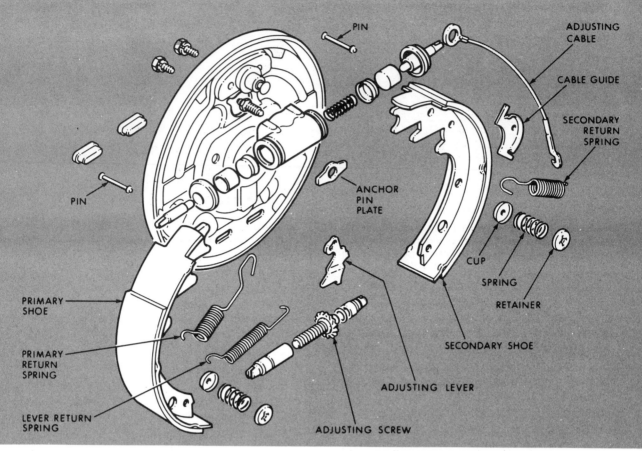

PIN

ADJUSTING CABLE

CABLE GUIDE

SECONDARY RETURN SPRING

PIN

ANCHOR PIN PLATE

PRIMARY SHOE

CUP

SPRING

RETAINER

PRIMARY RETURN SPRING

SECONDARY SHOE

ADJUSTING LEVER

LEVER RETURN SPRING

ADJUSTING SCREW

The parts of a typical drum brake assembly are shown in this drawing. Note the pins, springs, and retainers which hold the brake shoes in their places on the brake backing plate. It's a good idea to learn these.

away from the master cylinder. This is usually at the right rear wheel. Slip the tubing over the bleeder and place the opposite end in the jar. Open the bleed about ¼ turn and have your helper depress the pedal slowly. Fluid will be pumped into the jar. If you are bleeding the brakes following a change of fluid, keep bleeding until new fluid comes out of the tube and until no air bubbles appear. This may require several strokes of the pedal. Close the bleeder before having the pedal released, then reopening it for the next downstroke. If you are bleeding the system following repairs continue until no air bubbles are produced.

Be sure to keep the master cylinder reservoir filled while bleeding the brakes. On cars with dual master cylinders or dual brake systems the level falls rapidly since the individual reservoirs are usually rather small. Bleed the left rear, right front, and left front brakes and the job is done. If the brakes feel "spongy" there may still be

air trapped in the system. Bleed the brakes again until you are certain that the last bubble is out.

ADJUSTING

Disc brakes do not require adjusting. Most of today's drum type brakes are self-adjusting, but this feature sometimes fails to work properly. Cars having manually adjusted brakes must have their shoes advanced by hand periodically to prevent the brake pedal from getting too low. A low pedal is always a sign that brake adjustments are overdue or that they are not taking place automatically.

Some brakes are adjusted by inserting a screwdriver or brake adjusting tool through a slot in the brake backing plate. There are one or two star wheels within each brake assembly which must be rotated to move the shoes outward. Some cars, such as VW, have the adjustment opening in the face of the brake drum. Certain other cars may have a square lug projecting from the backing plate. Turning this with a wrench will advance or retract the brake shoes. Your owner's manual should show location of adjusters and indicate direction of rotation.

Self-adjusting brakes advance the star wheel each time the hand brake is used or whenever the brakes are applied with the car moving in reverse. If you never use the handbrake you may find yourself with a very low pedal. Stuck star wheels are the usual cause of failure in automatic brake adjusters.

The brake adjusters should be advanced until the shoes can be heard dragging against the drum as the tire is turned by hand. Press the brake pedal firmly to center the shoes in the drum and advance them again until they drag. When depressing the brake pedal no longer stops the shoes from dragging, advance the adjusters until it is hard to turn the wheel by hand, then back off the adjustments 1 or 2 notches or until the sound of the shoes dragging against the drum disappears.

CYLINDER REPAIRS

If the brake pedal continues to go down slowly until it finally reaches the floor there is a leak in the system. Check the hoses very carefully. Never keep a brake hose on the car which is cracked, gashed, or which has broken fabric or abrasion marks on its exterior. If no leaks are apparent, take off the brake drums and lift the rubber dust seal off each wheel cylinder. If fluid leakage is apparent the cylinder is faulty. Inspect disc brake calipers for signs of leaking fluid.

Usually, however, the above mentioned symptoms indicate a faulty master cylinder. If the car has over 50,000 miles on it it's usually best to merely install a replacement master cylinder since the cylinder walls may be worn past their useful life in the old unit. On low mileage cars it's economically sound to rebuild the master cylinder.

Obtain a rebuild kit and a brake cylinder hone. Remove the master cylinder from the firewell or from the power brake vacuum booster. Withdraw the

These are the integral parts of typical wheel or "slave" cylinder assemblies. Notice the shape and location of the bleeder screws. These must be loosened to bleed brakes. Again, you could learn these names.

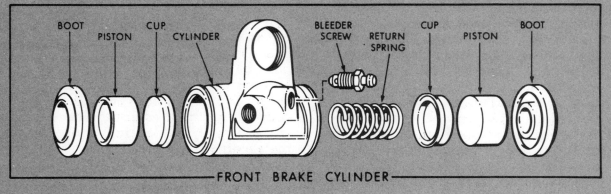

FRONT BRAKE CYLINDER

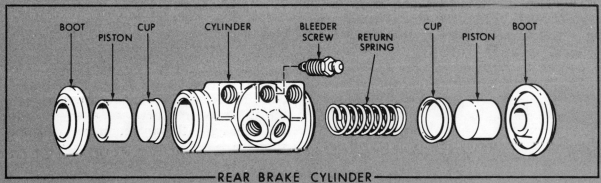

REAR BRAKE CYLINDER

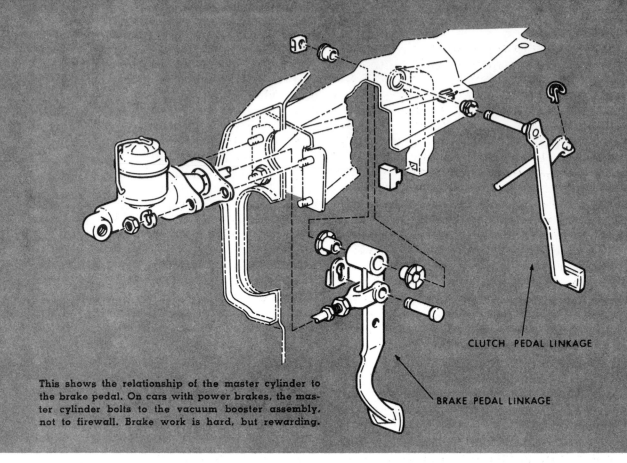

This shows the relationship of the master cylinder to the brake pedal. On cars with power brakes, the master cylinder bolts to the vacuum booster assembly, not to firewall. Brake work is hard, but rewarding.

CLUTCH PEDAL LINKAGE

BRAKE PEDAL LINKAGE

piston and lay the various internal parts out on a clean table in the order and position in which they were removed. Inspect the cylinder for pits and scoring and hone the cylinder until these disappear. Oversize rebuild kits are available to make up for the honing, but .005″ is the practical limit before declaring it a lost cause. Clean and deburr the small holes in the cylinder walls and blow out all abrasive dust after honing.

Wash brake parts with brake fluid or pure denatured alcohol. If the rubber seals appear swollen and spongy the fluid has been contaminated with fuel, oil, or kerosene. In such cases the entire system should be flushed out with 188-195 proof denatured alcohol and the wheel cylinder piston seals inspected for similar deterioration before putting in clean fluid.

Lubricate the piston seals with brake fluid as you install them in the cylinder. It's helpful to have a diagram of the cylinder to guide its reassembly, but such a drawing is included with most non-factory rebuild kits. When install-

ing the master cylinder make certain that there is at least 1/10″ of freeplay between the push rod coming from the pedal or vacuum booster and the master cylinder piston. A shop manual can provide accurate specifications for your particular car.

Wheel cylinders should be inspected for leakage periodically by lifting their dust covers. If faulty they can be rebuilt or replaced. New brake lines can also be obtained to replace any that show serious corrosion damage or dents caused by flying stones. The brakes must always be bled following any of the repairs described above.

DISC BRAKE LININGS

If you have disc brakes consider yourself lucky. It's possible to inspect the thickness of the linings without taking anything apart and replacing worn linings is a job that takes barely minutes. Some car makers recommend that the discs be replaced at every second pad change. However, many machine shops are now equipped to resurface the discs. Unless seriously scored they can be made to last the life of the car.

To replace the pads (linings) on disc brakes, take off the wheel and tire, then remove the anti-rattle spring clip or the retaining pins that lock the pads in the caliper. Insert a stiff wire hook through the opening in each brake pad's backing plate and pull the pads from the caliper. There are also thin metal shims that must come out. Replacements for these are included with the new linings.

Never depress the brake pedal while the pads are out. Wash away any dirt around the pistons with brake fluid and have the discs ground if they are scored deeply enough to make withdrawing the pads difficult. You'll have to unbolt the calipers and take the wheel spindle nuts off the front wheels to remove the discs, so be careful not to lose the wheel bearings. Rear discs normally slide off the axle flange after removing retaining screw.

The brake pistons will have to be pushed back into the caliper slightly to permit the new, thicker pads to slide in. A putty knife is a handy tool for this, but it's wise to remove some of the fluid from the master cylinder to prevent overflowing as the pistons are pushed in. Be sure to install the shims and pads so that any arrows marked on them are pointed in the direction of forward wheel rotation.

DRUM BRAKE LININGS

Drum brakes are very temperamental about the fit of their linings and on high-mileage cars or those with worn and scored drums the entire job is best turned over to a brake shop. Drums which have been scored by metal-to-metal contact with brake shoes or rivets will need to be resurfaced. This alone should provide the motivation to check lining thickness each 10,000 miles. If the linings are worn to within .002" of the rivets or if total lining thickness is 1/16" or less, replace linings.

Drums also need resurfacing if they are bellmouthed (often caused by overheating), out of round, or if normal wear has recessed the friction area more than about .005". The man at the

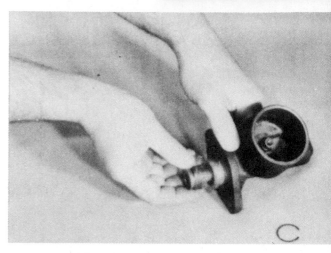

When rebuilding a brake cylinder the first step is to take it carefully apart and inspect the damage. The master cylinder has snap ring to remove but wheel cylinders usually not. Good inspection is important.

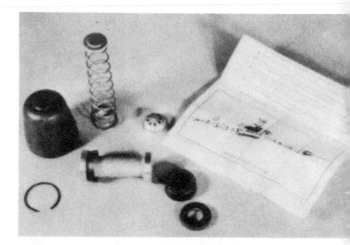

This is a typical master cylinder rebuilding kit. Notice that diagram of cylinder is shown on instruction sheet. Oversize pistons are available for excessively worn cylinders. But always read the instructions carefully.

A brake cylinder hone is needed to remove the scoring and pitting from inside the brake cylinder. A variable-speed power drill is the best tool for driving a cylinder hone. Use low RPM and you will achieve best effect.

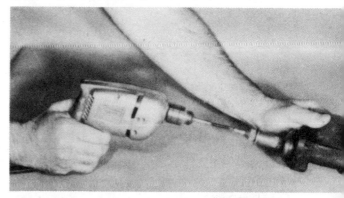

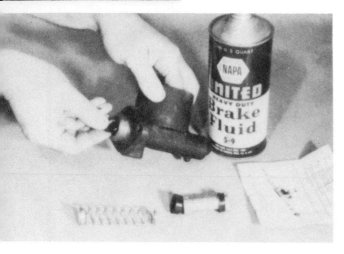

After honing, clean the cylinder and lube the new parts with brake fluid before you start to install them. Never clean or lubricate brake parts with petroleum greases or oil. Always use brake fluid and be thorough.

You will find removal and replacement of disc brake pads is a very simple operation. Pull out the lock clips and withdraw the pins that hold the brake lining pads and shims in place. You'll have no difficulty.

Once the retaining pins are out, the thin backing shims and the brake pads can be easily withdrawn from the brake caliper. Also do this when removing the caliper assembly. Work carefully, and it's simple.

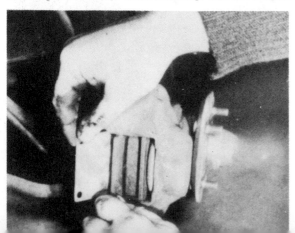

machine shop can tell you whether it's possible to recondition them or not. Reconditioned drums are slightly oversize, which means that their radius will not be quite the same as that of the new brake shoes. Special machinery is needed to grind the shoes to the new radius, so when drums are badly worn it's best to leave the whole job to a well equipped brake specialist.

Nowadays it's usually possible to trade in your old brake shoes for new ones with the linings already installed. There's a special lever-like tool used to pry off the retracting springs that link the two brake shoes of each wheel together and this item is well worth purchasing. Small cars, however, have light springs which can usually be removed by hand or with the help of a screwdriver.

The shoe retainer springs must also be removed. This is done by placing one finger behind the brake backing plate to hold the retaining pin in, then pushing on the retainer to compress the spring. Turn the retainer until the slots line up with the flattened end of the pin and the retainer and spring will come off, releasing the brake shoe.

Clean all dust from the brake parts with a stiff brush before installing the new linings. Never touch the linings or drums with greasy hands. Coat the areas of the backing plate against which the shoes rest with Lubriplate. Lubriplate may also be used to lubricate the adjusters and hand brake linkage. The brake adjustments must always be backed off when new linings are installed or the drums will not go on. Adjust the brakes after the drums are once again in place. If the car has automatic adjusters this can be done by moving the car in reverse and applying the brakes repeatedly.

Thanks to bonded linings, disc brakes, improved designs, and government standards for brake fluid, braking systems are becoming much more trouble-free and easier to service than they were in the past. If the fluid is kept clean and adjustments are made regularly, one or two changes of linings should be the only repair work required in 100,000 miles of driving with today's automobiles.